Medical Illustration in the Courtroom

Medical Illustration in the Courtroom: Proving Injury, Causation, and Damages educates the reader on how to communicate science visually—in personal injury, medical malpractice, criminal, and forensic cases—by creating art that utilizes medical records, radiographs, and computer software.

Medical illustration bridges the gap between complex technical, medical, and scientific concepts to clearly illustrate, and explain visually, a medical condition, negligence, or the causation of an injury or death to the lay person. Medical artists are frequently challenged with illustrating injuries and medical conditions that can't be seen by the naked eye. And while using medical photography and imaging for illustrative purposes can be helpful, to an untrained eye it can often be unclear or confusing. This is where the medical illustrator enters the equation. There are often patients who have recovered from an injury or infection that appear in good health. However, should an unforeseen injury or fatality happen, medical illustrators can reveal to people what's actually going on inside the person, an invaluable asset to attorneys in the courtroom—especially for personal injury and medical malpractice cases. While many attorneys utilize medical artists, nonvisual people don't always recognize the value of demonstrative aids until they see them first-hand.

When attorneys and their clients enlist the aid of medical artists, it quickly becomes apparent that properly conceived and executed artwork is invaluable to illustrating the facts—and medical impacts—of any number of scenarios: homicides by shooting, stabbings, vehicular accidents, in addition to medical malpractice and personal injuries resulting from surgery or possible negligence.

Presenting a myriad of services and computer technologies that can be utilized, *Medical Illustration in the Courtroom* provides demonstrative aids used in cases to illustrate personal injury and medical malpractice, employing "tricks of the trade" to create an accurate effective image. Such images are educational to attorneys, insurance adjusters, judges, and juries to help create a visual storyline, the goal being to help combine art and science to provide a clear illustration of events to help in adjudicate legal and forensic cases.

Lindsay E. Coulter graduated with a BFA in medical illustration from the Cleveland Institute of Art—with medical classes taken at Case Western Reserve University. She is also a board-certified medical illustrator (CMI). Coulter works as a medical illustrator and owns ION Medical Designs, LLC. ION Medical Designs is a boutique medical illustration company that specializes in custom medical illustrations, 2D and 3D animations, interactive applications, timelines, VR, and augmented reality. She creates medical demonstratives for medical malpractice and personal injury cases to assist attorneys with their demand packages, mediations, and trials. She helps to create visuals of complex surgeries and injuries that are compelling and educational for a broad audience. She has worked on high-profile and medically complex cases globally.

Medical Illustration in the Courtroom

Proving Injury, Causation, and Damages

Lindsay E. Coulter

CRC Press
Taylor & Francis Group
Boca Raton London New York

CRC Press is an imprint of the
Taylor & Francis Group, an **informa** business

Designed cover image: Lindsay E. Coulter

First edition published 2024
by CRC Press
2385 NW Executive Center Drive, Suite 320, Boca Raton FL 33431

and by CRC Press
4 Park Square, Milton Park, Abingdon, Oxon, OX14 4RN

CRC Press is an imprint of Taylor & Francis Group, LLC

ISBN: 978-1-032-37298-3 (hbk)
ISBN: 978-1-032-37294-5 (pbk)
ISBN: 978-1-003-33631-0 (ebk)

DOI: 10.4324/9781003336310

Typeset in Helvetica Neue and Avant Garde
by Apex CoVantage, LLC

I dedicate this book to my amazing children. Maximilian, who inspires me with his inquisitive nature and passion for reading, and Alexander for his cute curiosity about what Mom does for a living. My children inspire me to do my best daily. They are the reason I decided to branch out on my own. I couldn't get the flexibility I needed with my former employer. ION is what it is today partially because of my two boys.

I would also like to thank my parents, Michael, and Kathryn Matthews, for their love, encouragement, and for believing in me and supporting my education and career path.

To my brilliant clients who are acknowledged, for helping to develop me into the professional medical illustrator that I am today. Without them this book would not be possible!

Lastly, to my cherished friend Shannon Haury for her unwavering love and support. For supporting me through writing this book and all challenges in my life. I couldn't have dreamed up a better friend!

Contents

Preface *xi*
Acknowledgements *xiii*

1 Introduction to Medical Illustration 1
1.1 What Is Medical Illustration? 1
1.2 Patient Education 2
1.3 Law 5
1.4 Medical Device 7
1.5 What Does a Medical Illustrator Do? 13
1.6 Fields of Study 15
1.7 A Brief History of Medical Illustration 15

2 Medical Illustrations Enhance Trial Presentation 21
2.1 How to Take Complex Medical Information and Present It Visually 21
2.2 Colorized Radiology—Types and Visual Solutions 23
2.3 Presentation Method—How Is It Proposed? 30
2.4 How to Decide What Presentation Format Best Fits Your Case 32
2.5 Timelines and Fetal Monitor Strips 37
2.6 Why Are Accuracy and Client-Specific Anatomy Important? 39

3 Medical Illustrations for Personal Injury Cases 43
3.1 Case Study One—Worker's Compensation, Jack Walker 43
3.2 Case Study Two—Personal Injury/Wrongful Death, Matthew A. Lathrop 50
3.3 Case Study Three—Medical Malpractice, Attorney Howard Thigpen 59
3.4 Case Study Four—Medical Malpractice, Attorney Andrew Sibbernsen 65

4 Medical Illustrations for Medical Malpractice Defense Cases 73
4.1 Case Study One—Medical Malpractice Defense, John Sly 73
4.2 Case Study Two—Medical Malpractice Defense, Christina Billiet 93
4.3 Case Study Three—Medical Malpractice Defense, Kiely Keane 107

5 Medical Illustration—Interpersonal Violence 113
5.1 Forensic Nursing 113
5.2 Diagrams for Documentation 114
5.3 Diagrams for Documentation—Valerie Sievers, MSN, RN, CNS, AFN-C, SANE-A, DF-AFN 114

6 Illustrating Gunshot Wounds 123
6.1 Overview of Ballistics 124
6.2 Internal Ballistics 124
6.3 External Ballistics 124
6.4 Terminal Ballistics 124
6.5 Bullets Cause Tissue Damage 125
6.6 Atypical Entry Wounds 125
6.7 Ricochet 125
6.8 Case Study One—Mass Shooting,Justin Demerath, April Strahan, Thomas J. Henry Law, Marion M. Reilly 126
6.9 $230,000.000.00 Verdict! 145
6.10 In News Today—Department of Justice Set to Appeal—Victims Will Receive 144.5 Million Dollar Settlement 145
6.11 Case Two—Apartment Shooting—Civil Suit, Greg Bevel Wesley Gould, Rochelle McCullough, L.L.P. 146

7 Forensic Facial Reconstruction 149
7.1 Four Categories of Forensic Art 149
7.2 Three-Dimensional Facial Reconstruction of the Skull 150
7.3 Circumstances for Creating 3D Facial Reconstruction—Method 151
7.4 Technical Phase 152
7.5 Tissue Depth Markers 152
7.6 Tools and Materials 154
7.7 Modern 3D Facial Reconstruction with Artificial Intelligence (AI) 156

8 Medical Legal Illustrations Are Useful in Every Stage of Litigation—Not Just Trial! 162
8.1 Submitting Medical Demonstrative Aids to Trial 163
8.2 Find a Qualified Medical/Forensic Illustrator 163
8.3 Find a Qualified Medical Expert 164
8.4 Expert Witness Directories 164

8.5 Utilize Your Medical Imaging/Reports 165
8.6 Exchange/Submit the Demonstrative Aids 165
8.7 Know the Courtroom 166

9 Utilizing Focus Groups for Review of Demonstrative Aids 167
9.1 Advantages of Focus Groups during Trial Prep 167
9.2 How to Hire a Focus Group 168
9.3 Do Focus Groups Enhance Settlement Negotiations? 169
9.4 Having Your Medical Artist Listen in on the Focus Group 170
9.5 In Closing—Utilize Focus Groups! 177

10 How Media Has Affected Learning 178
10.1 The Tech Generation—Immediate Access 178
10.2 Community Strength through Social Media 179
10.3 The Technology "Wow" Factor 180

11 Conclusion 189
11.1 Thank You! 196

References *197*
Index *199*

Preface

I am a medical illustrator by trade and author at night. Due to my publications online, I was noticed by a publisher by writing about current trends and news in newsletters and blogs for my business. At this point in my career, I have the relevant experience to educate others in my profession and relevant fields.

As a young lady after graduating from high school, I planned to study medicine to become a bilingual pediatrician. I was enrolled in premed when a college flyer came in the mail from the Cleveland Institute of Art for a program in medical illustration. It was a combined program with Case Western Reserve University School of Medicine and Dentistry. I have always been interested and taken many advanced classes in art. My mother was an art teacher. She exposed us to all kinds of art and education. I decided then and there to apply to that program and was accepted.

After my college education I really wanted to create pharmaceutical advertising or cellular editorial artwork. I think that the microscopic cellular world is so beautiful. I wanted to work for a company called Anatomical Travelog. The artists in their company created a book titled *From Conception to Birth* that I was enamored with. The book had a series of photographs and illustrations of conception and then all the stages of human development until birth. I applied for a job there; however, the pay was certainly not enough to live in Manhattan! I then applied to a medical legal firm. I was offered a job and moved to Colorado to work there. The work was very fast-paced and chop shop, meaning you take work that has been created by other artists that work for the company and rework it to fit the case you are working on. As an artist I wasn't very enthusiastic about this. I then got a better job in the same field in Dallas, Tx. Although with this firm I did learn how to read radiology, which is a very useful skill in medical legal illustration. I learned a lot from this company; however, it was still what I would call chop shop and very fast-paced.

When my oldest son was born, I decided to fully branch out on my own. I needed the flexibility for my family, and I was finally able to create my own artwork. I create my work from start to finish. I start by reviewing all the pertinent records and writing up detailed proposals from the operative and surgical reports. I deliver quality, medically accurate artwork. This has always been a passion of mine. People suffering these catastrophic injuries deserve the attention and detail of customized work.

This book was written for attorneys, no matter the stage of their practice, for medical artists who want to learn how to break into the industry, and forensic nurses primarily. Really anyone with an interest in art, medicine, law, and forensic science would benefit from reading it.

The book touches on what medical illustration is, what medical artists do, the fields of study, and a brief history. It touches on learning styles, radiology, presentation methods, and services offered by medical illustration firms. We try and keep up with the latest trends in the industry and offer a wide range of services.

Chapter 3 is dedicated to trial attorneys who specialize in personal injury and medical malpractice for the plaintiff. There are actual featured cases that were taken on by the attorneys and then specific interviews about the cases from the attorneys.

Chapter 4 is dedicated to trial attorneys who specialize in medical malpractice defense. There are real cases featured in this chapter too. The attorneys were gracious enough to take the time to answer my interview questions and provide excellent answers.

There is a chapter about interpersonal violence and is geared towards the forensic nurse community. The chapter features some of the illustrations created for the Academy of Forensic Nurses and their standardized illustration packages. There are some sample injuries they would mark up for the victim to help represent them in court.

Mass shootings are represented and how to utilize medical illustrations to depict gunshot wound trajectories. The chapter focuses a little bit on ballistics as well as a few actual cases I worked on and illustrations utilized by the attorneys in trial.

Facial reconstruction is discussed, what it is and the types. Digital and traditional reconstruction efforts. The field trends and how facial reconstruction has evolved from bone and clay to AI assisted.

The benefits of focus groups, how to hire participants and the results from them. There is also a chapter that touches on how media affects learning through visual effects and technology and social media.

Then into the future. . . . AI and what that will mean for the industry. Please turn the pages to find out.

Acknowledgements

To my clients, without you this book would not be possible. Each of you have been a large part of my career development. You were handpicked to be featured in this book.

A very special thanks to the following clients for their contributions.

- Jack Walker

  Martin Walker Attorneys at Law

  Jack is a catastrophic personal injury trial attorney. He completed an interview for Chapter 3, regarding a personal injury case for the prosecution. Thank you so much, Jack. It is always an absolute pleasure to work with you!

- Matthew Lathrop, JD

  Law Office of Matthew A. Lathrop

  Matt is a personal injury trial attorney. He has completed an interview in Chapter 3, regarding a fatal injury case. He also contributed an interview that his law firm uses for potential focus group participants. Matt is a very thorough trial attorney and enjoyable to work with in all the stages of his cases, from the initial demand to the focus groups, mediation, and, of course, trial preparation.

- Howard J. Thigpen, Esq.

  Bachus & Schanker, LLC

  Howard is a trial attorney who specializes in medical malpractice and nursing home abuse cases for the plaintiff. He completed two interviews for this book, one interview for Chapter 3, regarding a fatal medical malpractice case, and another in Chapter 9, on focus groups. He is an excellent attorney, and I very much enjoy collaborating with him.

- Andrew Sibbernsen

  Sibbernsen Law Firm

  Andy is a trial attorney who specializes in personal injury and medical malpractice. He completed an interview for Chapter 3 on a plaintiff's medical malpractice case. The case written about in this book was my first case working with him. Hopefully there will be more to come!

- John Sly, Esq.

  Waranch & Brown, LLC

  John is a medical malpractice defense attorney. He completed an interview for Chapter 4, about a medical malpractice defense case. John is still an active partner at Waranch & Brown, however retired from trying cases. I very much miss working with you, John!

- Christina Billiet, Esq.

  Waranch & Brown, LLC

  Christina is a medical malpractice defense attorney. She completed an interview in Chapter 4 on a medical malpractice defense case. Christina is an amazing attorney that I very much enjoy working with!

- Valerie Sievers, MSN, RN, CNS, AFN-C, SANE-A, DF-AFN Forensic Clinical Nurse Specialist, Forensic Healthcare Consultant

  Medlaw Consultants, LLC

  Valerie is a forensic nurse who cares for victims of assault and interpersonal violence. She contributed her knowledge and expertise in Chapter 5 to accurately portray the field of forensic nursing. Also, to explain how injuries would be documented in court. Valerie is an amazing nurse and human being. Thank you so much for your contribution!

- Justin Demerath

  O'Hanlon, Demerath & Castillo

  Justin is a personal injury attorney that I had the opportunity of working on the Sutherland Springs Church Massacre case with. Justin helped me get permission from the survivors and families of the victims depicted on the illustration boards in this book. Thank you, I look forward to working with you on future cases!

- April Strahan

  The Ammons Law Firm

  April is a personal injury attorney that I worked with on the Sutherland Springs Church Massacre case. She represented many of the survivors and families of the victims. She helped me get the permissions needed to reproduce the injury illustration boards. Thank you, I look forward to working with you in the future!

- Greg Bevel and Wesley Gould

  Rochelle McCullough

  Greg and Wesley are personal injury attorneys for the prosecution. I wrote about an apartment shooting case in which they represented the victim in this book. It was a civil suit with no criminal charges due to security issues with the apartment complex. Thank you both for your contribution, and I look forward to our next case together!
- A huge thank you to the survivors and the families of the victims of the Sutherland Springs Church Massacre. I appreciate you allowing me to reproduce yours and/or your family members' injury illustration board. Hopefully the illustrations will help to educate others on how to illustrate/represent this type of case in the future. Wishing you all health, happiness, and support in your lives now and in the future.
- I would like to thank all the survivors and families of the victims who gave me permission to reproduce their injury and/or fatal injury boards. Hopefully these images will help the attorneys represent your injuries to the best of their ability in all stages of the cases.
- Dr. Sarah Chen for the 3D print graphic and study behind her 3D print. She utilizes her knowledge of anatomy and 3D printing to help improve laparoscopic surgery.
- I would like to thank Oscar Nilsson for allowing me to feature his forensic reconstruction images. I am floored by the detail and beauty of his work!
- I would like to thank the Brazilian graphics expert Cicero Moraes for allowing me to feature his computer graphics work of reconstructing Vistegutten's jaw and completing his skull.

TO MY TEAM

Thank you, Ken Coulter, MFA. Ken is a developer and is responsible for creating our applications. Without him, we wouldn't have our advanced technology.

I would like to acknowledge our contract artist, Jennifer Darcy, MS, CMI, FAMI, for creating some of the medical art as well as our graphic design. She amazes me with her talents!

And finally, our office assistant, Joe. He is a great asset to our team, helps to organize our files, and is an all-around wonderful person!

CHAPTER 1

Introduction to Medical Illustration

1.1 WHAT IS MEDICAL ILLUSTRATION?

Medical illustration is the intersection where art meets science to visually convey complex ideas and concepts relating to medicine and the biological sciences. The art is meant to teach through visual storytelling, particularly in ways photography cannot. Medical art is a highly specialized technical field of illustration requiring advanced knowledge of the human body, anatomy, and biology while utilizing artistic skill and technical skills on a computer. A medical artist may also be well-versed in biotechnologies and pharmaceuticals. Medical artists use a myriad of mediums to convey these concepts, in addition to working across a wide variety of fields. The medical field offers illustrators a broad choice of career opportunities such as research, healthcare, publishing, education, law, medical device, and pharmaceutical companies.

To follow are some sample pieces of artwork that represent the aforementioned categories:

DOI: 10.4324/9781003336310-1

1.2 PATIENT EDUCATION

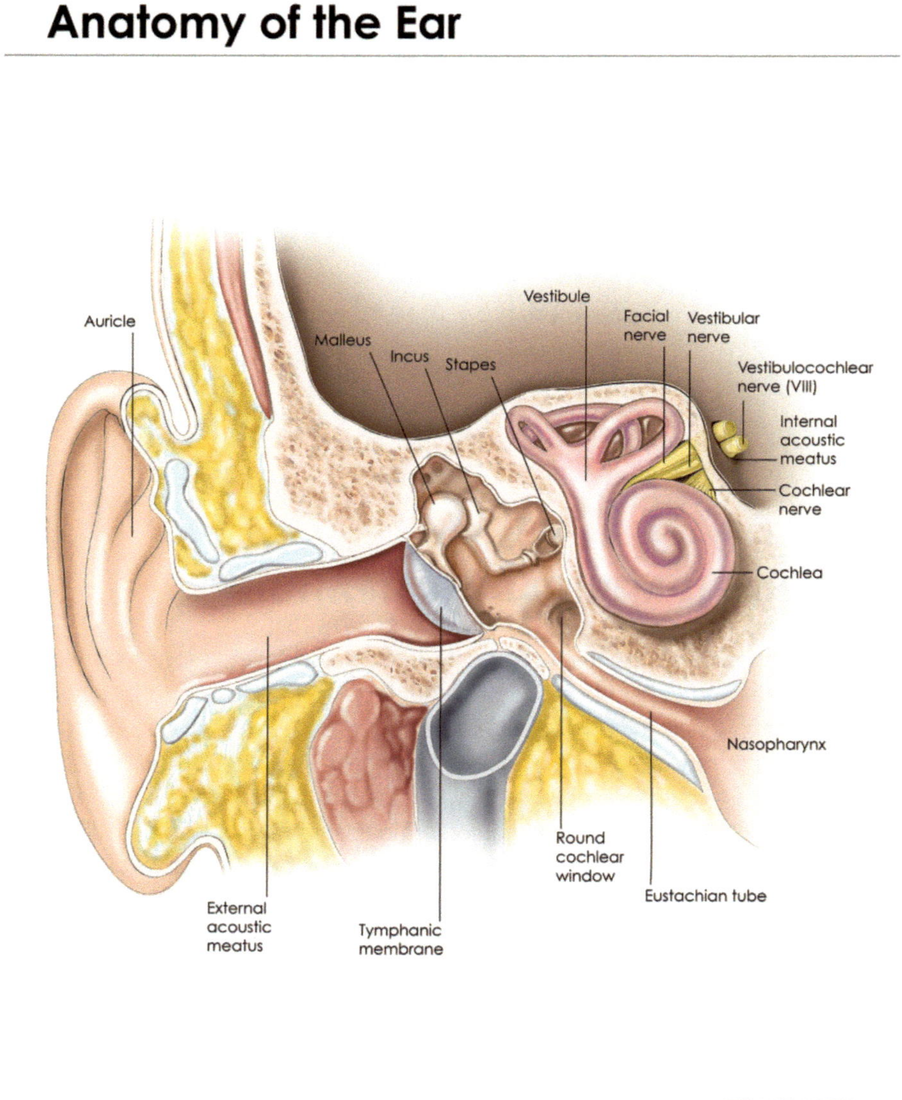

FIGURE 1.1 This anatomical poster of the ear was created for an ENT (ear, nose, and throat) doctor and utilized as a patient education poster to teach patients the external and internal anatomy of the ear.

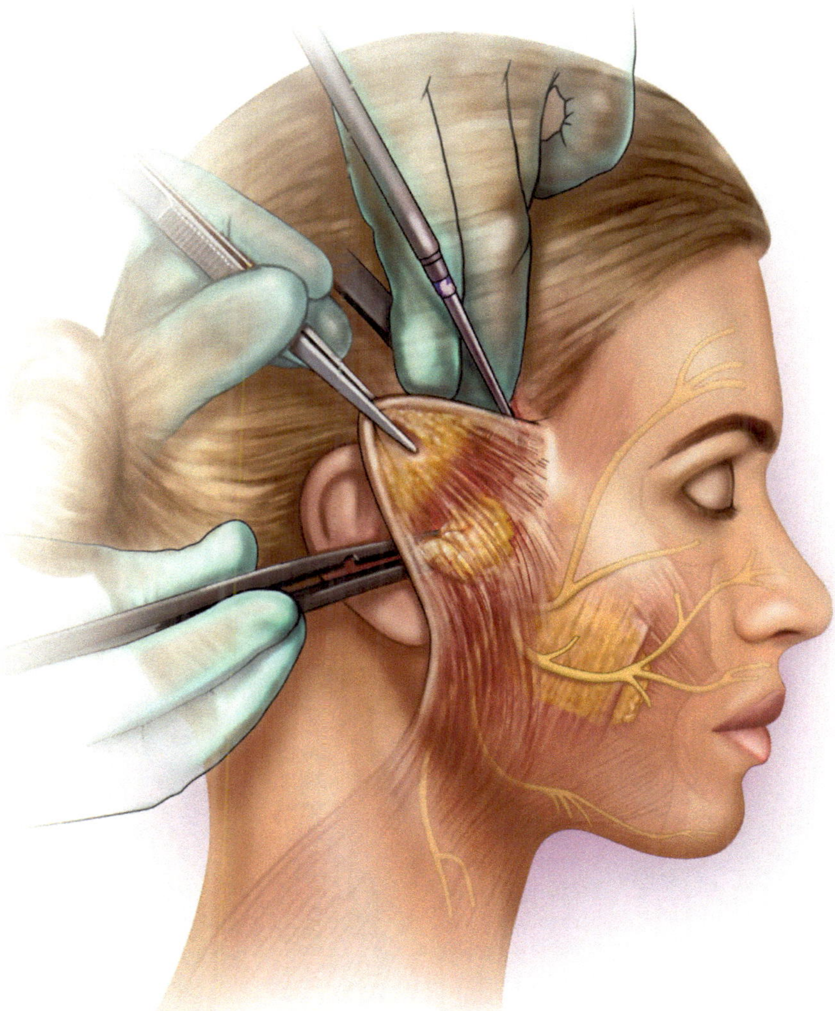

FIGURE 1.2 The illustration was created for a prominent maxillofacial plastic surgeon, showing the buccal fat pad being repositioned for a facelift. This is one of a series of medical illustrations created for this procedure.

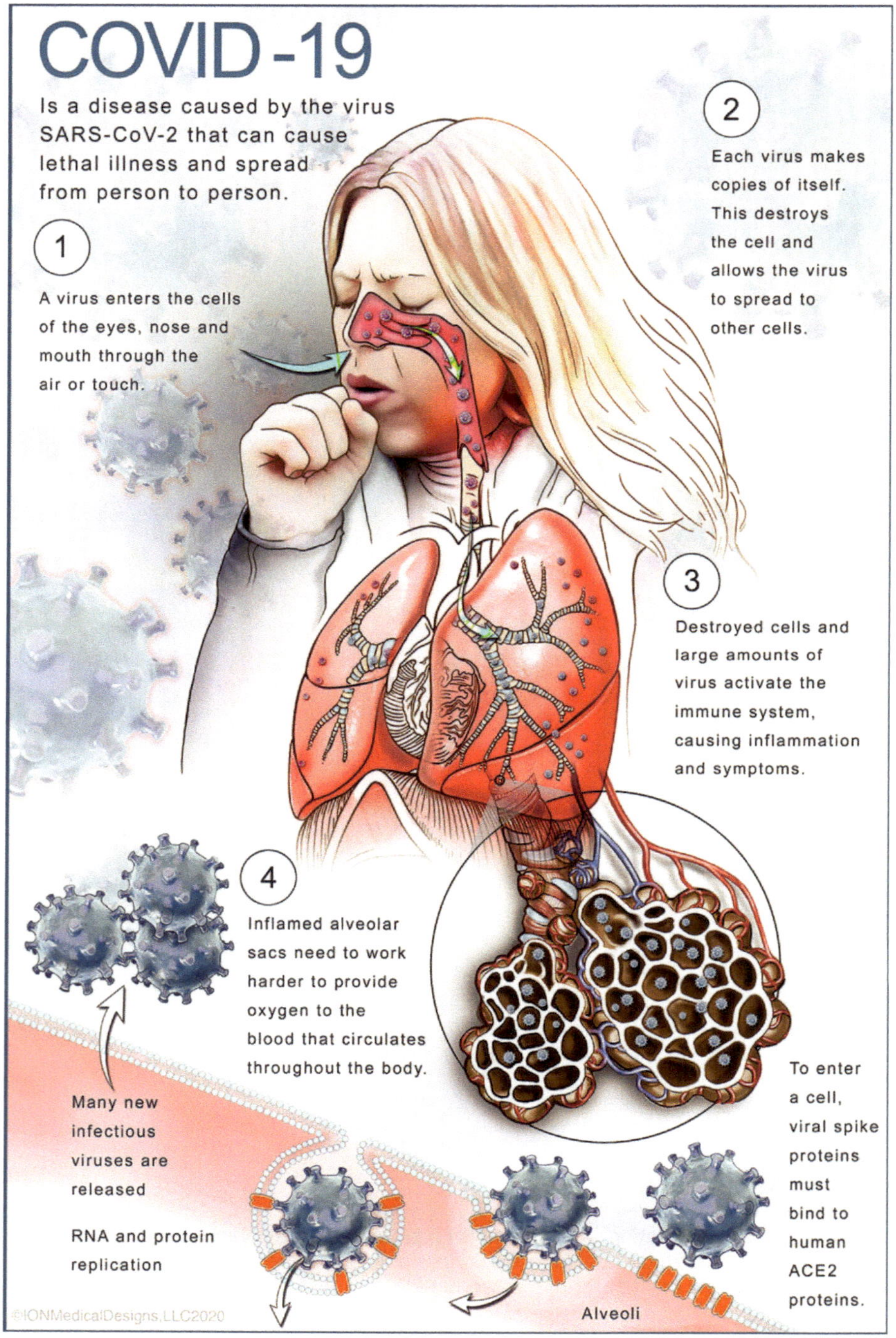

FIGURE 1.3 The illustration was created for the public to depict how Covid-19 enters your body and infects the lungs. The bottom of the page represents how the virus binds to the receptor sites and replicates inside the lung tissue.

1.3 LAW

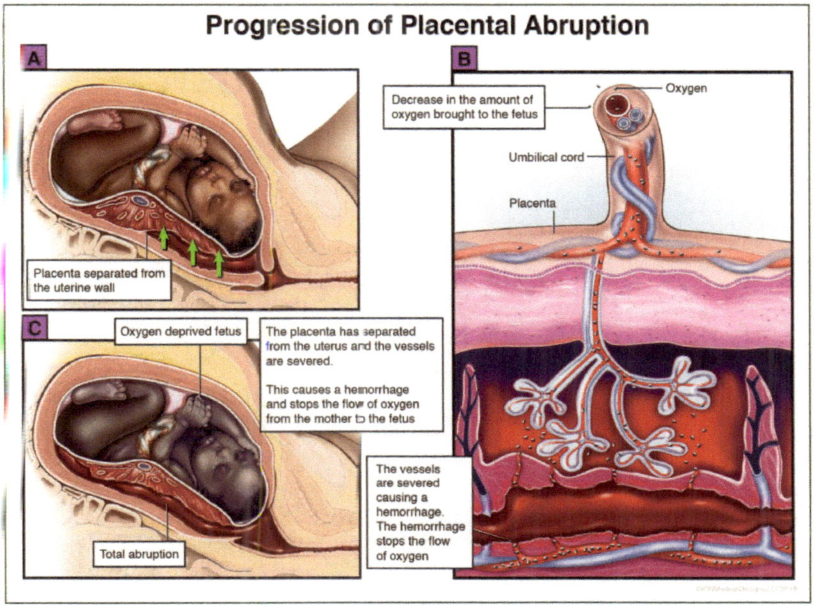

FIGURE 1.4 The illustration was created for defense counsel to show the progression of placental abruption.

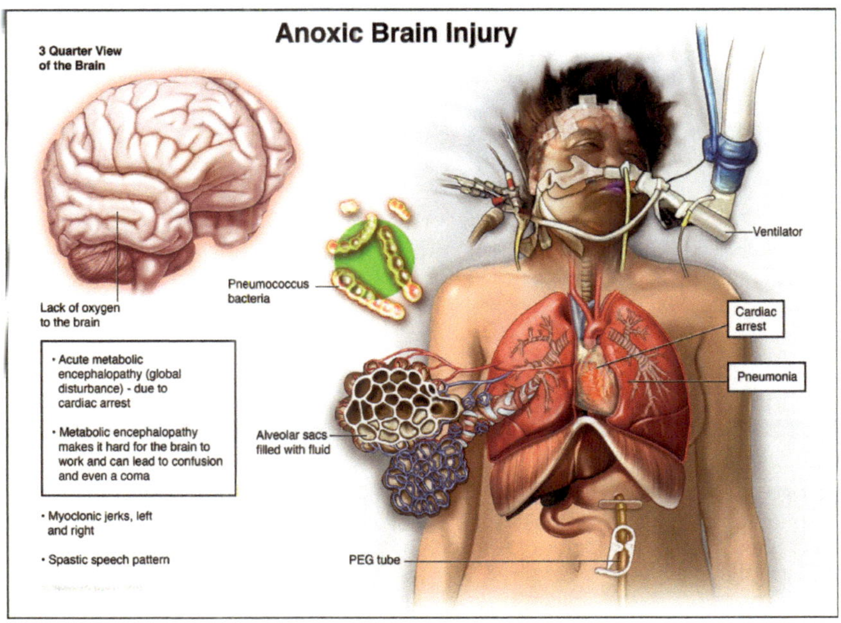

FIGURE 1.5 The illustration was created for plaintiff's counsel to depict an axonic brain injury causing the brain function to decline. She also suffered from pneumonia. The artwork was made to depict the condition of the plaintiff.

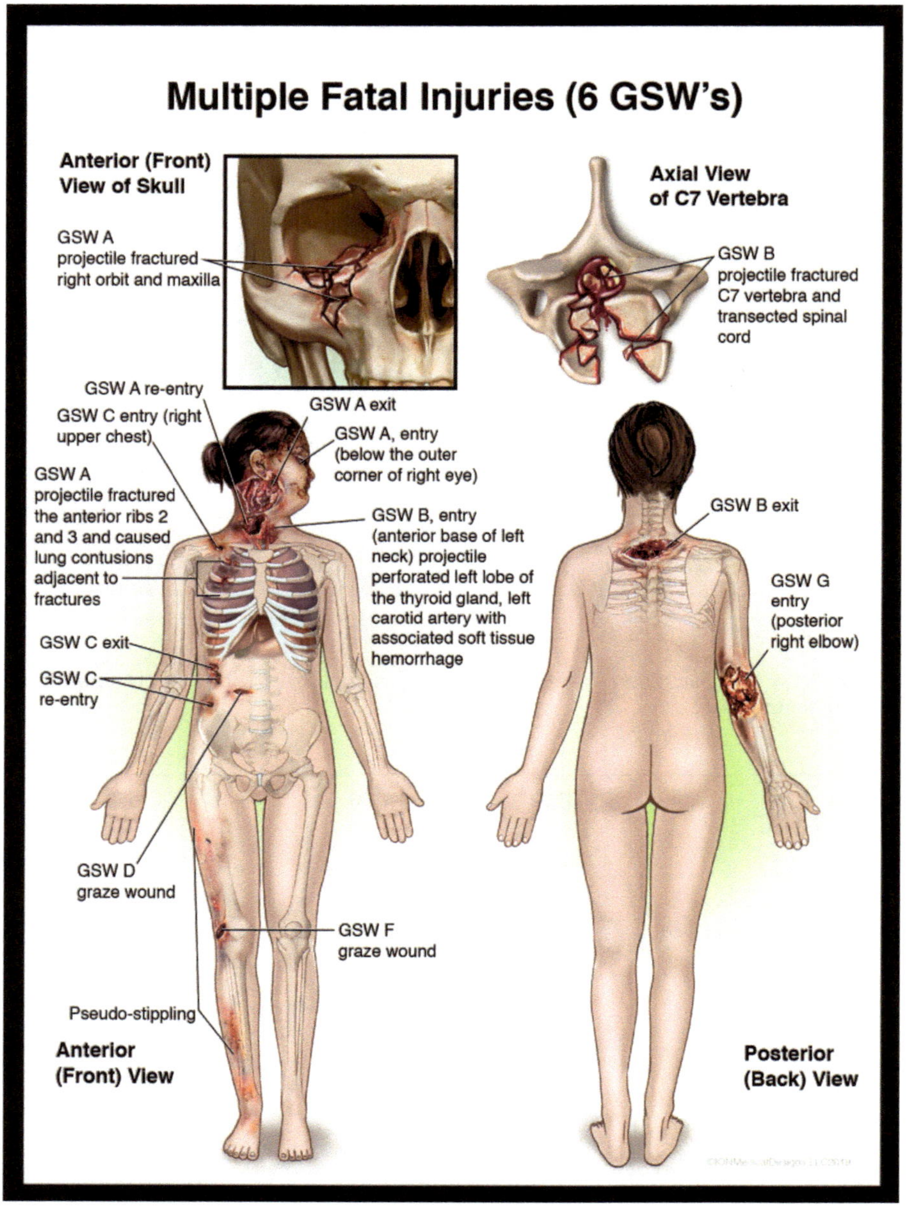

FIGURE 1.6 The illustration was one of many illustrations created for the prosecution to help represent victims in a mass shooting at a church in Sutherland Springs, Tx. They were created to help the doctors to explain the bullet trajectories to the judge at the bench trial they had for this case.

1.4 MEDICAL DEVICE

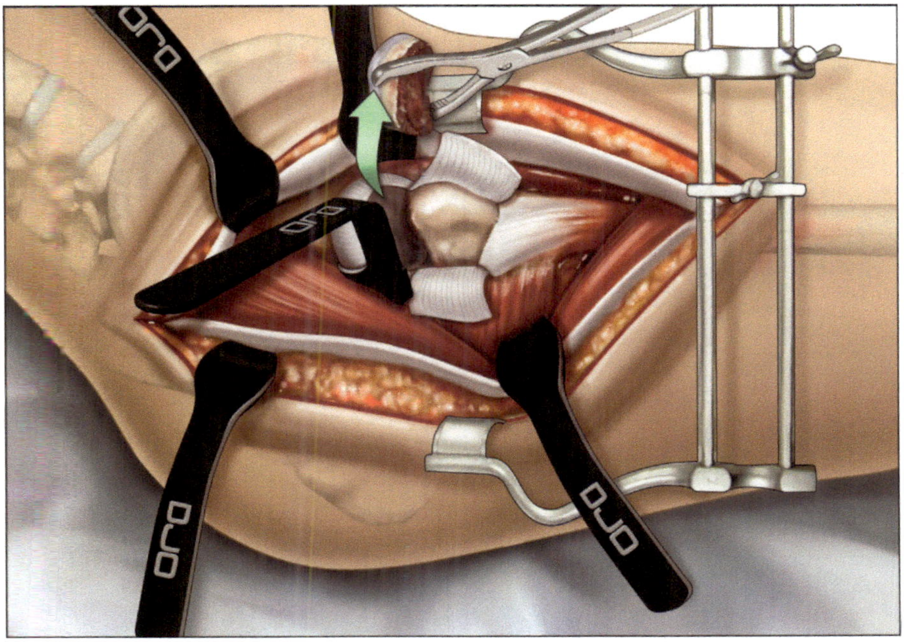

FIGURE 1.7 The illustration was created for DJO surgical. They are a medical device company, and the purpose of the illustration was to feature their new surgical retractors.

For the purposes of this book, we will be focusing on the specialty of medical art as it relates to legal and forensic demonstrative aids for court. Medical legal art is utilized to help attorneys, medical experts, and legal/forensic nurses visually depict injuries to help to inform juries and judges and prove causation and any rulings on damages. Medical illustrations can depict injuries, surgeries, anatomy, or anatomical landmarks.

Medicolegal cases can hinge on a variety of factors. Interpretation of radiological imaging, language utilized on the illustration board such as "hole vs tear," and medical case strategy are important for medicolegal cases. Attorneys have specific strategies for their cases, parts they want highlighted and parts they don't. There is extensive in-depth research on medical conditions or diseases that have multiple causes to create reasonable doubt and are backed up by medical publications and expert opinions. On the plaintiff personal injury and/or medical malpractice side, attorneys highlight extensive injuries and corrective surgeries to prove liability and damages for their clients.

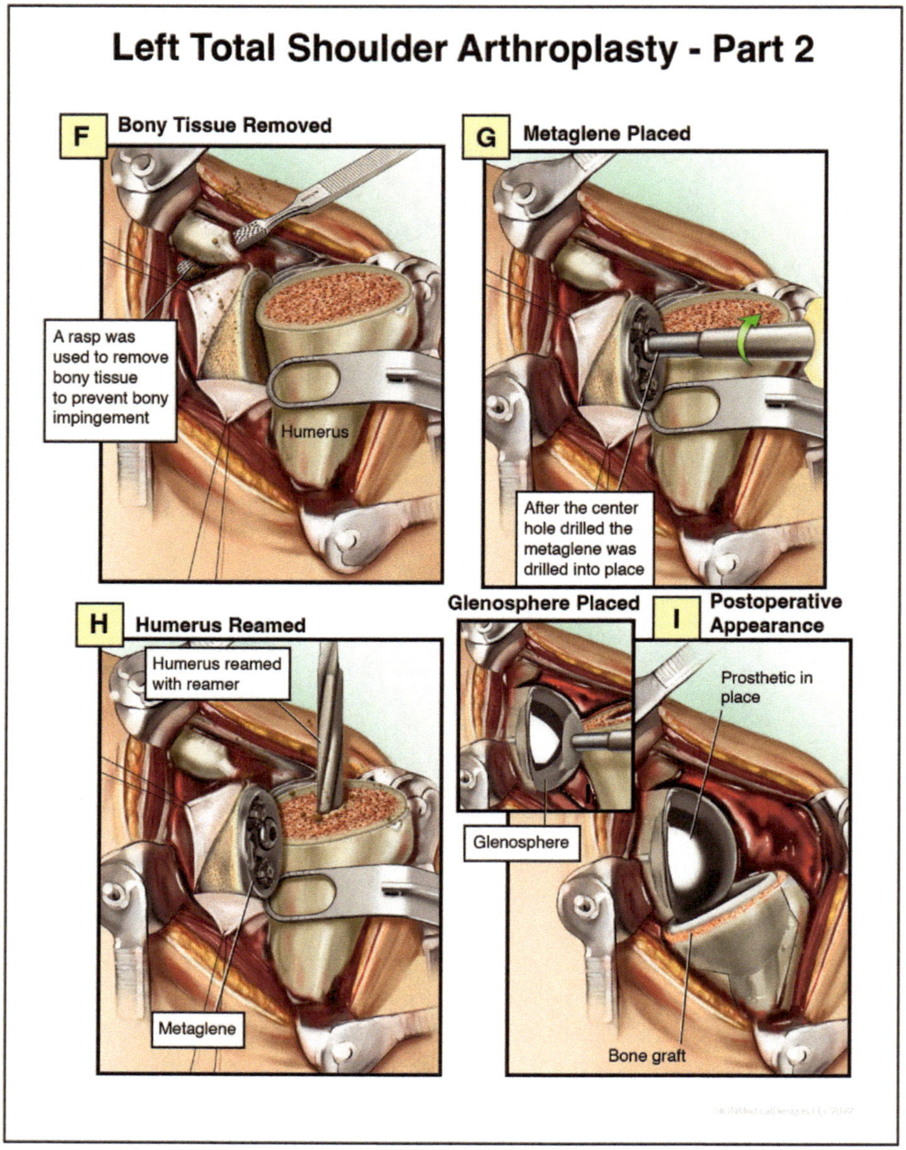

FIGURE 1.8 The illustration was created for the prosecution to depict a total reverse shoulder replacement. The purpose of the illustration was to help the expert witness doctor explain the surgery and for the jury to understand all the pain and suffering this plaintiff went through.

Personal injury and medical malpractice attorneys appreciate a case review from the medical artist, meaning a thorough review of medical records and medical imaging as well as a detailed outline/proposal of the injuries and/or surgeries sustained

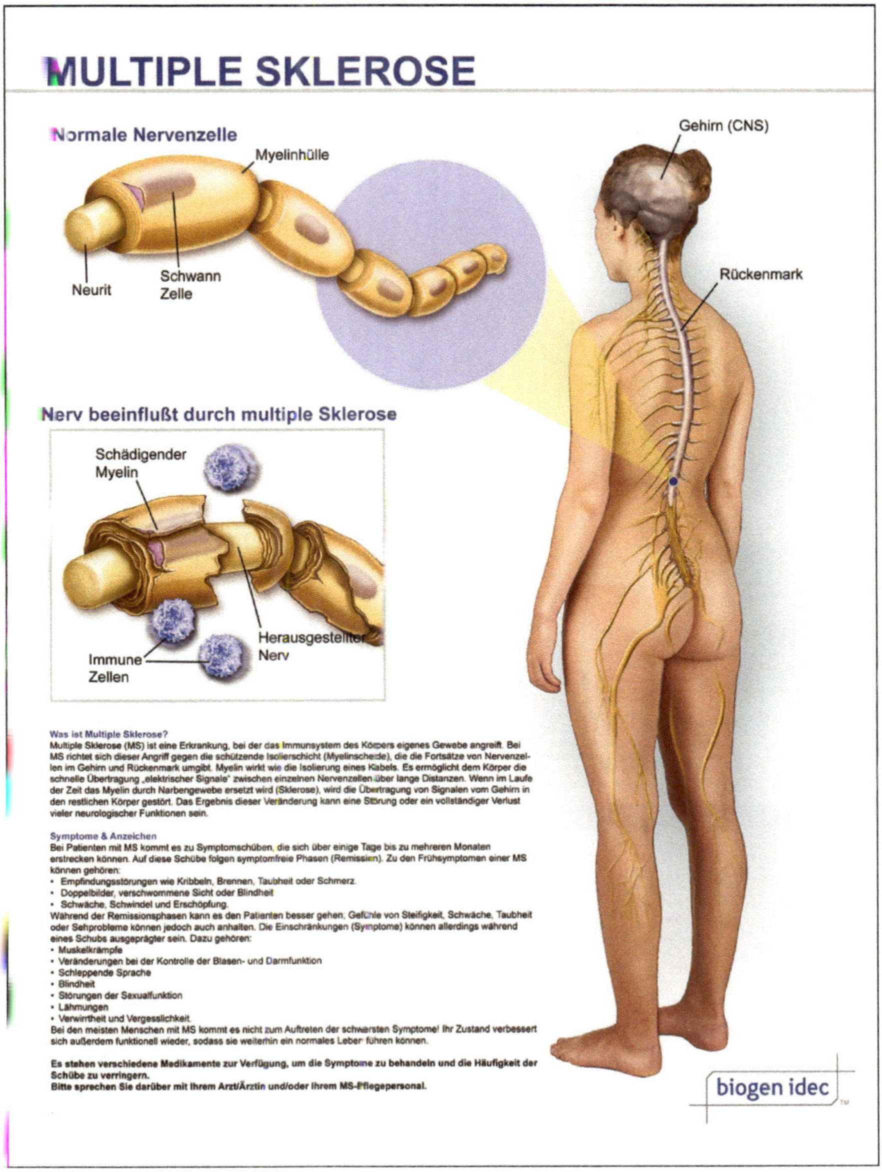

FIGURE 1.9 The illustration was created for Biogen to depict multiple sclerosis. It was translated into several different languages.

by the injured party. Proposals help describe how medical artwork will enhance their cases by bringing the records to life with imagery.

Plaintiff and defense attorneys are wildly different in strategy and approach, relying on expert professionals to help them present their case to a mostly medical lay audience.

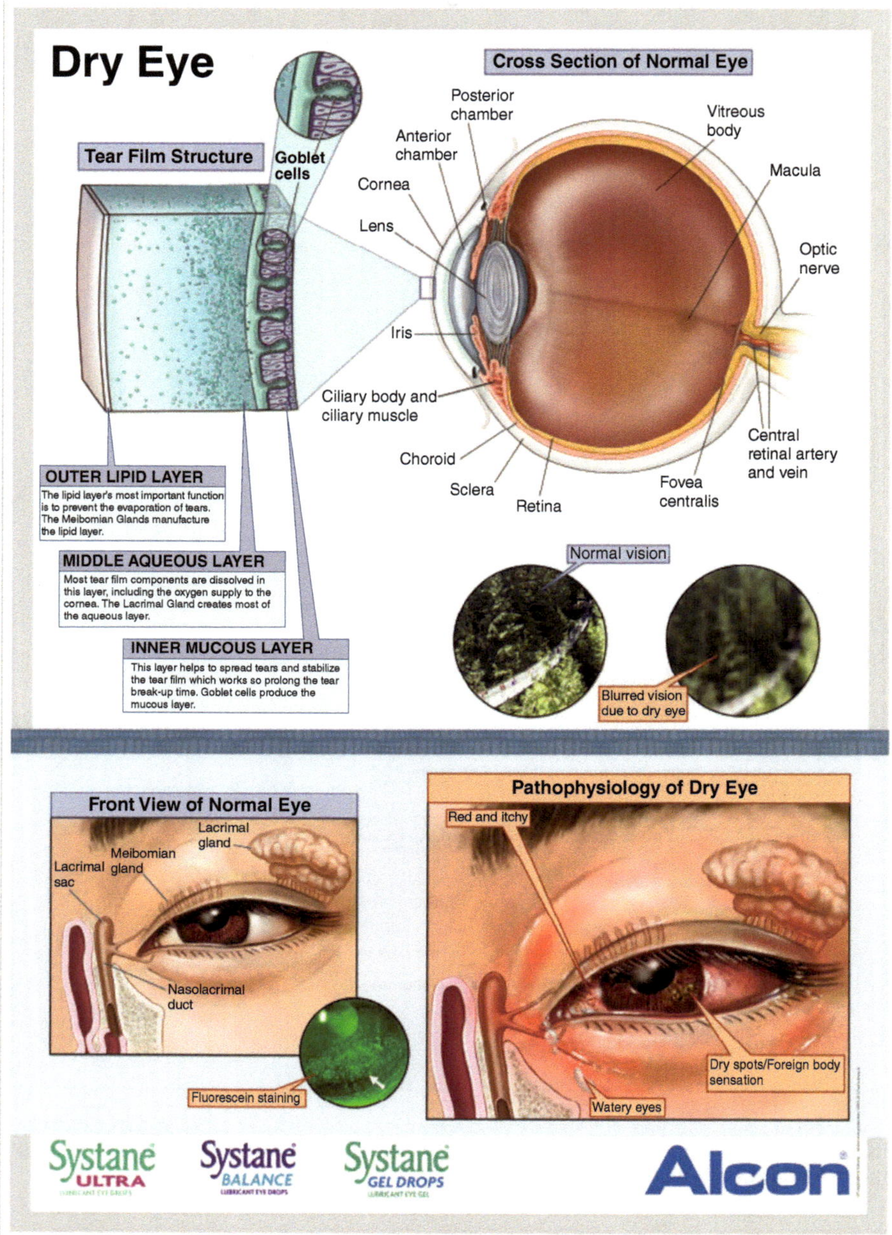

FIGURE 1.10 The illustration was created for Alcon and depicts a normal/healthy eye and then the pathophysiology of dry eye as well as their product Systane eye drops.

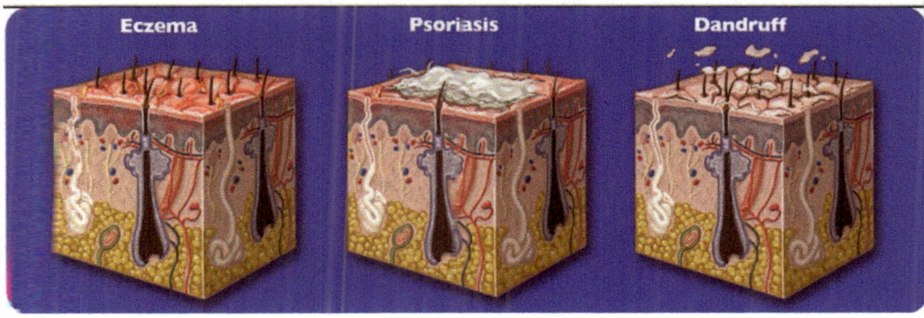

FIGURE 1.11A The illustration was created for Mediceuticals, depicting eczema, psoriasis, and dandruff. These skin conditions are a few of what their product helps to treat.

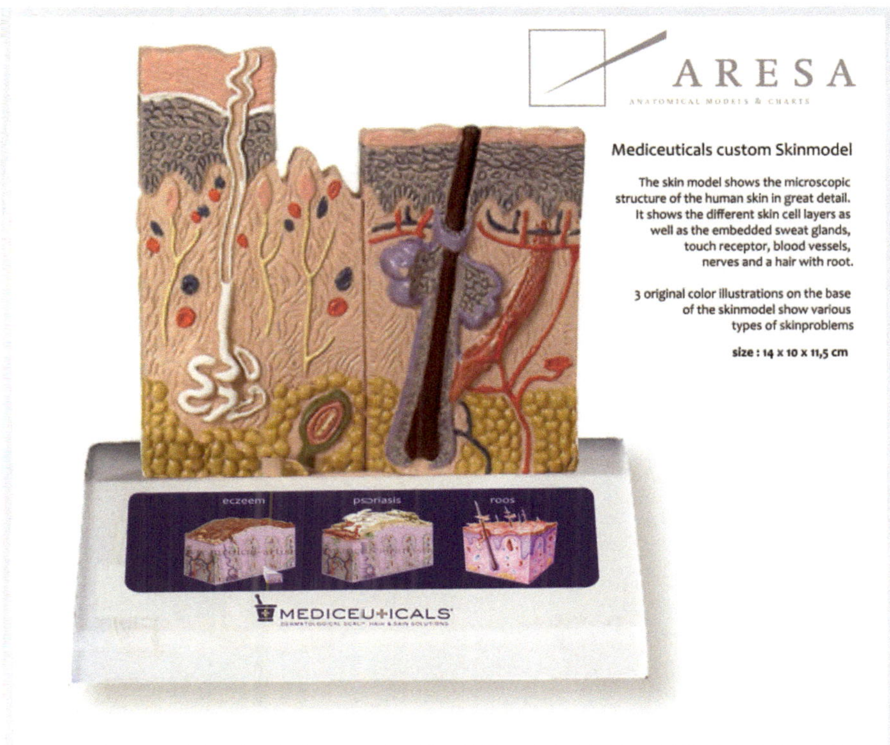

FIGURE 1.11B The illustration of the skin cube was converted into a plastic tangible model created for Mediceuticals, depicting eczema, psoriasis, and dandruff. These skin conditions are a few of what their product helps to treat.

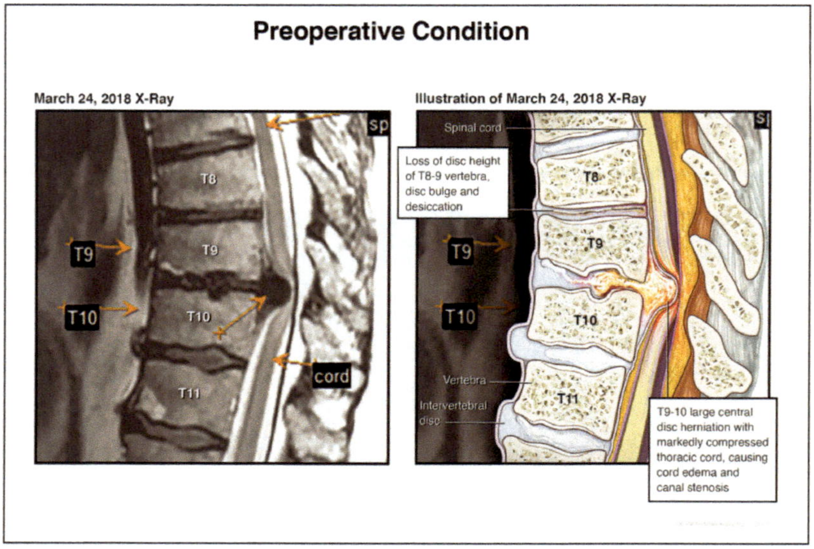

FIGURE 1.12 The illustration is an example of an x-ray colorization created for defense council to show how occluded the plaintiff's spine was preoperatively. It was one of several illustration boards. Defense attorneys will highlight the condition of plaintiff before an operation if the condition is emergent or typically hard to treat. As you can see in the colorization, this person's spinal cord is nearly occluded at the T9–10 level. He collapsed in the hospital, walking in for treatment.

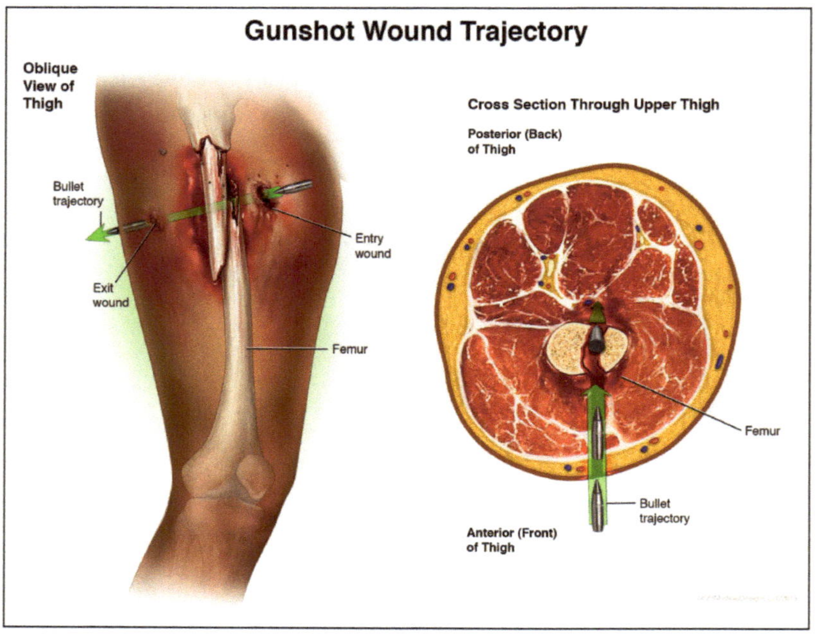

FIGURE 1.13 The previous illustration is an example of a gunshot wound and its trajectory. It depicts a femur fracture caused by the bullet, residual shrapnel, and soft tissue injuries sustained.

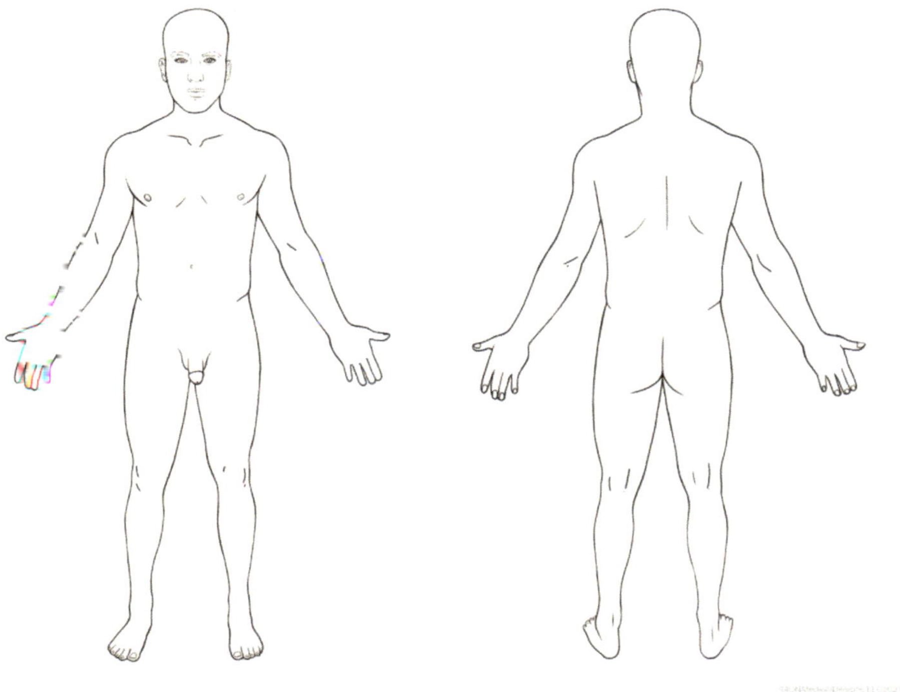

FIGURE 1.14 The illustration is one of a series of illustrations created for the Academy of Forensic Nurses. The illustration packages are being utilized as a standard way of marking injuries to help the prosecution in court.

Medical illustrators are often called upon, and enlisted, to support expert testimony in criminal and civil cases. Illustrations of gunshot wounds and trajectories are helpful to show the trajectory path and what organs the bullet traversed. They can be utilized to visually support explanations of pain and suffering, or cause of death. By example, images could illustrate whether a bullet has left shrapnel and, if so, how that affects the body. Forensic nurses frequently use anatomical charts to document instances of interpersonal and intimate violence.

1.5 WHAT DOES A MEDICAL ILLUSTRATOR DO?

A medical illustrator is a professional artist who typically has advanced education in both life sciences and visual communication. They regularly collaborate with scientists, physicians, nurses, and other specialists, pharmaceutical companies, publishing companies—or small studios specializing in several of these areas—with the aim of transforming complex medical information into visual images.

The field is constantly changing due to discoveries in science and technology, and there is frequently the need for continuing education in the industry.

The recent history of medical illustration began in large medical centers, aka hospitals, medical schools, and publishing companies, where there was need for publications, such as scientific journals and medical textbooks illustrated, as well as instructional videos and presentations.

Over the years the field became broader, and medical artists started working for medical device companies illustrating the latest medical devices. They can help create prosthetic limbs and eyes (orthotist and prosthetist).

Small studios of artists were formed to create pharmaceutical advertising and animation work or working in the legal field to create medical demonstrative aids.

A lot of medical artists are freelance, subcontracting for large and small companies alike, creating many forms of medical artwork.

There are forensic artists working on facial reconstructions both digital and physical. They can work in morgues, documenting faces and injuries, or in the field photographing evidence.

Advancements in computer graphics and technology, such as electron microscopes, allow medical professionals to visualize cellular processes. Computers and research papers written by scientists allow medical animators to depict subcellular processes. Medical illustrators have access to protein databases, allowing them to download scripts that can be turned into 3D models for visualization.

The scientific data acquired is then used to create artwork for journal covers, textbook illustrations, and molecular animations created by the medical animators.

Medical artists can produce a wide range of visual content—that serve a broad number of purposes—though a variety of media, that include the following:

- Presentations
- Magazines
- Advertising
- Film and television
- Web and interactive applications
- Mobile media
- Health games
- Tradeshows
- Museum exhibits
- Court room visual aids and graphics

- Medical simulation trainers
- Augmented and virtual reality applications

These days, 3D computer programs can be utilized to create 3D graphics for animations, illustrations, and interactive applications. Likewise, 3D printers can create a 3D printed physical model from a patient's CT scans. The 3D prints can be utilized in court as real evidence since they are created from a person's medical imaging. With such emerging technology, the use and application of such technology is expanding rapidly and virtually (literally.) limitless.

1.6 FIELDS OF STUDY

An aspiring medical illustrator must love the fields of art and science, specifically biological science. Coursework includes biology, anatomy, pathology, microanatomy, physiology, embryology, neuroanatomy, as well as fine art classes and surgical illustrations. Basic and advanced computer classes are also taught. The ideal approach to the career would be a bachelor's degree in fine arts combined with biological science (premed), followed by a master's degree in medical illustration. There are only a few universities in the United States that offer it. There are a few in other countries if you are up for an abroad experience.

After a few years practicing in the field, a board certification is recommended. The industry standard credential for medical illustration is a certified medical illustrator (CMI). The Board of Certified Medical Illustrators (BCMI) administers an exam including a science, art, and business practices section. Along with the written exam, a portfolio of professional artwork is required for review (*Learn About Medical Illustration*, n.d.).

1.7 A BRIEF HISTORY OF MEDICAL ILLUSTRATION

People have always been fascinated with human anatomy and physiology. For thousands of years artists have been depicting it with illustrations, paintings, and even intricate dissections. Think *Body Worlds* (a traveling exposition of dissected human bodies, animals, and other anatomical structures of the body that have been preserved through the process of plastination). Gunther von Hagen developed the preservation process, which unites subtle anatomy and modern polymer chemistry (late 1970s).

Hellenic Alexandria during the fourth century BC or early third century is where medical illustration instruction first appeared in documented historical writing. The illustrations were produced on papyrus, a paper that is still made today. Such Hellenic illustrations covered anatomy, surgery, obstetrics, and plants of medicinal value.

Medical illustration further progressed, and really took off, during the Renaissance. There were many innovations, with artists studying cadavers and performing detailed dissections.

In art in general during this time, dramatic figures posed against landscapes were more anatomically accurate and representative.

Leonardo da Vinci, an artist of the Renaissance and, for all intents and purposes, the first "medical illustrator," famously studied and documented (through both drawing and painting) the human figure, including dissections, with incredible skill and accuracy. Leonardo eventually pursued his own anatomy book with over 800 illustrations. His illustrations remained unpublished until the 1800s.

One of the major first published anatomy atlases are *De Humani Corporis Fabrica Libri Septem* by Andreas Vesalius (1514–1564). When *De Humani Corporis Fabrica Libri Septem* was first published, the ancient texts of Aristotle and Galen were still being taught in the European medical schools. As Vesalius studied and performed his own dissections, he noticed and noted errors in the ancient author's teachings. While Vesalius finding errors in the ancient texts initially caused problems for the medical schools, it ultimately won him respect and admiration. Integrated into the text are over 200 woodcuts created by a group of artists that may have included one Jan Steven van Calcar. Jan Steven van Calcar studied in a workshop under Titian. Not much else is known about the illustrators of the atlas other than the fact that they were most likely affiliated with Titian's circle. It may be the most well-known anatomy atlas in history, and it was influential to medical illustrators and their work for centuries.

In 1725, Berhard Siegfried Albinius and Jan Wandelaar spent 28 years producing two books, *Tables of the Skeleton and Muscles of the Human Body* and *Tables of the Human Bones*, with a focus on the musculoskeletal system. The engravings were full-length poses with lush backgrounds and were praised for their beauty and accuracy.

With advances and refinements in color printing techniques in the nineteenth century allowing, this allowed illustrators to work in a variety of media, making it easier to print and distribute anatomy atlases to the public.

A few examples of current anatomy atlases:

- Pernkopf Atlas, Eduard Pernkopf, 1933
- Atlas of Human Anatomy by Frank Netter, 1989
- Gray's Atlas of Anatomy (many editions)
- *Grant's Atlas of Anatomy* (many editions)

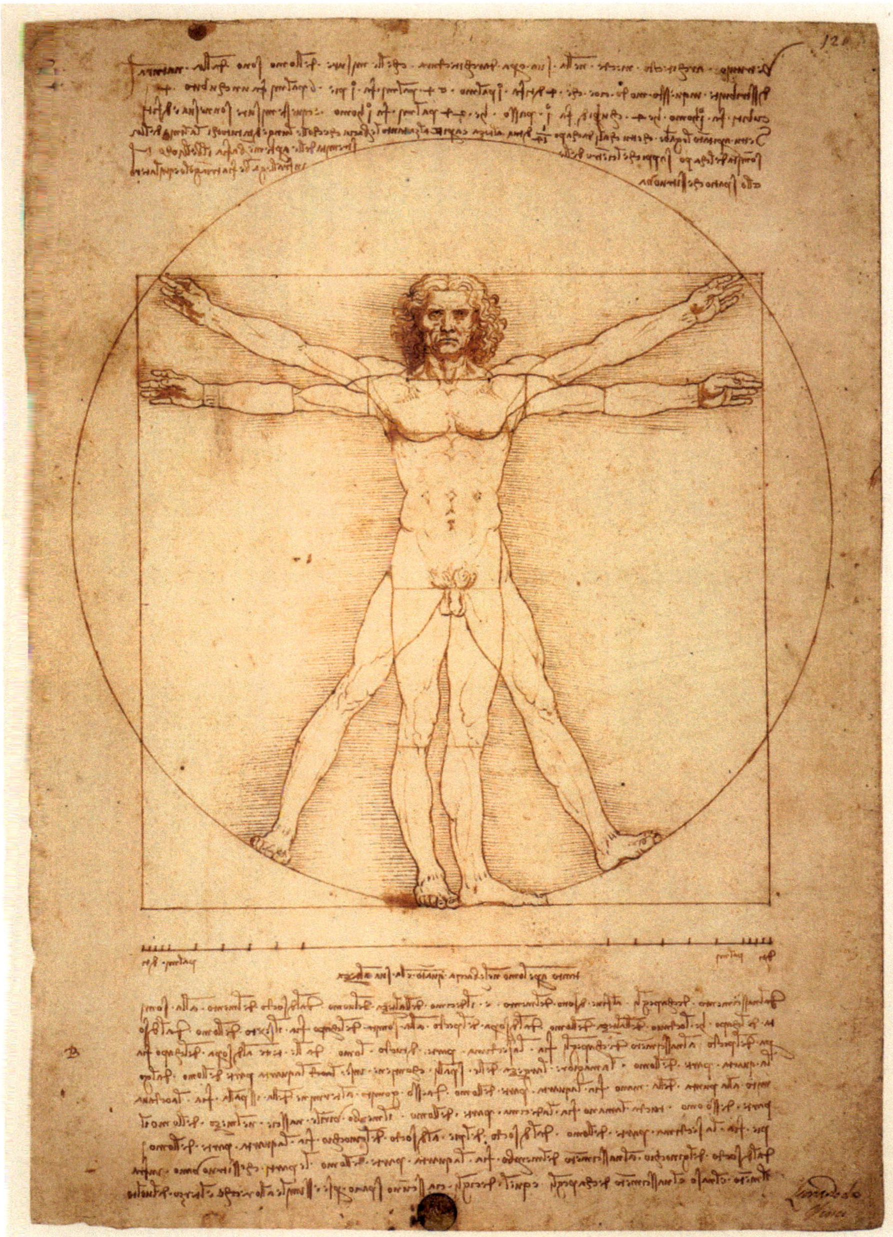

FIGURE 1.15 *Vitruvian Man* by Leonardo da Vinci is supposed to represent human proportion (*The Metropolitan Museum of Art*, n.d.).

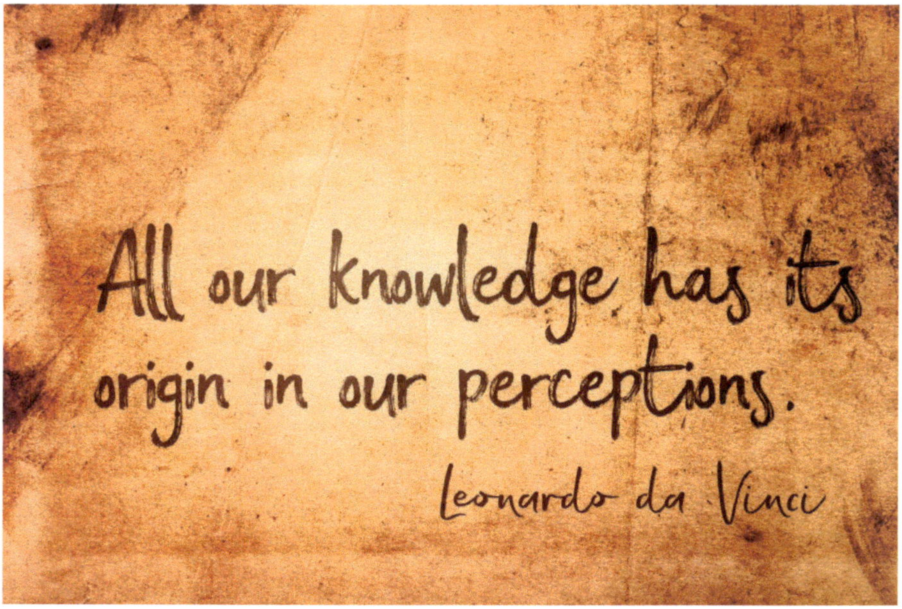

FIGURE 1.16 Leonardo DiVinci sketch (*Source: www.shutterstock.com*).

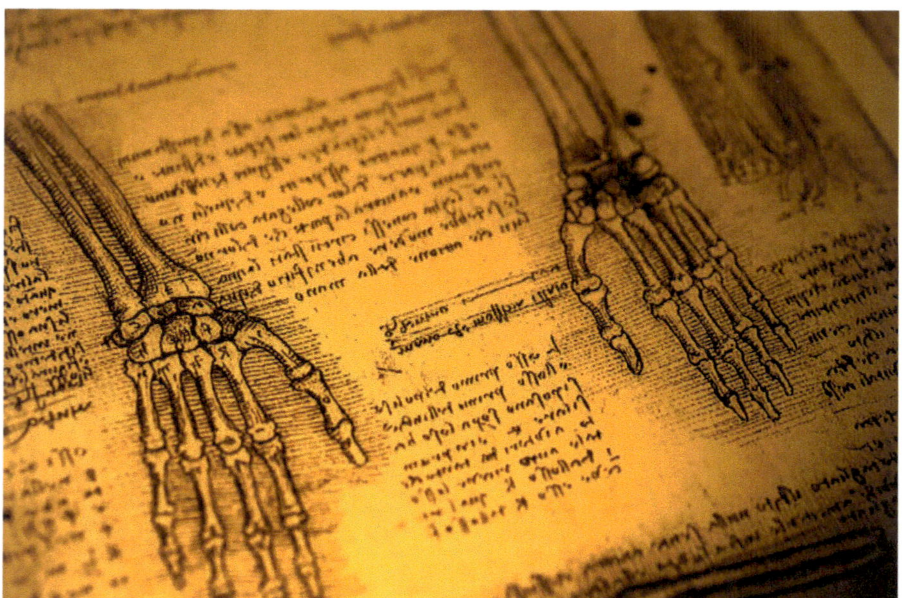

FIGURE 1.17 Leonardo da Vinci sketch (*The Metropolitan Museum of Art*, n.d.).

And, inevitably, the foundations of medical illustration emerged in the United States as well. Born in Germany, Max Brödel was a medical illustrator who had studied fine arts at the Leipzig Academy of Fine Arts. While working for Dr. Carl Ludwig, he gained basic knowledge of medicine and was recognized for his detailed medical illustrations.

In the 1880s, Brödel came to Baltimore Maryland to work for Harvey Cushing, William Halsted, Howard Kelly, and other physicians at Johns Hopkins School of Medicine. After working as a prolific medical illustrator, Brödel started the first department of art—as applied to medicine—at Johns Hopkins School of Medicine in an era before affordable immediate photography. Brödel's illustrations were in high demand among Johns Hopkins faculty for their anatomical correctness and exquisite realism. The department still thrives today! The program's graduates have spread across the world, having themselves formed several academic programs at other institutions.

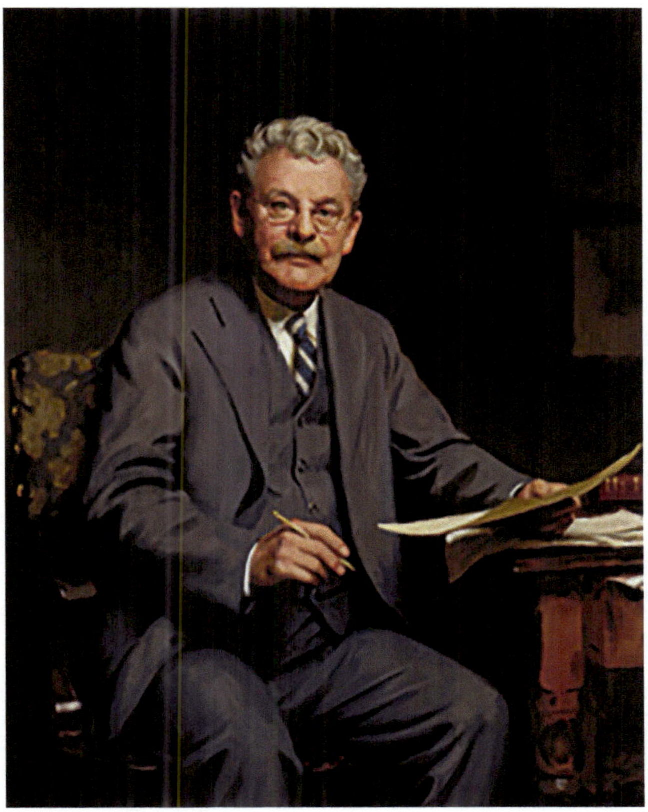

FIGURE 1.18 Portrait of Max Brödel—Thomas C. Corners 1938 painting (Brödel, n.d.).

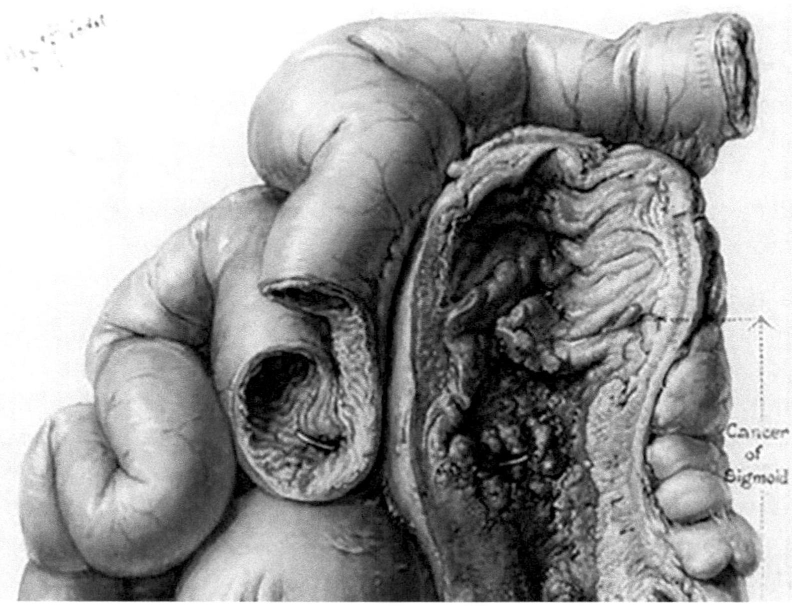

FIGURE 1.19 Johns Hopkins—illustrations by Max Brödel.

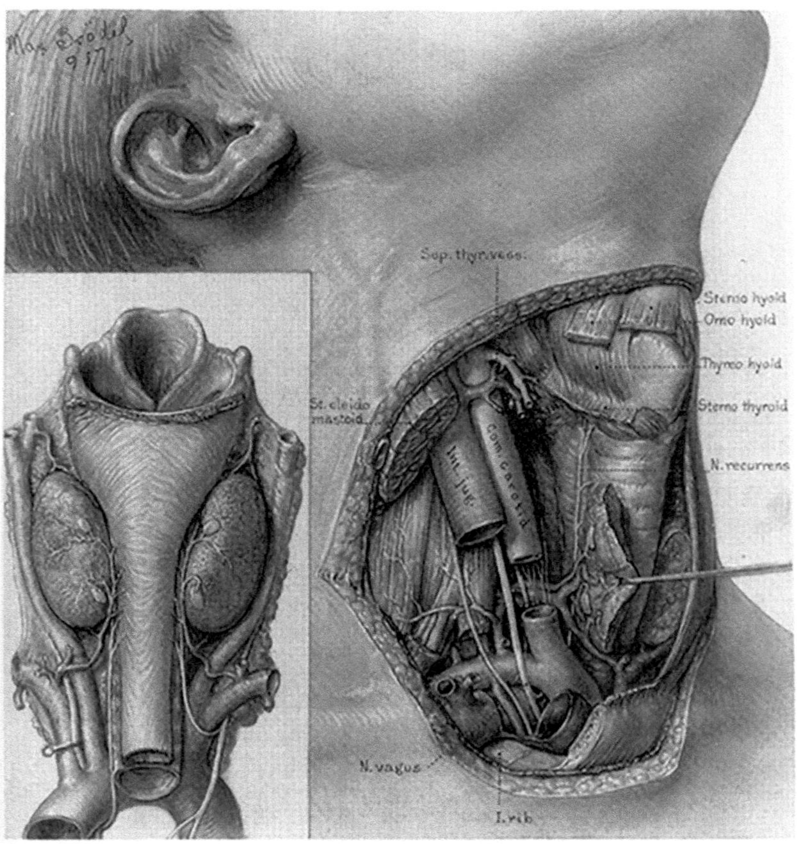

FIGURE: 1.20 Johns Hopkins—illustrations by Max Brödel—Anatomy of the Neck (Milesmartin, 2018).

CHAPTER 2

Medical Illustrations Enhance Trial Presentation

2.1 HOW TO TAKE COMPLEX MEDICAL INFORMATION AND PRESENT IT VISUALLY

When faced with a new case and a pile of medical records to read through, you may wonder how to present the case to a jury.

Academic research suggests that there are several types of learning styles that can help people to retain information presented to them:

- Visual
- Auditory
- Reading and writing
- Kinesthetic

There are general characterizations that can be ascribed to each of these various learning styles.

Visual learners retain information best when it is presented to them with pictures, illustrations, animations, charts, graphs, and diagrams. Visual learners thrive with clear images of the information presented.

Auditory learners prefer to have information presented to them vocally. They work well in group settings and may prefer to read to themselves aloud.

DOI: 10.4324/9781003336310-2

Reading and writing learners thrive when given written information such as worksheets, written presentations, and text-heavy resources. They are generally note-takers and often learn best when they can reference written text.

Kinesthetic learners are physical role-takers that are hands-on and engage their senses while learning. They typically do well in science and scientific fields where lab work is a component.

While people typically learn through some combination of all of these styles, oftentimes one learning method is usually dominant over others (Petoi, n.d.).

Presentations with medical graphics, animations, and interactive applications incorporated into them cover the four learning styles. In today's world, visuals are key in presenting evidence for those with short attention spans, especially the "tech generation" where everything is available within minutes and shows like *CSI* exist.

When presenting medical concepts to laypeople and those with no training, medical graphics can be very beneficial to the jury, and by bringing details and case specifics to light with art. Especially regarding injury summary illustration boards or surgical illustrations, such graphics help the jury to relate to the trauma that a person may have undergone.

For the medical artist, reviewing pertinent medical records, imaging, and radiology reports is the first step in the creative process. Once the case is thoroughly reviewed, a case-specific proposal is written. The proposals should be extremely detailed to list all the relevant information.

The optimal presentation method mostly depends on the type of injury, cause of injury, surgery, and/or budget set. It also depends on the client's comfort level with technology, or lack thereof. There are many types of presentation methods including the following:

- Colorized radiology—Illustrated radiology clarifies previously black and white radiographs so that anatomy and injured anatomy can be clearly delineated and understood. (Figures: 2.1, 2.2, 2.5, 2.7, 2.8.)
- Traditional illustration boards (print)—Large 36″x48″ prints of illustrations exhibit for trial. (All example figures can be printed.)
- Digital illustration—Digital files that would be inserted into your trial presentation software, for example, Trial Director, Exhibit View, PowerPoint, etc. (All example figures can be digital.)
- Interactive digital applications—PC, Mac (executable), iPad, and android applications. (Figures: 2.3, 2.9.)
- 2D and 3D animations—Presentations where motion graphics are helpful to outline surgeries with many steps and/or scientific theories, or to otherwise educate the jury on a particular subject. (Figures: 2.11, 2.12.)

- Timelines (static or interactive)—An interactive timeline can organize important dates and visually highlight medical records. Medical records can be blown up, as well as additional illustration work added. (Figures: 2.15, 2.16, 2.17.)
- 3D printing—Helpful in depicting fractures, vessels, hardware, or anything that would be visualized in 3D as a tangible model. 3D prints from CT scans are considered real evidence and can be submitted as so. Real evidence, meaning these 3D models are based on the patient's actual CT or MRI scans. They would be an exact replica of their anatomy, whereas an illustration is a demonstrative aid. Real evidence, meaning (material, physical) evidence. Something that can be touched and brought back to the war room for the jurors. It must be relevant, fair, and accurate, and jurors may touch and inspect them in deliberation (Figure: 2.19)!

2.2 COLORIZED RADIOLOGY—TYPES AND VISUAL SOLUTIONS

Client-specific illustration can be produced and utilized on a case-by-case basis using client-specific medical records, radiology, and photos. Having experts use general and/or typical healthy anatomy to explain how injuries occurred can be confusing to the audience, especially when cases relate to unique and/or specific medicine and injuries.

To follow in Figure 2.1 is an example of a presentation utilizing colorizing/illustrated over radiology (medical imaging) to enhance the illustrative and explanatory aspects of the radiograph.

MRI and CT scans are taken from feet to head, so the patient's right is the left side of the image and vice versa—the left is the right side. In other words, images would present backward to the viewer. Drawing over radiology can highlight the anatomy and injuries to clarify the scans. The scans can be reproduced adjacent to the image for reference. X-rays are typically used to visualize bone to find and diagnose fractures. These sample colorizations would be made two-dimensionally as illustration boards.

CT and MRI scans can be colorized and placed in a three-dimensional model head, as shown in Figure 2.3. When placed in a 3D space, the scans are then read correctly (left is left, right is right). This modality is especially helpful in situations where a person has multiple anatomical levels of brain hemorrhages, damage, or skull fractures.

Medical imaging software programs such as Osirix, InVesalius, and others can utilize sets of scans and recreate raw data 3D models of patient's scans. This data can be used as reference for a 2D illustration or to create 3D models (Figure 2.4).

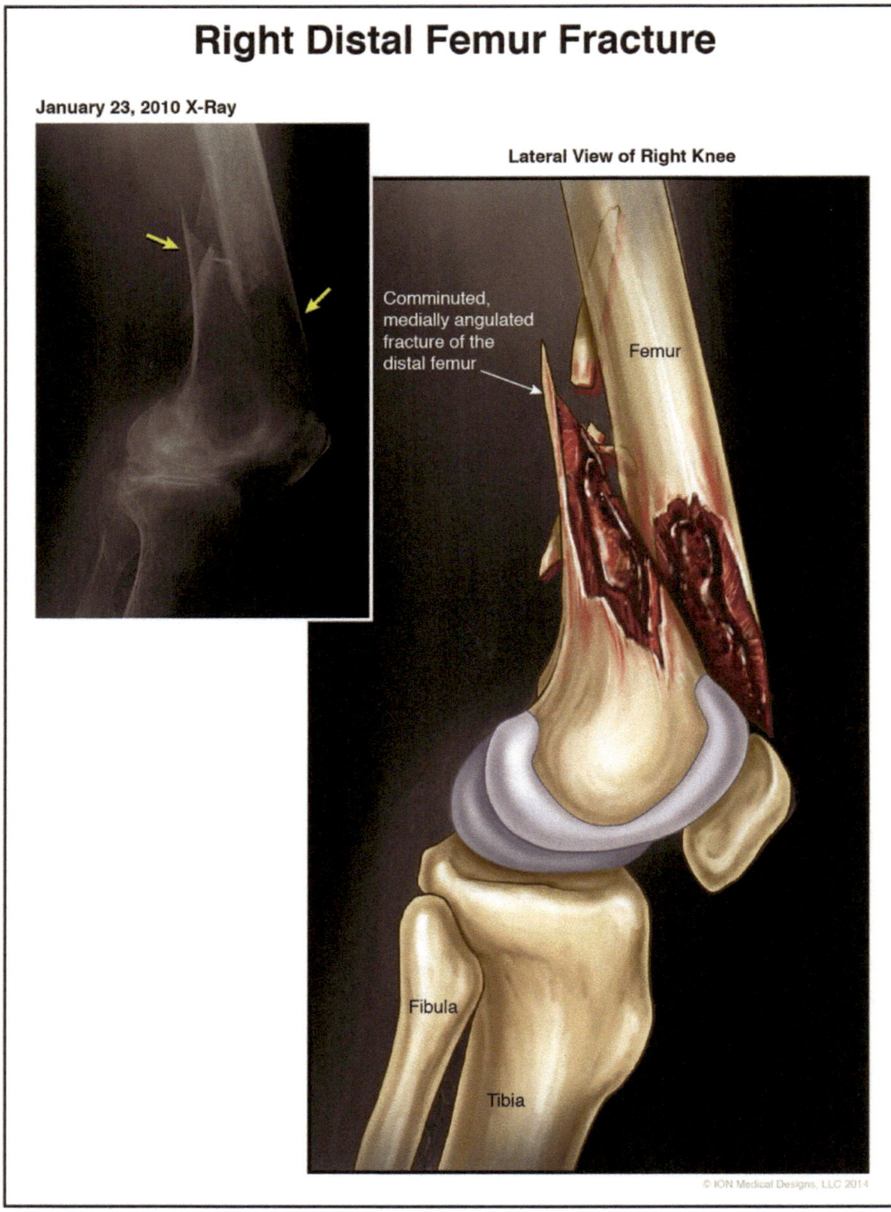

FIGURE 2.1 The illustration is an example of a colorized x-ray depicting a femoral shaft fracture.

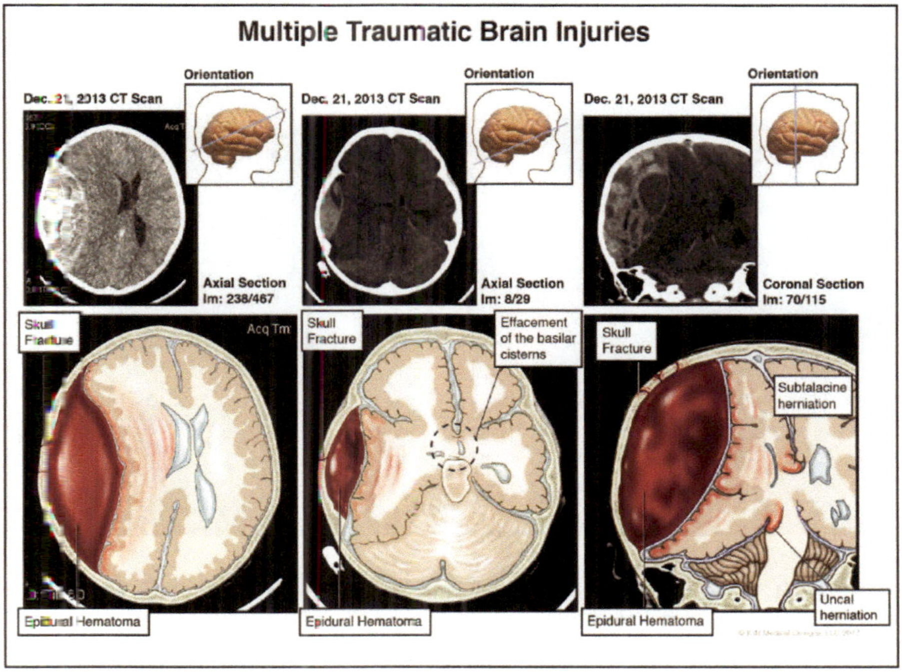

FIGURE 2.2 The illustration is an example of a colorized MRI depicting brain hemorrhages a child sustained from a slip and fall on slippery tiles at a hotel pool deck.

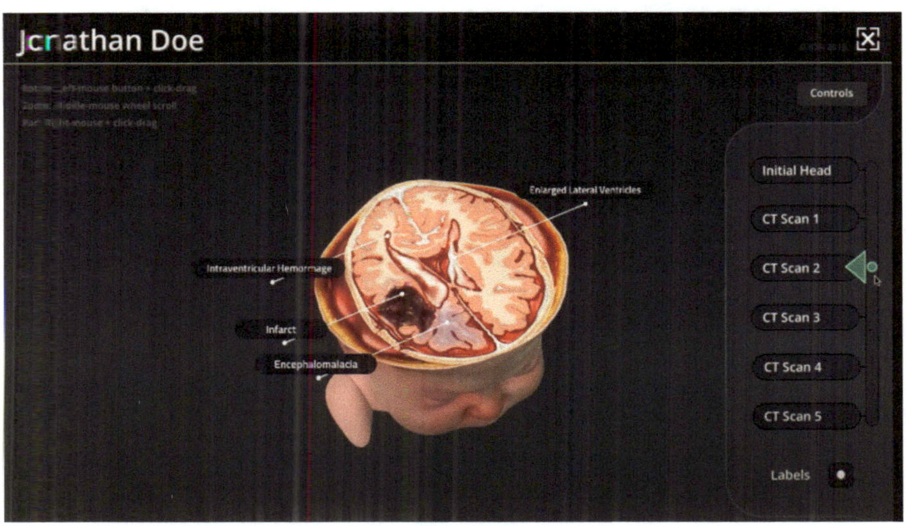

FIGURE 2.3 This is a screenshot of a 3D interactive project depicting skull fractures and brain hemorrhages from a forceps delivery.

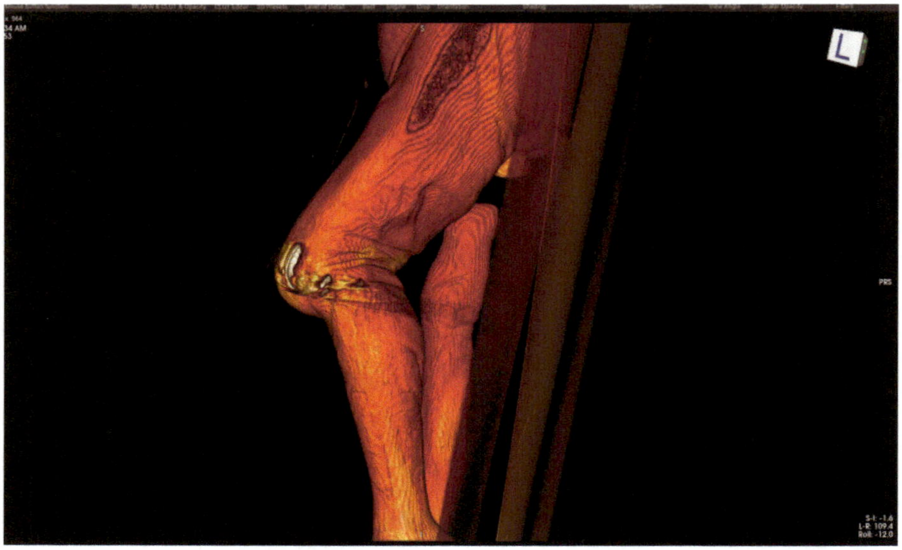

FIGURE 2.4 This is a screenshot of a volumetric rendering created in Osirix from CT scans of a nursing home fall case.

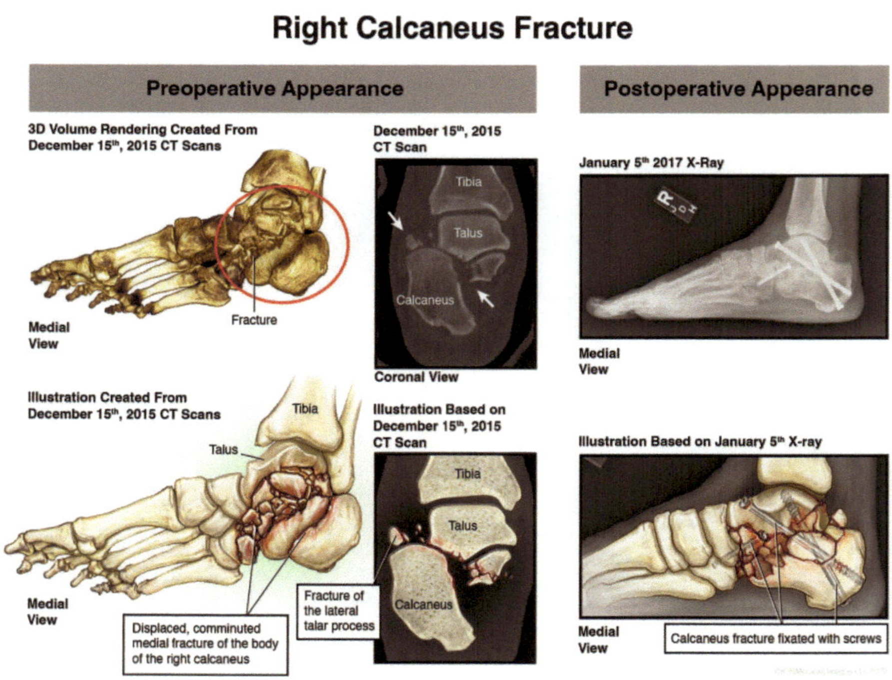

FIGURE 2.5 This is an illustration created from CT scans and x-rays and is a great example of a colorization. You can see how the illustration brings the radiology to life.

An MRI (magnetic resonance imaging) is a medical imaging technique that uses a magnetic field and computer-generated radio waves to create detailed images of the organs and tissues of your body (soft tissue).

Let's discuss the types of medical imaging technology used to study the human body. Such information should provide a better understanding of what types of medical imaging are used diagnostically and what type of medical art may be best suited in each case.

An MRI machine is a large tube-shaped magnet. When lying in an MRI machine, the magnetic field temporarily realigns water molecules in your body. The radio waves cause the aligned atoms to produce faint signals that are used to create MRI slices. MRI machines can also produce 3D images that can be viewed from different angles.

MRIs are a noninvasive way used to view organs, tissues, and the skeletal system. The images are high resolution and help to diagnose a variety of medical conditions.

MRIs are most frequently used to test the brain and spinal cord. They are often performed to diagnose the following conditions:

- Aneurysms of cerebral vessels—angiograms work well for this too
- Eye and inner ear disorders
- Multiple sclerosis
- Spinal cord disorders
- Stroke
- Tumors
- Brain injury from trauma

A functional MRI (fMRI) is a special type of MRI that produces images of blood flow in certain areas of the brain. It examines how the brain handles critical functions.

As an example, the fMRI helps to identify language and motor control areas of the brain in people who are being considered for brain surgery. fRMI scan also be used to detect damage from head injuries or disorders such as Alzheimer's disease.

MRIs of the heart and blood vessels are used to assess the size and function of the heart's chambers, thickness, movement, and extent of damage from heart attack or heart disease. They also assess structural problems of the aorta, aneurysms, dissections, inflammation, and arterial blockages.

MRIs can be used to detect tumors and other abnormalities of organs, bones, and joints. MRIs of the breast can be used with mammography to detect breast cancer in women with dense tissue who may be at higher risk.

For illustrative purposes, MRIs are great for visualizing soft tissue injuries—for example, rotator cuff tears, brain hemorrhages, and intervertebral disc herniations.

A computerized tomography (CT) scan combines a series of x-rays taken from different angles, around the full circumference of the body. Computer processing technology is used to combine such images to create cross-sectional images (slices) of the bones, blood flow, and soft tissues inside the body. This scan can provide much more detail than an x-ray.

While there are many uses for CT scans, they are typically used for quick examinations for people who were in car accidents or who have otherwise suffered trauma. However, a CT scan can be utilized to visualize nearly *all* parts of the body and is used to diagnose disease or injury as well as to plan medical, surgical, or radiation treatment.

CT scans may be recommended for the following:

- Diagnosing muscle and bone disorders, tumors, and fractures
- Pinpointing location of tumor, infection, or blood clot
- Guiding procedures—surgery, biopsy, and radiation therapy
- Detecting and monitoring diseases and conditions such as cancer, heart disease, liver nodules, and cancer
- Monitoring treatments
- Detecting internal injuries and internal bleeding

For illustrative purposes, CT scans would be a helpful reference for injury summary boards, tumors, and fractures (since volume renderings can be generated from these) (*Top-ranked Hospital in the Nation—Mayo Clinic*, n.d.).

The invention of x-rays

Wihelm Conrad Rontgen (Figure: 2.6) was an eighteenth-century physicist who received the first Nobel Prize for Physics, in 1901, for his discovery of x-ray. Such discovery revolutionized diagnostic medicine and is widely used today.

Portrait of Wilhelm Röntgen

Wihelm Rontgen's research included elasticity, conduction of heat in crystals, capillary action of fluids and absorption of heat by gases, and piezoelectricity.

On November 8, 1895, while experimenting with electric current flow in a partially evacuated glass tube (cathode-ray tube), Röntgen noticed that a screen of barium platinocyanide located far from the tube gave off light while in operation. His theory was that when the cathode (electrons) struck the glass wall of the tube, an unknown radiation was formed as it traveled across the room, struck the chemical, and caused the fluorescence. Upon further experimentation, Röntgen discovered

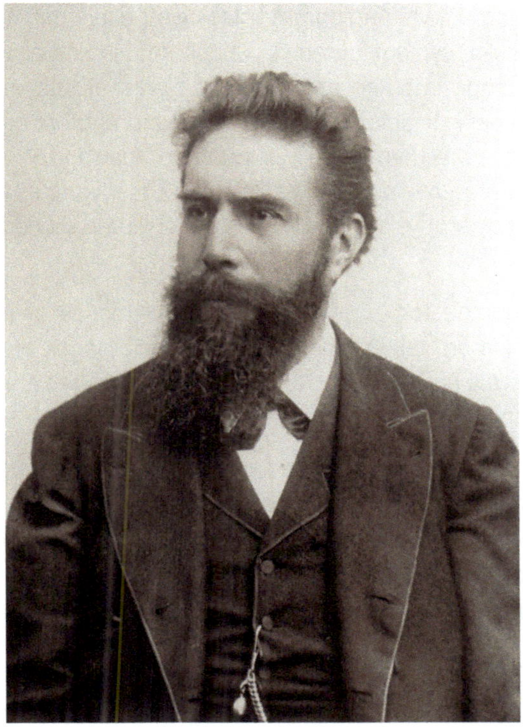

FIGURE 2.6 Wilhelm Röntgen, pictured here in 1900.

that paper, wood, and aluminum was transparent to this new form of radiation. It did affect photographic plates and didn't noticeably exhibit properties of light, such as reflection or refraction. He thought the rays weren't related to light. That was an inaccuracy in his research. Because of the radiation's uncertainty, he named it x-radiation. Among his first x-ray were photographs of the interiors of metal objects and bones of his wife's hand.

X-rays quickly were used in medicine; the first use was for diagnosing cancer just weeks after Röntgen's discovery in 1896.

X-rays are utilized for medical purposes. Following are the types of radiology used in the twentieth century:

- Projectional radiographs—This is the traditional form of radiology where an image is formed when diagnostic-range x-ray energy interacts with an electron cloud of human tissue (bone, soft tissue, air). It is great for visualizing bones, specifically fractures and skeletal system pathologies. Gas trapped in the lungs can be visualized, and soft tissue pathologies such as bowel obstructions and kidneys stones (calcified and hard). Calcifications and/or hard tissue shows up in white, and air in black.

- Angiography—Angiogram imaging is used to visualize the cardiovascular system (arteries, veins). An angiogram is created when an image is taken of the specific area of interest. Iodine contrast material is injected into the patient and another image is taken. The images are then digitally subtracted, leaving the iodinated contrast outline of the vessels. The radiology images are then compared and read by a physician (radiologist) to evaluate damage or blockages to the vessel.
- Computed tomography (CT scan)—A series of multidirectional 2D images are taken. The cross-sectional images are then placed into software and visualized in 3D. These CT images are used for diagnostic and therapeutic purposes.
- Fluoroscopy—An imaging technique used to capture radiology images in real time. Modern fluoroscopy uses a computer monitor and x-ray image intensifier to transfer the imaging to a CCD video camera to record and play the images in real time on the monitor. Cardiac catheterization and coronary artery blockages are a few procedures where fluoroscopy would be utilized.

For illustrative purposes, x-rays can be used for comparing pre- and post-operative imaging (popular and to the point), detecting pneumonia or pneumoperitoneum, abdominal obstructions, post-accident emergency imaging (injury summary), vascular blockages, aneurysms, and stents.

In short, there are a lot of great medical demonstratives that can be created from medical imaging. Hopefully, from reading these previous sections, there is a better understanding of the different types of medical imaging options and what images to request when assessing your case.

2.3 PRESENTATION METHOD—HOW IS IT PROPOSED?

There are many considerations to think about before choosing what type of presentation method to move forward with. The following tips would be helpful to know as the presenter (attorney) or the creator (artist). Professional designers will tell you to consider time, money, and quality. If something is needed quickly, a 3D animation is out of the question, unless there is a stock animation to buy that already exists. 3D animations are generally not easy on the wallet either.

If time and money are tight, a proposal for a traditional digital illustration or a stock image would be recommended. This recommendation would also work for those who might not be comfortable with technology. Illustration boards can be printed large 36″x48″ as well as in 8″x10″ format, with the smaller versions handed to the jurors and the large prints left up in the courtroom.

Attorneys, if there is sufficient time and motion graphics would work well for the case, ask for 3D animation. 3D animation is at the top price point.

To obtain a professional quote from a medical design company and/or medical artist provide the following:

- All relevant medical records—surgical reports, radiology reports, medical summaries, and emergency room reports
- Medical imaging—x-rays, MRIs, CT scans, and angiograms
- Relevant photography—scene, autopsy, or close-up of face for injury boards
- Relevant depositions—expert testimonies, expert theories
- Expert reports—life care plans

After providing this information, a medical artist will provide a thorough case evaluation. From there, a detailed proposal would be provided to the lawyer, describing how to best present their case visually. The proposal would include a description of the person's injuries, surgeries, or mechanism of injury (liability and damages) based on the legal strategy and how it would be illustrated, animated, or created into an interactive presentation, and associated costs would be provided. The proposal should then be reviewed and discussed by both parties (attorney and medical/forensic artist) before moving forward.

When the proposal is agreed upon, drafts of the demonstrative aids are created by the artist and sent to the attorney for approval.

If animations are requested by an attorney, make sure there is the appropriate amount of time for storyboards. Timing is everything with animations! Storyboards are still sketches provided by the medical artist, but they are multiple ones laid out that show how the sequence of events will play out visually—the views, zooming effects, etc. Review the storyboards thoroughly and make revisions before the process to animation begins.

If an interactive application is created, a link would be provided to the attorney, and it could be exchanged and shared with opposing council and similarly disclosed to experts (medical doctors).

Traditional digital illustration can be emailed, exchanged in person, or disclosed. Encourage comments from the medical expert(s) at the draft stage of this process. Most medical artists will work directly with the medical doctors for revisions. It helps to do this to eliminate third-party confusion.

After the drafts are reviewed, changes can be made to the artwork. Again, with animations, look closely; changes take time to revise with animation. For a quality animation, allow at least one month, preferably two, for animation and interactive work to be created. There is a lot of computer programming involved in higher-technology presentations.

For higher-technology presentation attorneys, you may want to allow yourself time to practice with the animation or interactive presentation in the courtroom. Make sure to have all the requisite hardware to run your presentation in the courtroom.

Having illustration prints to hand out to the jury is a nice supplement to an interactive presentation or animation.

For illustration work, allow at least five business days. Most professionals will charge rush fees if the artist is given less time than that to create illustrations.

Illustration boards can be printed large (36″ x 48″) to present with in the courtroom. Allow at least three days for the printing process and delivery of large illustration boards. It is a good idea to have the printer test print a small version or part of an illustration for you to view before the final is printed. That way there is time to view the illustration proofs (drafts) for color corrections and mistakes, should there be any. Most professional medical artists will either set up the files for printing or have in-house printers.

2.4 HOW TO DECIDE WHAT PRESENTATION FORMAT BEST FITS YOUR CASE

Deciding what presentation format to use depends on time, budget, and comfort level with the computer software/hardware and technology. There are trial presentation companies that will help run presentation software within the courtroom. There are medical art companies that create applications that are very user-friendly too. Meaning you run it yourself. Think about how to engage the courtroom with the presentation. Attorneys are professional presenters by nature, and, as such, they should make sure they have a well-thought-out and cohesive presentation. Using illustration, videos, and similar supplemental displays to convey concepts should be no different.

For cases with a lower budget, try x-ray colorizations. Pre-operative and post-operative appearances presented side by side, as shown in Figures 2.5 and 2.18, are impactful. MRIs and CT scans (Figure 2.2) can also be drawn over for a much clearer presentation to a jury, especially when guided by a medical expert.

For middle-of-the-road budgets, use illustration boards, interactive applications, or a combination of the two. Combining illustrations into an interactive application is a very effective and easy way to present concepts. Stills (single illustrations) can be provided and presented—with the interactive application as well as printed—and left up to reference (Figures: 2.13, 2.14, 2.15, 2.16). Timelines, static or interactive, fit into this category too.

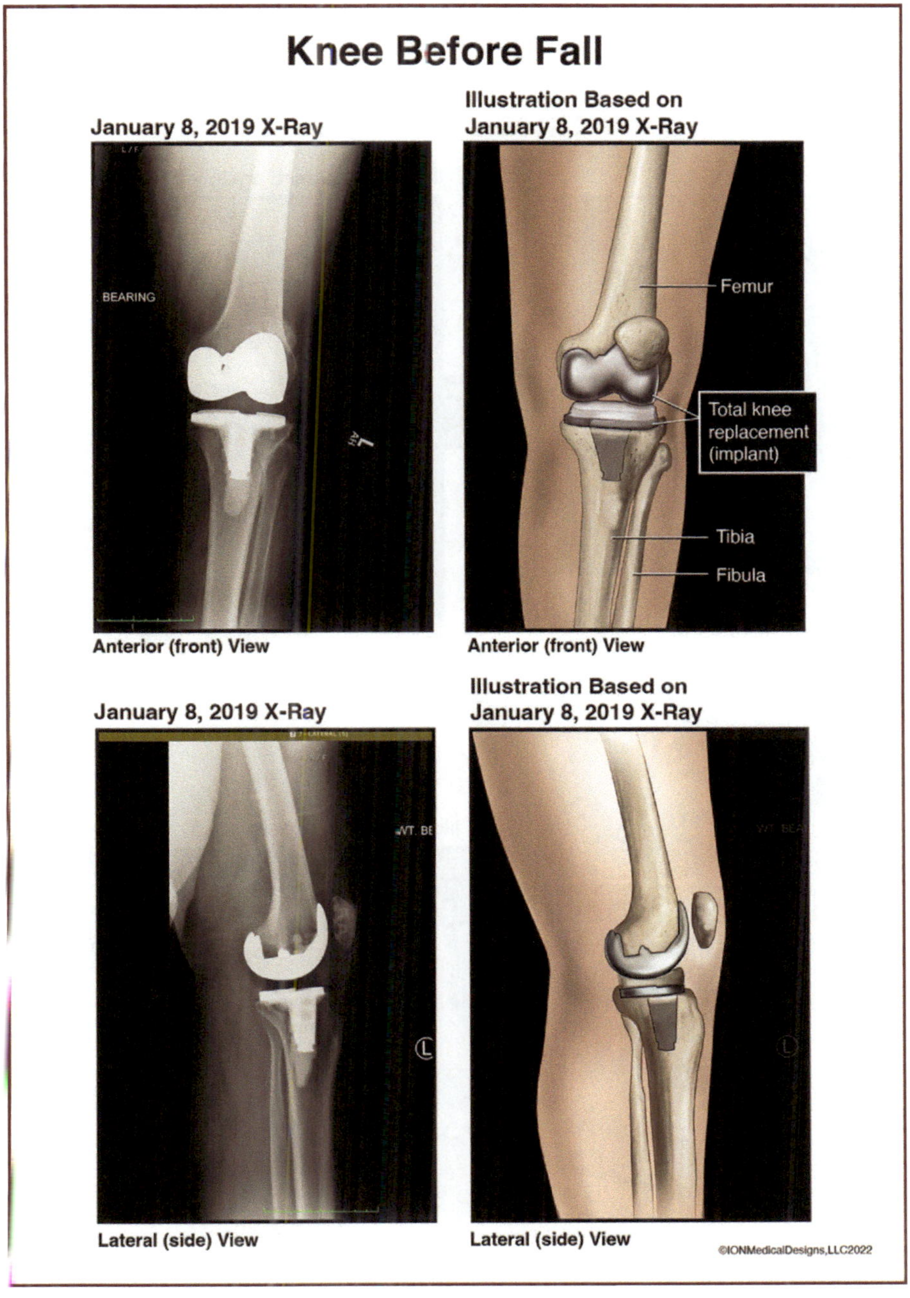

FIGURE 2.7 The illustration represents the pre-operative condition (pre fall). This was created to compare to the post-fall illustration.

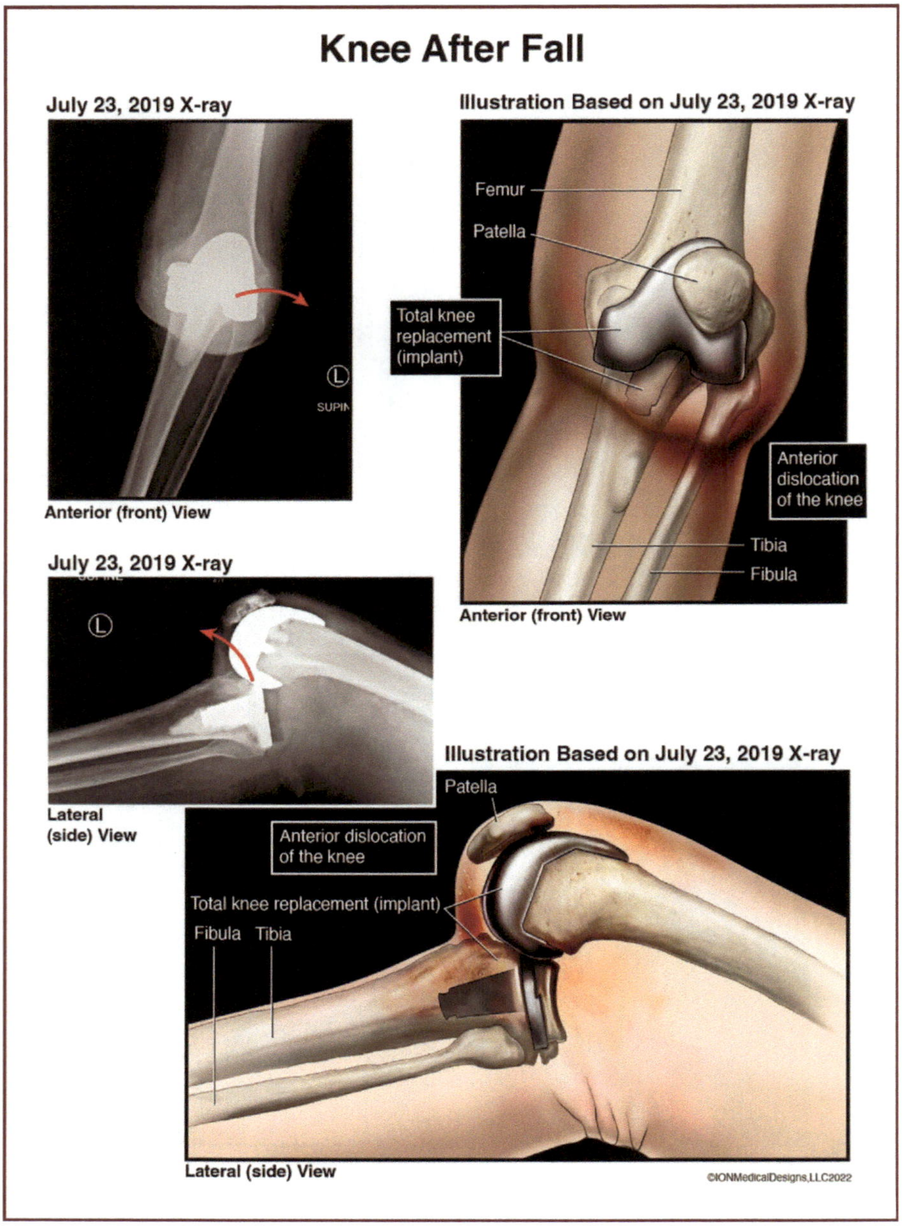

FIGURE 2.8 The illustration represents the post-operative condition severe anterior dislocation of the knee (post fall).

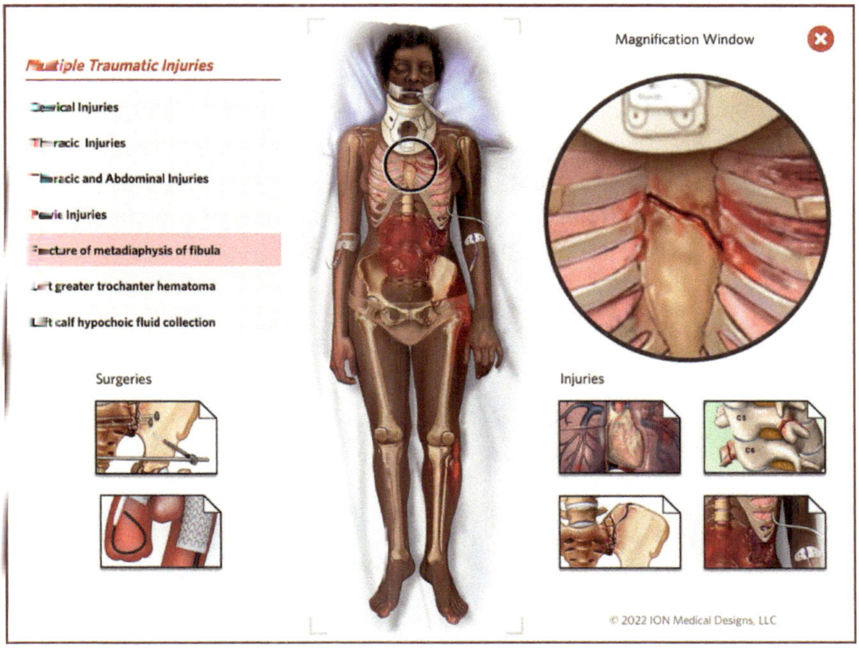

FIGURE 2.9 This is a still shot of an interactive iPad application of an injury summary board. All the plaintiff's injuries and surgeries are included in this self-sustaining application.

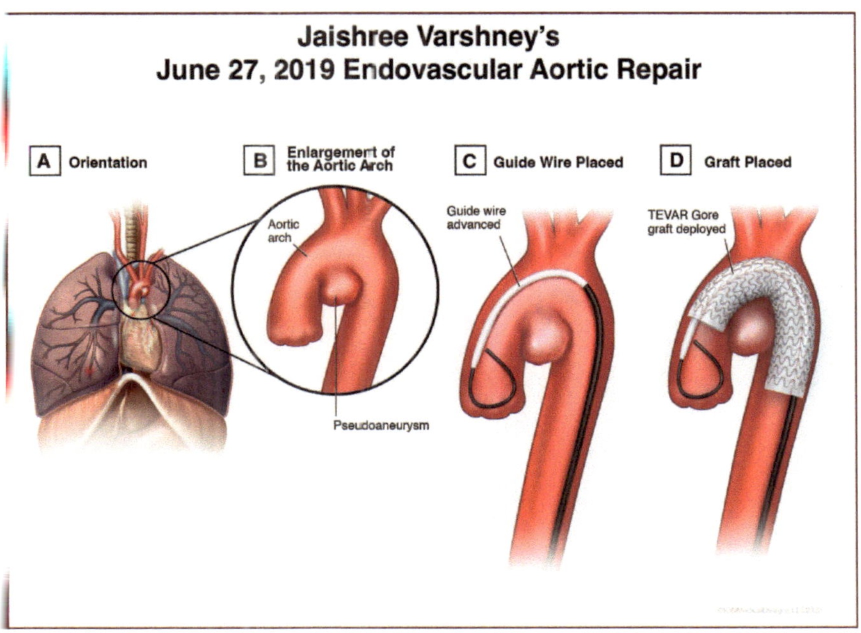

FIGURE 2.10 This is an illustration still from the same interactive application. The illustration depicts an aortic stent that was placed to strengthen the plaintiff's aortic arch since there is an aneurysm.

Medical artists, when you have mid- to high-budget cases, that motion graphics would enhance the presentation, consider proposing 2D and 3D animations, or a 2D animation with 3D components to the attorneys. 2D animations with 3D components give you a nice illustrative look with added 3D pizzazz (Figure: 2.11). The 3D components would be mostly medical tools or surgical instruments, implants, retractors, etc. (Figure 2.12) Attorneys, when asking for an animation, make sure to get a storyboard created (series of sketches) first, and allow for plenty of time for revisions. 3D animations can take up to a day to be revised and re-rendered.

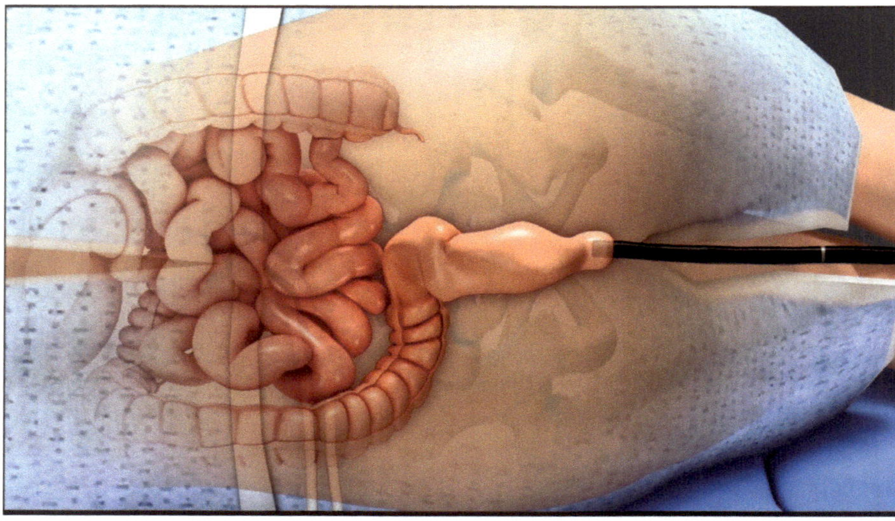

FIGURE 2.11 This is a still from a 3D animation of a colonoscopy procedure.

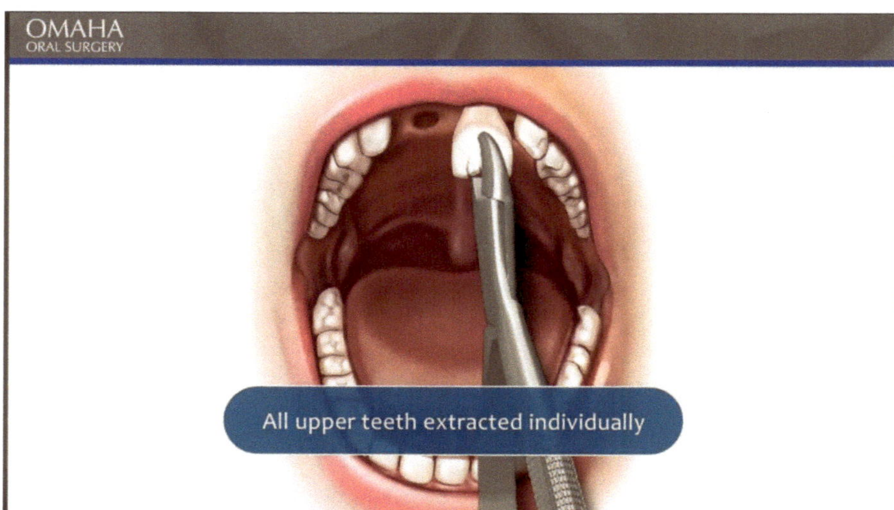

FIGURE 2.12 This is a still shot of a 2D animation with 3D components of a full zirconium bridge created for an oral surgeon.

2.5 TIMELINES AND FETAL MONITOR STRIPS

Attorneys and medical artists alike, if you find that you have a case with an injured person who has had a long stent in the hospital with many specific medical events that need called out/enlarged, or if you have a birth case that has a fluctuating heart rate, you may want to proceed with a timeline of events or fetal monitor strip.

Timelines can be static (not interactive) to call out specific events (Figures 2.13 and 2.14). Static timelines are good for a case that may have a few pages of events that need to be highlighted within a shorter amount of time.

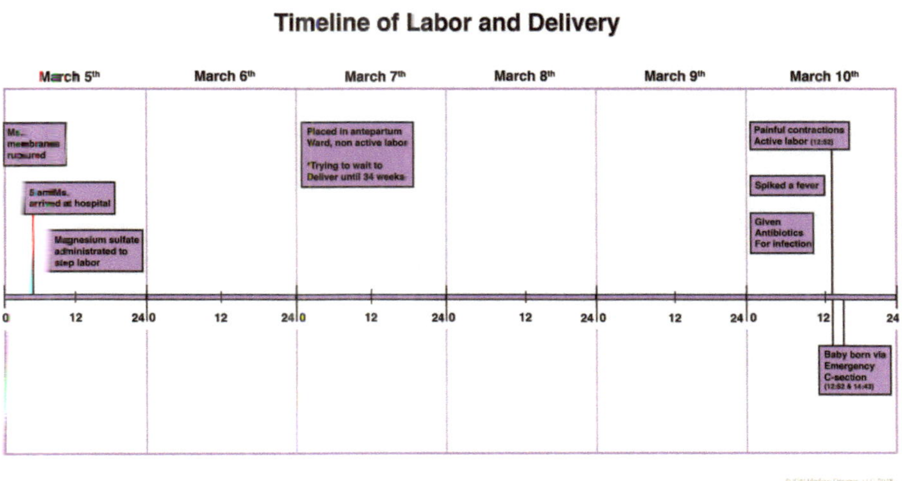

FIGURE 2.13 This is an example of a static (not interactive) timeline for a labor and delivery. The attorney wanted to highlight specific events that occurred during the labor and delivery.

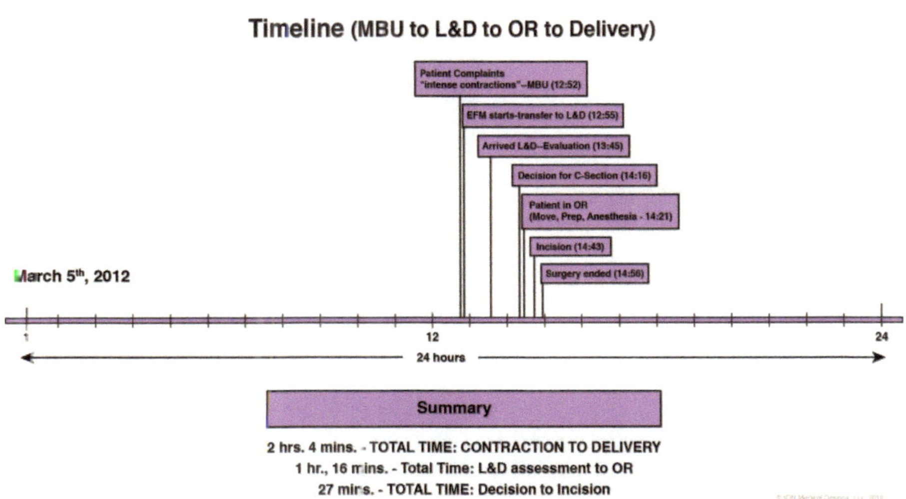

FIGURE 2.14 This is an example of a static (not interactive) timeline for a labor and delivery. The attorney wanted to highlight specific events that occurred during the labor and delivery. Part 2 of the timeline for the same case.

An interactive timeline would be best for cases with a lot of medical records that would be called out to blow up that can be opened and closed with touch. Specific events from the medical records can be called out and highlighted. See figures 2.15 and 2.16.

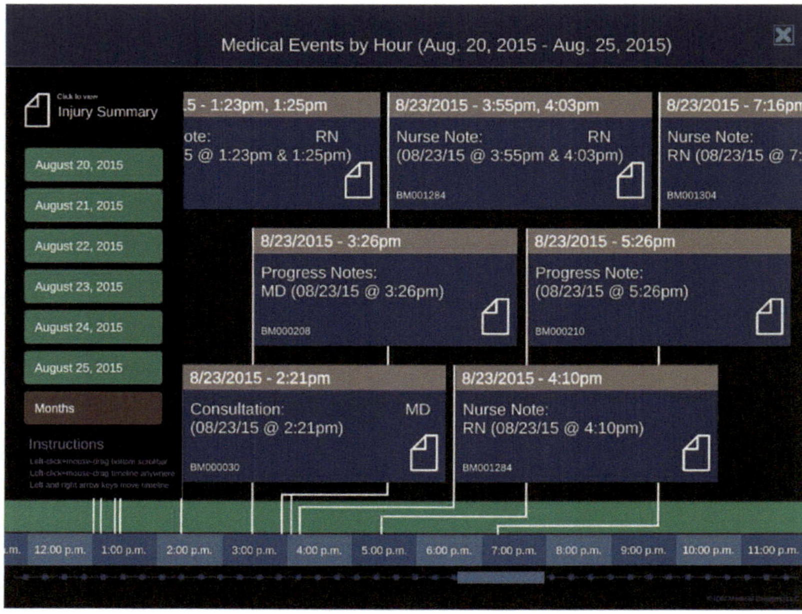

FIGURE 2.15 This is an example of an interactive timeline. The application can be run on a Mac or PC laptop, iPad, or Android device.

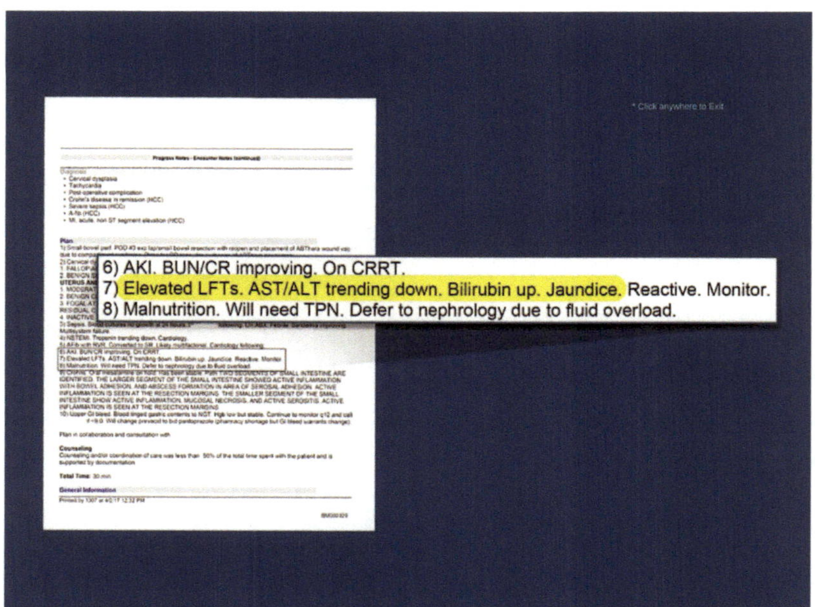

FIGURE 2.16 This is an example of an interactive timeline application. The application can be run on a Mac or PC laptop, iPad, or Android device. A blowup of part of a medical record is shown. Pieces of this can be highlighted and then opened and closed by the user.

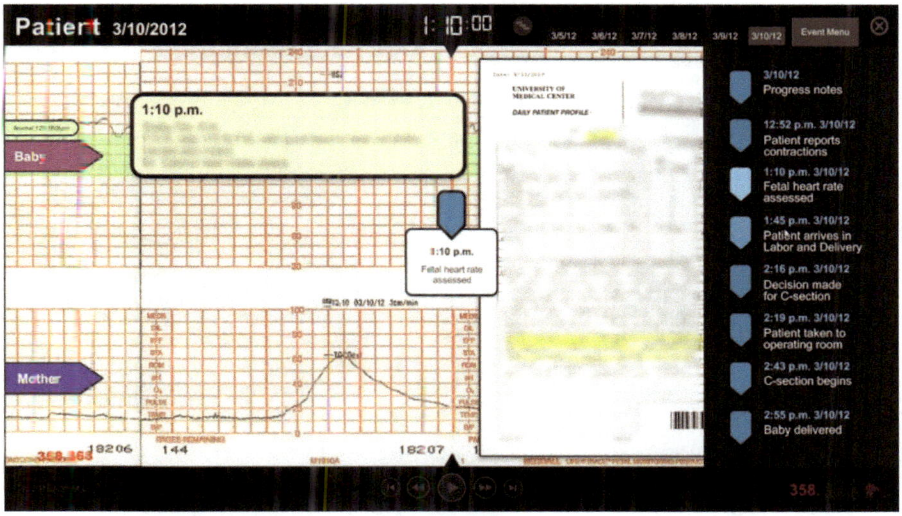

FIGURE 2.17 This is an example of a fetal monitor strip interactive application. The application can be run on a Mac or PC laptop, iPad, or Android device. A blowup of part of a medical record is shown when you click on the tabs. Pieces of the records can be highlighted and then opened and closed by the user when clicked on.

2.6 WHY ARE ACCURACY AND CLIENT-SPECIFIC ANATOMY IMPORTANT?

As with many things, success is all in the presentation. Don't use general anatomy (textbooks, Netter) or images taken from the Web to present the client's unique and/or distinctive injuries. Having a client-specific cohesive presentation will help the case substantially.

Using general and/or uninjured (healthy) anatomy juxtaposed next to case specific demonstratives is a lot more helpful for your client (injured person) (Figure 2.18). That way when presenting in the courtroom, the jury will be able to see what the uninjured anatomy looks like compared to your client's anatomy. Most companies have stock images for sale or standard anatomy posters for lower-budget cases.

Uninjured/healthy anatomy can also be included on the same illustration board as the injured anatomy.

Illustrations based on the injured person's scans, with the scans reproduced adjacent, is more impactful to a jury. It evokes an emotional response if that's what you're going for.

A new technique that has emerged recently is 3D printing (Figure 2.19). With 3D printing, models are created from slices of CT scans and/or MRIs and can be submitted as real evidence* instead of a demonstrative aid.

Real evidence, meaning a physical, tangible model created from a person's CT or MRI scans using CAD software. The workflow involves receiving DICOMs (medical

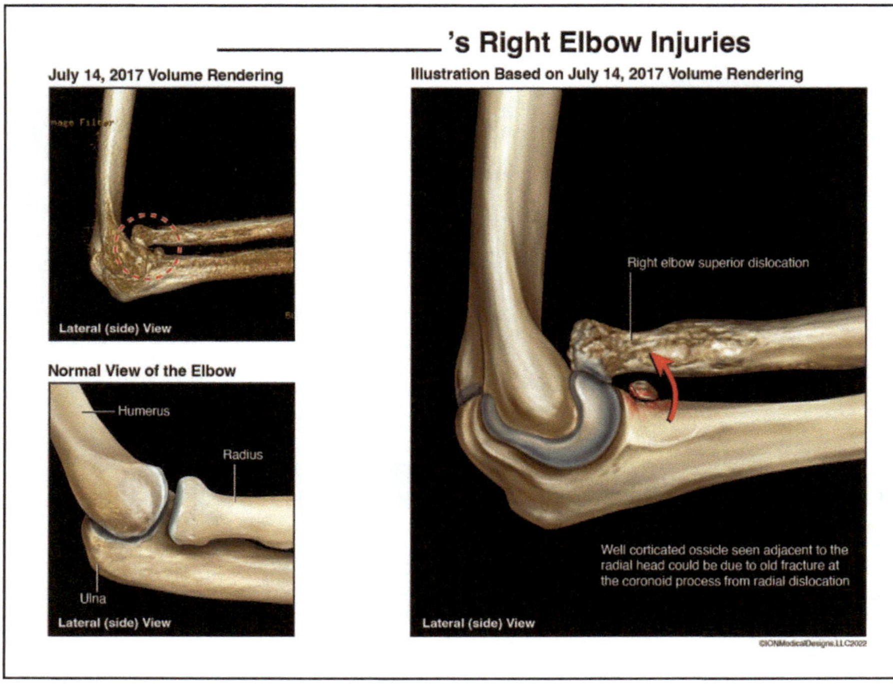

FIGURE 2.18 This is an illustration drawn from a volume rendering with a normal (healthy) anatomy view included.

imaging), uploading them to segmentation software, segmenting requested anatomy to export as StereoLithography (STLs) cleaning up the scans, labeling, ensuring the model is structurally sound for printing, uploading the scans to the 3D printer, printing, and post-processing. The turnaround time is around two to five days. Models can be printed and layered with color resin (Figure 2.19). For instance, if there is a client with a middle cerebral infarct, a clear brain could be printed, and the arteries printed in a different color to easily identify the pathology.

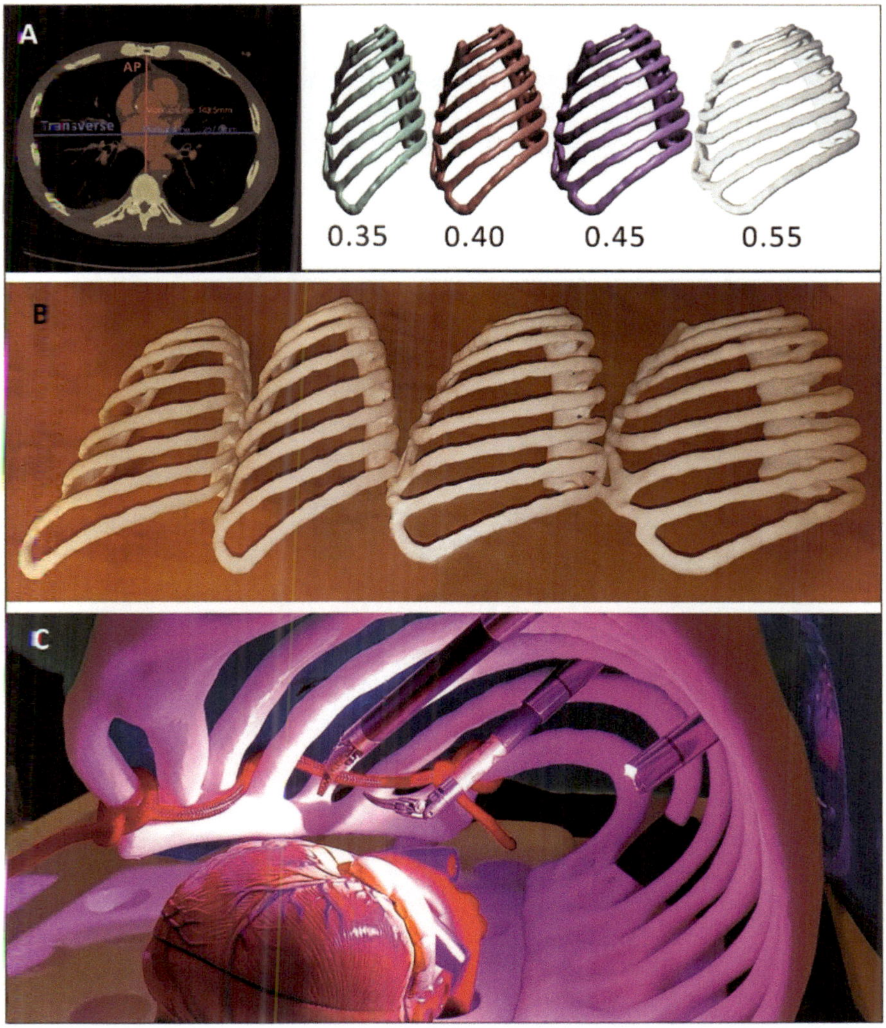

FIGURE 2.19 Sarah Chen, MD, utilized 3D printing technology to determine the feasibility of robotic left internal thoracic (LITA) harvesting. The study investigated the anteroposterior distance to transverse distance ratio. Several life-sized hemi-ribcage models were created based on a CT scan of an average adult-sized chest. The models were used for simulation using the da Vinci (Intuitive, Sunnyvale, CA, USA) robotic trainer to mimic LITA takedown. The conclusion was that LITA takedown is possible with an AP to transverse chest wall lower than proposed as long as the port placement is precise and there is sufficient LAD to chest wall distance. Custom 3D printed models help determine chest wall extremes and determine eligibility for cardiac procedures. (Images used courtesy Sarah Chen, MD).

Good uses for 3D prints include the following:

- Patients with unusual anatomy (young or old)
- Cases with tactile components—fractures, extrinsic tumors, infarcts
- Cases involving foreign bodies—objects left in the body cavity, implants, and hardware

*Real data = real evidence

Real evidence, meaning (material, physical) evidence. Evidence that is tangible, it must be based on the client's radiology. 3D prints from a client's scans are considered real evidence as opposed to exhibits.

Example: Clear and colored layering

All in all, using client specific anatomy is a better for an accurate and more cohesive representation for the client.

CHAPTER 3

Medical Illustrations for Personal Injury Cases

This chapter features actual cases and describes the work that was done to depict injuries, what was visualized, and how the artwork was utilized. In addition, an interview with the representative attorney, to coincide with each case, will also be provided. The chapter will focus on personal injury cases, specifically those in which attorneys are working on behalf of the plaintiff.

3.1 CASE STUDY ONE—WORKER'S COMPENSATION

Jack Walker and Martin Walker, PC Attorneys at Law

Jack and I have had a great working relationship for eight years! Jack has experience working with medical illustrations, so he knows the process and what to ask for. He typically schedules a phone call to review his case and sends the requisite materials for me to review before our call. I listen to him describe his case and visualize what he has in mind before I make my suggestions. I will read and review all the requisite materials to see if I have any suggestions such as an additional surgery or pre- and post-operative appearances. If it is a big case with a lot of injuries, I typically suggest our stand-alone applications for the iPad or laptop computer. It is a convenient way to have all the materials together in one stand-alone application.

That being said, the featured case was a worker's compensation case accident at a warehouse, where an employee was driving a forklift—the plaintiff was hit by

DOI: 10.4324/9781003336310-3

another employee driving a cart while on the job (Figures: 3.1–3.3) According to the warehouse safety regulations, when crossing intersections in the warehouse, employees are required to honk the cart's horn to let the other employees know that they are approaching each intersection. In this accident, the employee in the cart crossing the intersection forgot to honk and collided with a coworker, the forklift operator (the plaintiff), and caused significant injury to her left ankle. (Figures 3.1 to 3.3) to view the mechanism of injury (how the person was injured) and the injury board (what happened to the ankle) because of another person's negligence.

A proposal was written with three deliverables: mechanism of injury illustration boards, (how the injury occurred), an illustrated x-ray, and a surgical illustration board. I made the decision to illustrate these due to what Jack requested to depict, which was how the accident occurred (Figures 3.1–3.3), the damage to her ankle (Figure 3.4), to cause the injury that resulted in the plaintiff having her left ankle amputated (Figure 3.5). If there is a significant fracture such as what occurred in this case, ideally there would to be CT scans or MRIs taken of the fracture, however in this case, there were only x-rays. The x-rays were utilized to draw from and the surgery was illustrated from the plaintiff's operative reports.

Attorneys utilize demonstrative aids to help them prove injury, causation, and damages. Mechanism of injury illustrations help to prove causation in a personal injury case such as this. Causation referring to whether the defendant's actions caused the plaintiff's injuries. In this case, the action of the cart hitting the plaintiff's left ankle was shown from multiple views utilizing 3D models and illustrating the bones of her ankle.

The following illustrations are the mechanism of injury boards (Figures 3.1–3.5).

In this personal injury case, Attorney Jack Walker deemed it best to prove injury by illustrating the injuries caused by the cart based on radiology and medical reports and injury photographs. The purpose of drawing over the x-rays is to show the jury how extensive the injuries are more clearly, as you can see in Figure 3.4.

In the illustration, the accident caused a significant fracture that isn't visualized very clearly with the medical image (x-ray) alone. Given this, the illustration is drawn to overlay the x-ray image and provide the most accurate representation possible.

Please see the following illustration of the ankle injuries.

All three of the illustrations would help to prove damages. However, the left below-the-knee amputation (Figure 3.5) is very compelling for that! Because the plaintiff sustained significant ankle injuries, the surgeon was unable to save her foot. As a result, she had to undergo a left below-the-knee amputation (Figure 3.4).

Mechanism of Injury

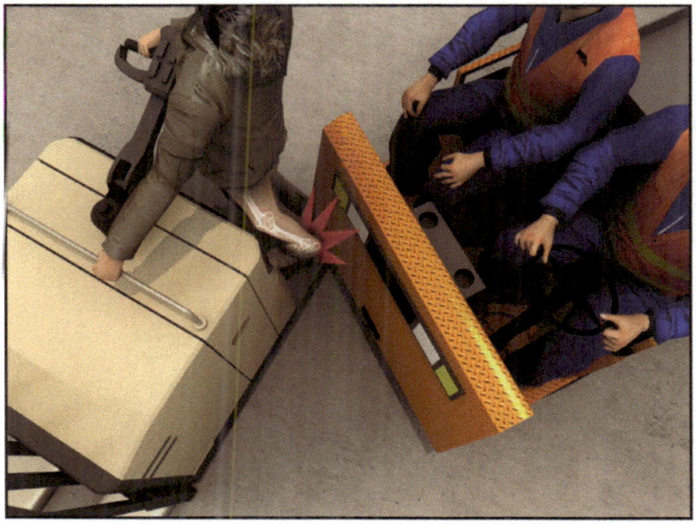

FIGURE 3.1 Mechanism of injury board showing one point of view of the accident where the cart hits her ankle and fractures it.

Mechanism of Injury

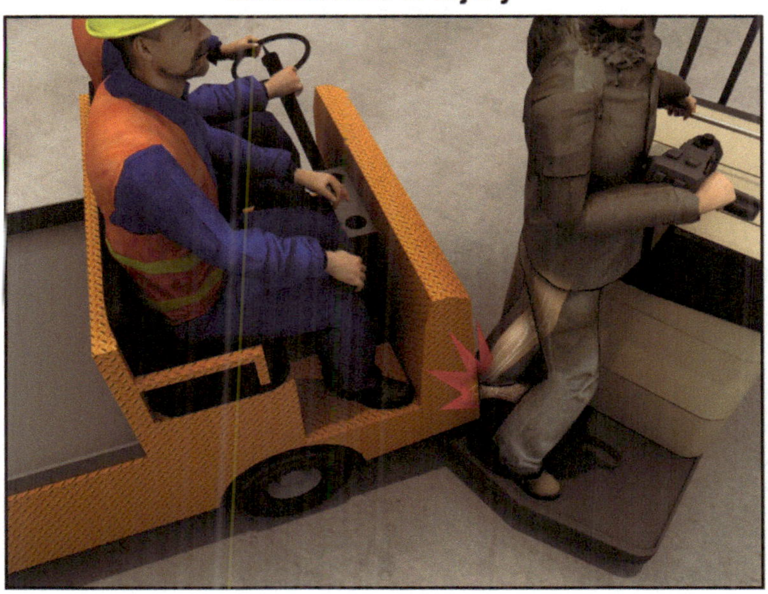

FIGURE 3.2 Mechanism of injury board showing an above (bird's-eye) point of view of the accident where the cart hits her ankle.

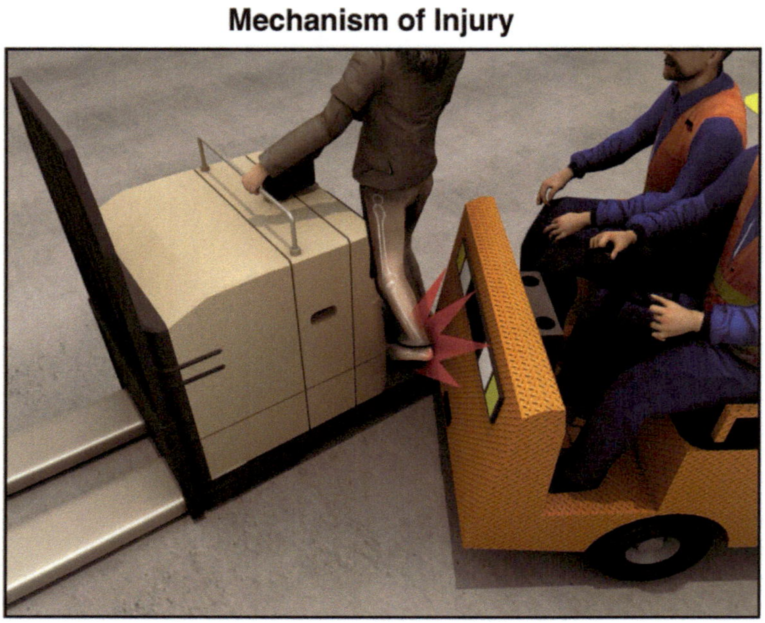

FIGURE 3.3 Mechanism of injury board showing a lateral (side) view of the accident where the cart hits her ankle and fractures it.

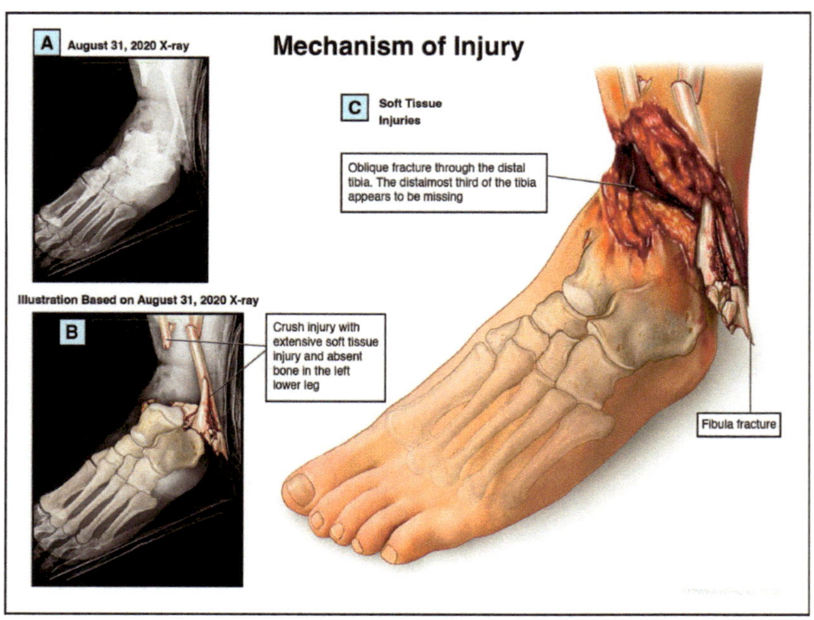

FIGURE 3.4 This is the illustration board describing a severe open ankle fracture. Box A is her x-ray, box B is the illustrated x-ray, and box C is the fracture with the soft tissue open wound. The illustration board is all based on client specific anatomy and relevant medical records.

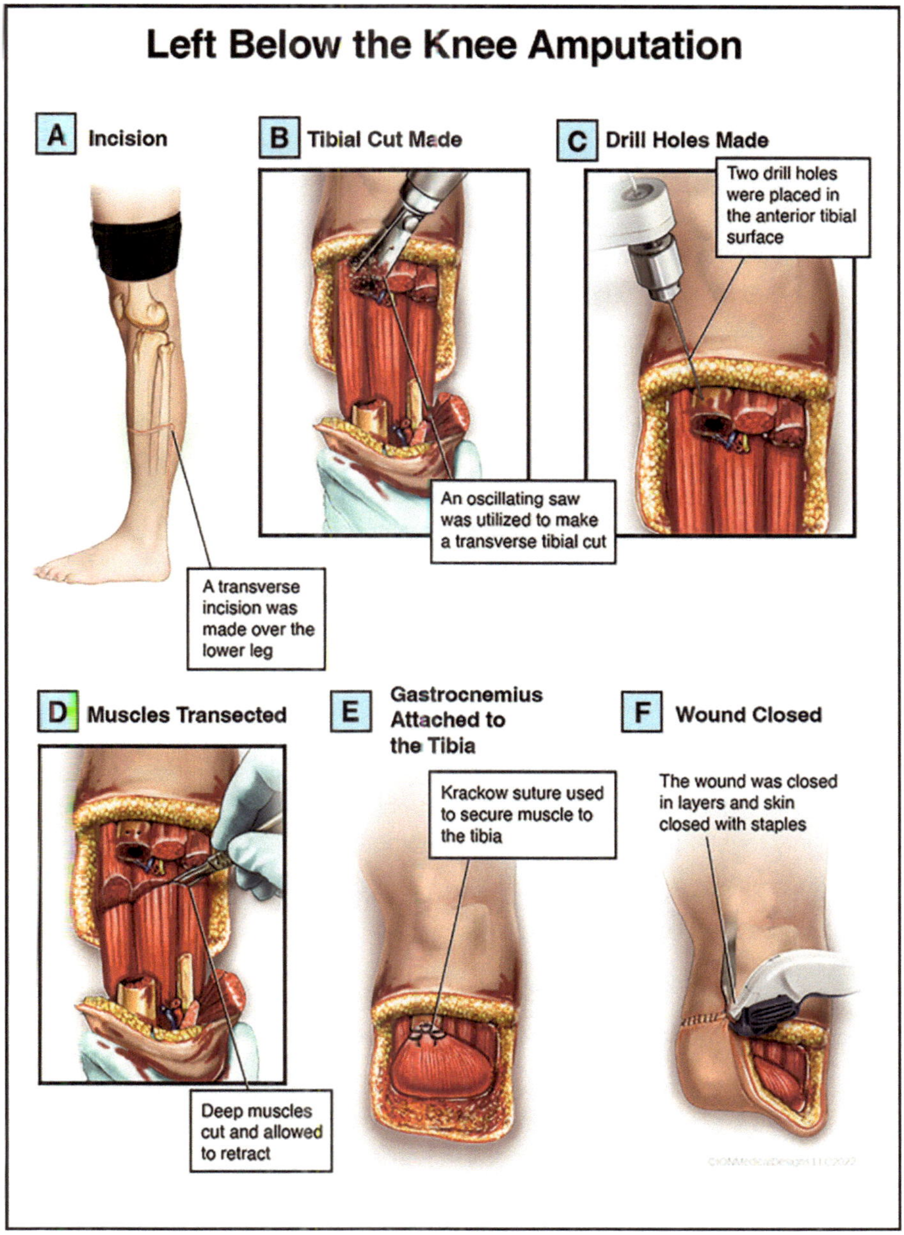

FIGURE 3.5 This is a surgical illustration board depicting the left below-the-knee amputation that was performed due to the severe fracture she sustained to her left ankle.

Attorney Jack Walker—interview questions and answers:

1) What is the process in which you use the illustrations for exchange, depositions, mediation, trial?

   I make the decision to get illustrations early on in my cases. They are very useful at trial, but I also utilize them in depositions of treating physicians as well as experts and attach them as exhibits to the depositions. I will also use the illustrations in demand letters and mediation position statements to help better explain the injury. At trial, I use the illustrations in my opening statement PowerPoint presentations, when examining witnesses, and during my closings.

2) How do you decide what cases you think would benefit from medical illustrations?

   An illustration is always helpful in allowing the jury to envision the full extent of the injury or damage pertaining to the cause of action. In most of our medical malpractice cases, the medicine is complicated and, unless you have a medical background, can be very confusing. An illustration teaches the jury and allows them to visualize the extent of the damages. I have also noticed that having a visual aid helps the jury retain the information better.

3) How do you use the artwork in the courtroom?

   I typically have the illustrations enlarged and mounted on a board. I use an easel to display them in front of the jury. I will also have a digital image to present on a screen in the courtroom. I find that having them mounted on boards that can stay up for a good amount of time is helpful in allowing the jury to refer to the boards during testimony.

4) What medical art service have you tried, for example, illustration, animation, interactive application, timeline?

   We have used illustrations and timelines.

5) Is the artwork well received in the courtroom?

   In my experience, the artwork is the tool that teaches the jury and judge why we are there. It is a way to not only tell them about our case but show them exactly what happened, and I believe it is very well received.

6) Do you find the artwork educational to the jury? In what ways do visuals help experts to educate?

   I believe the artwork helps educate the jurors about the anatomy of the injury. Our experts generally refer to the illustrations during testimony and teach the jury about the injury right there in the courtroom with a visual aid.

7) How often do you utilize medical artwork with your cases?

I find the illustrations so helpful that I am currently utilizing the artwork in all my cases that have complicated medical issues.

8) What type of medical art demonstrative aids have you used?

I have used illustrations and timelines.

9) What is your level of comfort with more advanced applications? What factors determine what you decide to go with as demonstrative aids: technological capability/comfort level, price, ease of getting the illustration approved?

I am very comfortable using the advanced applications. I have no problem with getting these approved.

10) Does opposing counsel have medical illustrations when you do? If so, how does that play out?

I have not had experience with opposing counsel using medical illustrations.

11) Please choose a case in which you used medical demonstrative aids and describe how it was helpful. Did they help you to achieve a verdict higher than expected?

Our firm used medical illustrations and a timeline in a very complicated GI case. A hospital's surgical team failed to properly coordinate the care of our client after an initial procedure failed. Evidence presented at trial demonstrated that the hospital did not follow its own bylaws and allowed a doctor without privileges to abandon the patient. A doctor from another facility was eventually called in to save the patient's life. A calendar-type illustration was used to indicate the lack of care the patient received while in the hospital. It proved that our client went days with no treatment at all while he lay there dying. The medical illustrations made explaining the medial condition much easier, and our experts were able to literally point to the problem and explain things step-by-step. In a case where the injury was hard to image from a layman's point of view, it made it visual and easy to understand. Our use of visual aids in the trial of this case earned our firm the No.1 Medical Malpractice Verdict in Texas in 2018.

3.2 CASE STUDY TWO—PERSONAL INJURY/ WRONGFUL DEATH

Matthew A. Lathrop, Law Office of Matthew A. Lathrop

This featured case is a personal injury/wrongful death case in which a truck, with a cattle guard attached to it, hit a runner. The individual was running on the wrong side of the road in a very rural area. He heard the truck coming but didn't have enough time to move out of the way before being struck by it. The truck struck the runner at ~50 mp, hitting the runner and throwing the victim over the hood of the truck and into the grass alongside the road (Figure 3.6).

I have worked with Matt for many years now, and he is an academic who knows what he wants. He elected to go with multiple services for this case. He first chose to illustrate the mechanism of injury, meaning how the injury occurred (Figure 3.6). It was important to show the jury how he sustained the significant fatal injuries. There were three sequential illustrations created of the truck hitting the plaintiff's head and neck (Figure 3.7), with the associated injuries that resulted from that. Then the truck hitting the torso, with the associated injuries (Figure 3.8), then, lastly, the truck hitting the legs, with the associated injuries (Figure 3.9). Each illustration board has an inset of where the truck struck the runner as well. The final illustration showed the victim's fatal injuries in detail (Figure 3.10). These illustrations are extremely important and help the jury to see the person from the inside out. To show the pain and suffering and everything the person went through. They help to clarify and depict the words.

The illustrations were then combined into an iPad application that was professionally programmed and comprised of all the digital illustration files. The illustrations were also provided to opposing counsel, the jury, judge, and medical experts to assist them in trial. They were used individually digitally and printed to present the plaintiff's injuries (Figure: 3.11).

Attorney Lathrop is strategic and thorough; he hires focus groups to provide feedback and, thus, improve his illustrations by making them more illustrative and impactful to the jury. The focus group is comprised of people from different ethnicities, professions, and socioeconomic backgrounds. The focus group is presented with the demonstrative aids and asked to interpret them for understanding and accuracy, as well as to provide any additional feedback they may have. When a focus group is hired to review cases, they often struggle with the language (medical terminology) on the illustration boards. It is helpful to utilize the language from the medical reports for accuracy and redundancy if debated by defense counsel and having the jury understand the material presented to them. In my experience, having a healthy balance of simplified language and medical report reflection with the medical expert to help explain the language is key to the best visual representation.

Medical terminology and radiology are specialties that people untrained in the medical field have a difficult time understanding, and that's another reason why demonstrative aids are so important.

In resolution to this case, Attorney Lathrop and the team of experts were able to obtain a sizable settlement for the victim's widow and their three children.

Injury, causation, and damages were shown with the following demonstrative aids and iPad application (Figures 3.6–3.11).

Maybe have a screenshot of the application on an iPad.

Attorney Matt Lathrop—interview questions and answers:

1) What is the process in which you use the illustrations for exchange, depositions, mediation, trial, etc.?

   My decision to get illustrations is something that I do as part of pre-trial preparation. I think you could say that I get illustrations only for trial.

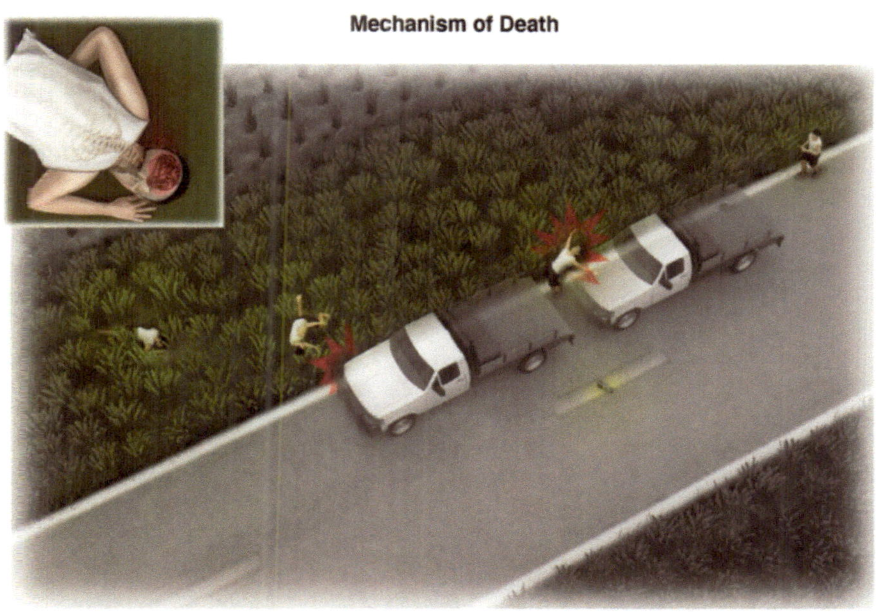

FIGURE 3.6 The plaintiff's mechanism of injury illustration board. This illustration depicts the direction the truck was traveling. It strikes the plaintiff, and his body tumbles over the hood of the truck and subsequently lands in the grass. The blowup in the upper left corner shows where he landed in the grass and his brain injuries. This illustration board gives the audience an understanding of how the prosecution thinks the victim was injured.

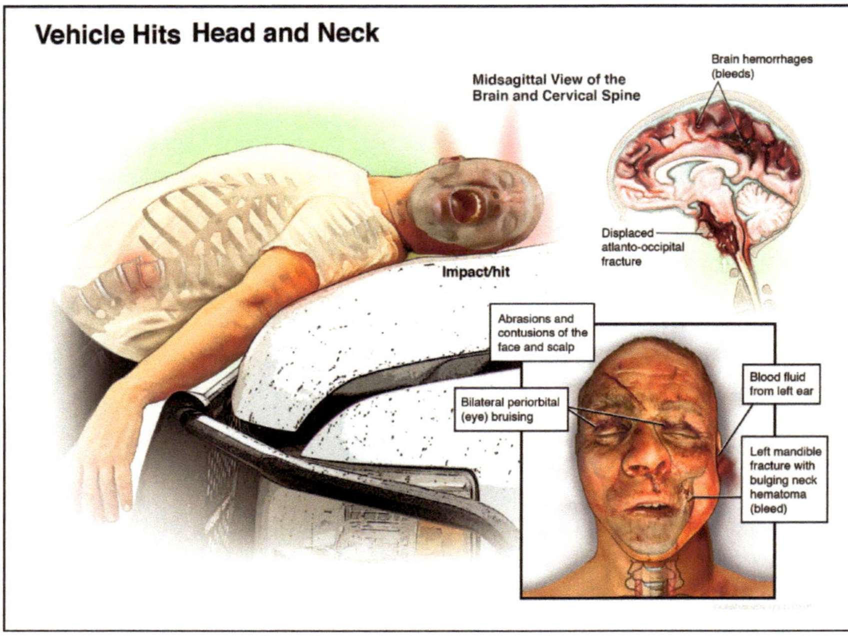

FIGURE 3.7 This illustration board shows how the plaintiff's head and neck hit the truck and the injuries caused by the impact. This is a sample of a mechanism of injury illustration.

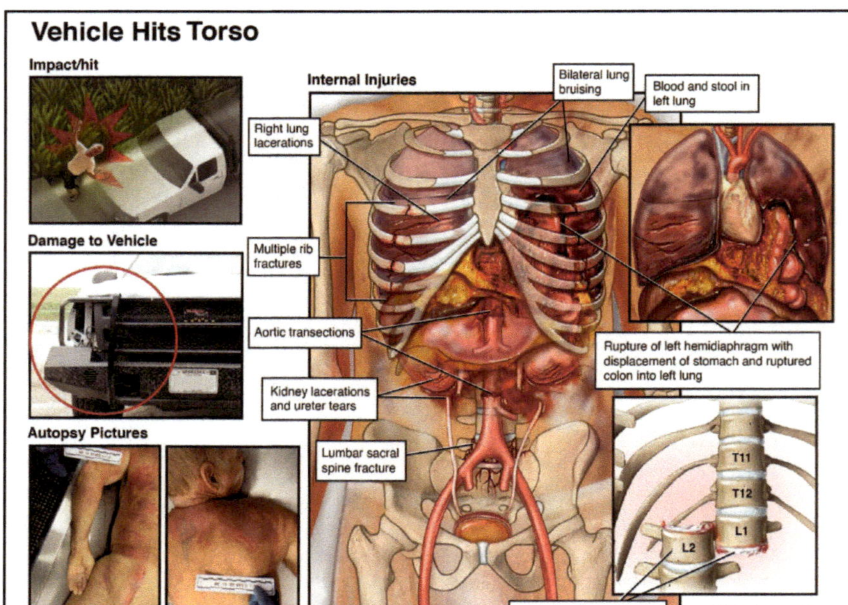

FIGURE 3.8 This illustration board shows how the plaintiff's torso hit the truck and the injuries caused by the impact. This is a sample of a mechanism of injury illustration.

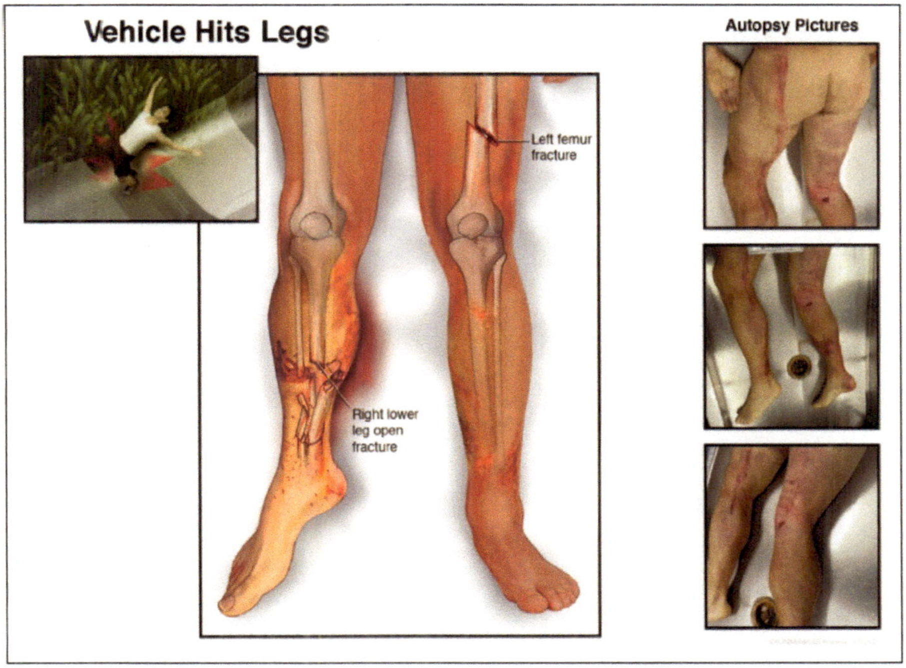

FIGURE 3.9 This illustration board shows how the plaintiff's legs hit the truck and the injuries caused by the impact. This is a sample of a mechanism of injury illustration.

However, once I have them, I do use them throughout the trial preparation process. I will use the illustrations with my medical experts in discovery depositions, taken by opposing counsel, to better explain the injury or the mechanism of injury. I will use them in depositions that I take of the experts hired by opposing counsel. This is also effective in explaining the injury, even if the opposing medical expert doesn't agree with the injury, the causation of the injury, or even the extent of the injury. And it's useful in having opposing medical experts agree that the illustration accurately depicts my client's anatomy, even if they don't agree that the injury depicted was caused by the event.

Illustrations that explain how the injury was treated, or how the injury healed, are also very important to my practice. Illustrations of these procedures, such as surgeries, scopes, and injections, paint a visual description of processes that are surprisingly violent—or otherwise depict procedures which look dangerous or painful. Again, I can use these illustrations during the testimony of my own doctor, or during cross-examination of an opposing medical expert. The expert may not

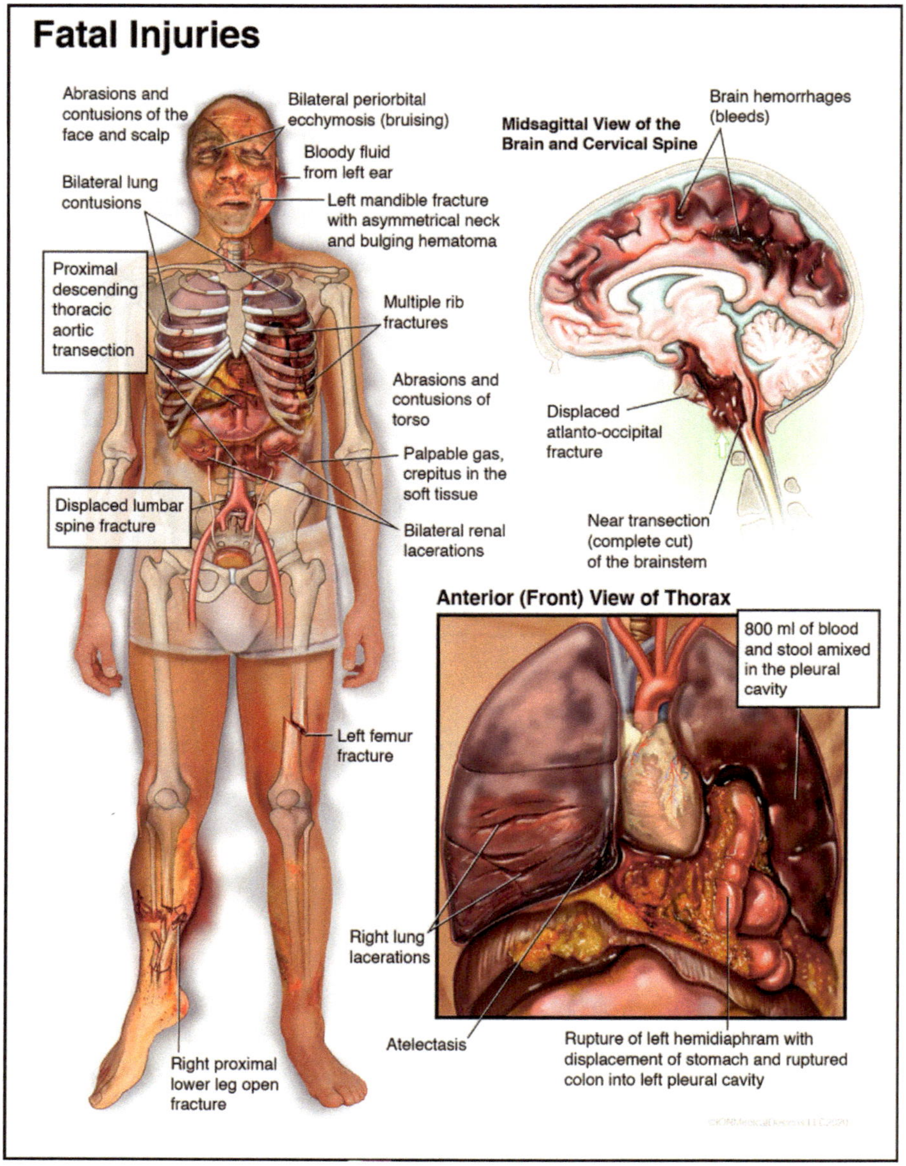

FIGURE 3.10 This is a fatality board illustrating all the plaintiff's injuries at the time of death. It is based off the autopsy report and pictures. There is a client likeness and blowups of the organs that are severely damaged so that the viewers can see them in larger scale.

agree that my client's surgery was necessitated by the event, but that same expert almost always agrees that the illustration depicts the procedure my client went through.

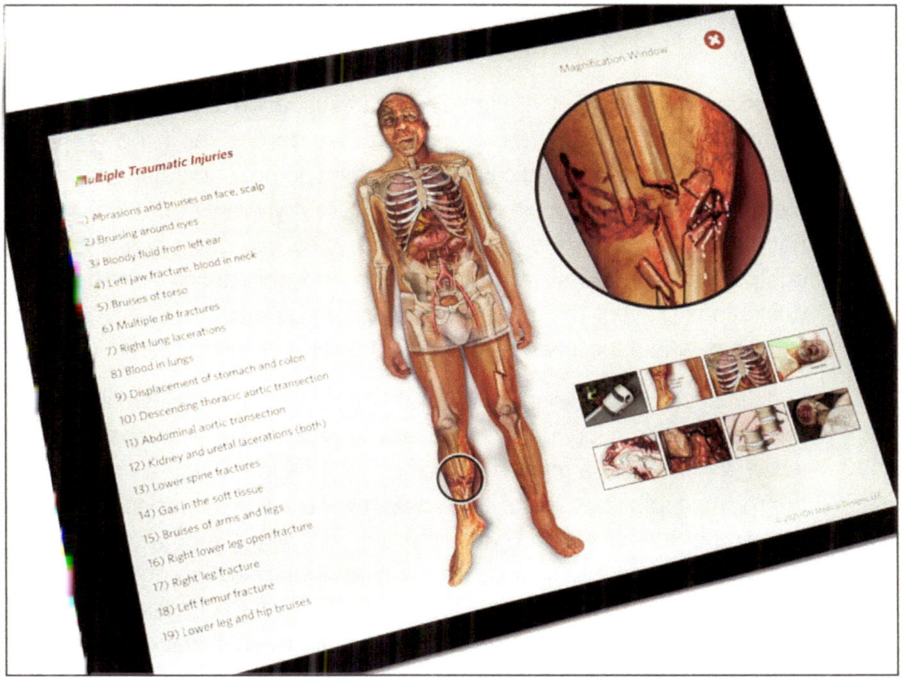

FIGURE 3.11 This is a screenshot of the interactive iPad application created for the attorney (client). All the images are included in this stand-alone application that is user-friendly and can be run in the courtroom by the attorney.

I also use the illustrations in mediations. I do not schedule or agree to a mediation unless the case is ready for trial. Therefore, although I had the illustrations produced to prepare for trial, they are also effective in depicting my client's injuries to a mediator. Ultimately, in a mediation, the audience I must reach is the adjuster or the defendant. The illustrations are strong visual depictions of the harm caused by the negligent conduct.

Finally, I have used medical illustrations to prepare my clients for their own depositions or for trial testimony. When clients can see and understand their own injury better, their ability to testify clearly and accurately about those injuries, and about how those injuries affect them, is enhanced.

2) How do you decide what cases you think would benefit from medical illustrations?

Many times, the injury itself is too difficult to understand without illustrations to aid the jury and, frankly, my own understanding. Those are the easy cases and the obvious cases when I decide to get an illustration done.

However, many times I learn that I need an illustration after forming a focus group, and I am told by the group that they do not know the anatomy; they do not know the medical condition; they do not understand the treatment intervention; or their understanding of my client's problem's does not accurately reflect the physical difficulty that my client has. Here, the illustrations simplify my task of informing and persuading. Likewise, the illustrations prevent me from having to serve as teacher, or instructor, in situations where the jury may feel like I'm talking down to them.

Even in cases where an injury is well-known, such as whiplash, a medical illustration helps a jury understand exactly what happens to the anatomy when, for instance, a muscle is strained or sprained. When a jury can see the microscopic changes to the tissue, they are more open to an understanding of the full extent of the problem. In reality, the cost of a medical illustration to depict an injury is almost always justified. The illustrations are powerful, and they can be repeatedly put in front of a jury, especially during a long trial, to remind them of the permanent physical change caused by the defendant's conduct.

3) How do you use the artwork in the courtroom?

From a logistics point of view, I have the illustrations printed up and mounted on foam boards as large as is necessary for the jury to easily see them from any placement in the courtroom. Digital images are certainly nice as well and are very effective to use in courtroom presentation televisions or monitors. However, once those images have been shown, I may need to present other evidence on the monitor, and this results in having to take down the illustration to use the viewer. There's just no substitute for having the physical, printed illustrations in the courtroom that can be put up and left up, even when other evidence is being presented to the viewers.

My goal is to have all medical illustrations on display for as much of my trial as I can. Once they have been admitted and shown to the jury, I try to leave the boards up in the courtroom until, and unless, opposing counsel asks to have them taken down.

Once admitted, illustrations can be set up during medical testimony, during the testimony of physical therapists, during the testimony of family and friends who have seen the effects of the injury on the client.

4) What medical art service have you tried, for example, illustration, animation, interactive application, timeline?

I have used each of them at various points—illustrations, animations, interactive applications, and timelines.

5) Is the artwork well received in the courtroom?

My experience is that juries not only appreciate medical illustrations, but in this age, they expect medical illustrations. As I have stated earlier, I also form focus groups to test my medical illustrations. The purpose of this is to get the exact answer to this question. Even if I have spent a lot of money on a medical illustration, if a focus group tells me that it is bad, or it doesn't portray what I'm trying to convey, or it's too graphic, I want to know that and determine if there is any way to fix the problem, or if the illustration should just never see the light of the courtroom. Ultimately, the illustrations that I present to a jury have been vetted, and, as a result, I know that they will be well received.

Once the artwork has passed this test, my experience is that juries do like the illustrations. Judges are glad to have the illustrations to help them better understand the medical issues involved. In mediations, mediators tell me that the medical illustrations have a much stronger impact than most other documentary evidence presented or discussed during a mediation.

6) Do you find the artwork educational to the jury? In what ways: visually displaying events or injuries, helping experts to educate them, or the whole presentation overall?

My purpose for getting medical illustrations is to educate the jury, in some respect, regarding my client's injuries. Either I am trying to explain a complicated medical problem or procedure, or I am trying to explain why an injury causes pain, limitation, or impairment. I may need the illustration to explain how one event could lead, through a chain of physical changes, to another problem that is unexpected or difficult to conceptualize. The goal, for me, with illustrations is always to educate. If the illustration does not educate, it is not necessary, or it requires revision.

7) How often do you utilize medical artwork with your cases?

I try to use medical illustrations in almost every case. All my clients have personal injuries, and the illustrations help show either how the injury occurred, or the nature and extent of the injury that was caused. Sometimes generic illustrations can be reused and don't require customized art. These could be things such as a muscle strain or sprain, cervical whiplash, or other common injuries.

8) What is your level of comfort with more advanced applications? What factors determine what you decide to go with as demonstrative aids: technological capability/comfort level, price, ease of getting the illustration approved?

I am more comfortable with static medical illustrations. These are easy to manipulate, and the procedure for getting them admitted is simple. There are plenty of cases out there that explain the process of using just about any kind of demonstrative aid. Ultimately, if the tool is useful to the expert in explaining or illustrating testimony for the jury, the court will allow the expert to use the tool as an adjunct to the testimony.

As far as difficulty in using the material, if the media is a challenge to use but is effective, I will take the time necessary to become facile enough to use it in court.

When it comes to price, I do pay attention to the cost. Sometimes animations or 3D renderings may have a lot of pizzazz, but they are not cost-effective. In addition, too much flash can put off a jury. Simpler is always better.

9) Does opposing counsel have medical illustrations of their own? If so, how does that play out? It's rare that opposing counsel (defense counsel) gets their own medical illustrations. I believe the reason for this is because medical illustrations clarify an issue rather than obfuscate or befog an issue. Confusion and uncertainty about a medical condition is a significant reason why juries either do not connect an injury to an event, or a jury does not consider an injury to be significant or life-changing. Helping a jury understand a medical issue is somewhat counterproductive to the goals of my opposing counsel.

10) Please choose one of your cases in which you used medical demonstrative aids, and describe how it was helpful. Did they help you to achieve a verdict and award higher than expected?

Yes, I'll elaborate on the case you've included in this book. I represented the family of a man who was struck by a car while jogging on a country road. In that case, we alleged that the decedent was aware of the impending collision just before impact. We had very strong medical testimony from the pathologist who conducted the autopsy on the decedent. However, that testimony required a jury to connect physical signs on the decedent's body to the environment around him, including the vehicle that struck him. The pathologist's testimony was clear and very detailed. But when the illustrations were completed, and paired with the testimony of the pathologist, the evidence was easy for anyone to see and understand. For instance, the illustrations were able to match up bruising, cuts, and marks on the body, with parts of the truck that hit him. The illustrations were able to show the position of the decedent at the time of impact, relative to the truck. The illustrations were able to show that at the time of impact, the decedent was in a physical position that would have been unnatural to an unsuspecting jogger, struck from behind, without warning. His injuries were a clear sign that he was looking over his shoulder when he was struck—unquestionably looking at the oncoming vehicle, aware but unable to save himself.

This illustration certainly helped with proving our allegations of pre-death fear. This evidence was used throughout the case, with our pathologist's testimony, and during mediation, and it drove the value of the case higher, without question.

3.3 CASE STUDY THREE—MEDICAL MALPRACTICE

Attorney Howard Thigpen Bachus & Schanker

Attorney Thigpen and I met on LinkedIn, a professional social networking platform, and chatted for a few years before I took him to coffee where I presented our services to him. He is very intelligent and has a vision for his cases most of the time; however, he encourages me to review all the requisite case materials and provide my professional insight. For the featured case, he and I combined our ideas to create the demonstrative aids. Attorney Thigpen is unique with his reference callouts (medical record citations). When working on a surgical illustration, he references relevant reports on the lower left corner of the page. These are callouts to the records referenced to create the illustration boards. They assist the medical expert on where the material was derived from.

This case is a medical malpractice case in which a young woman arrived at an urgent care facility presenting signs and symptoms of sepsis, including a very low oxygen saturation level, fever, high blood pressure, and trouble breathing (Figure 3.12). The treating physician blamed her low oxygen level on her acrylic nails. Even though her oxygen level was very low, he could've taken her O^2 saturation level another way. After an exam, the doctor sent her home with instructions on how to treat acute sinusitis. She passed away later that evening of bronchopneumonia, leading to sepsis (Figure 3.13). The physician later stated in his deposition that he didn't know what sepsis was.

Attorney Thigpen chose to illustrate her illness, pathogenesis of sepsis, and the different ways to take blood oxygen saturation levels.

The injury illustration depicts the signs and symptoms of bronchopneumonia, leading to sepsis, based on her in clinic report. As stated earlier, she had many signs of sepsis, including critically low oxygen saturation level and trouble breathing, during the medical examination (Figures 3.12, 3.13).

Attorney Thigpen and team achieved the medical malpractice policy limits for this case.

Please see the following demonstrative aids used in this case (Figures 3.12–3.14).

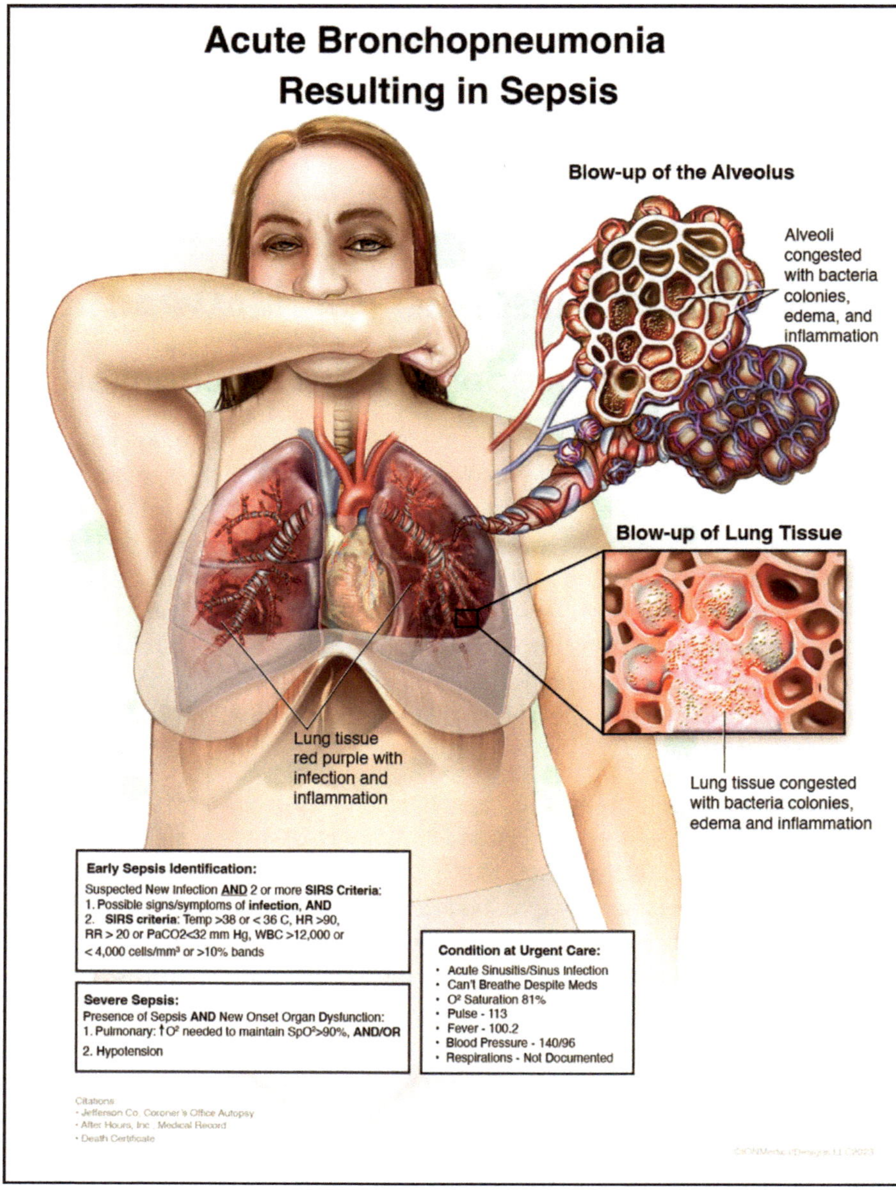

FIGURE 3.12 This illustration depicts bronchopneumonia (infection of the bronchiole tubes and alveoli). The charts on the left are from Stanford on early detection and the detection of sepsis (blood poisoning), and the chart in the middle is the decedent's vital signs in the clinic.

The following illustration board depicts injury, causation, and damages (death) showing the pathophysiology of septicemia, that is, blood poisoning (infection in blood). The infection started in her lungs, then traveled to the bloodstream, affecting her liver, heart, and kidneys, eventually causing multiple organ failure.

The following illustration is based on her autopsy report.

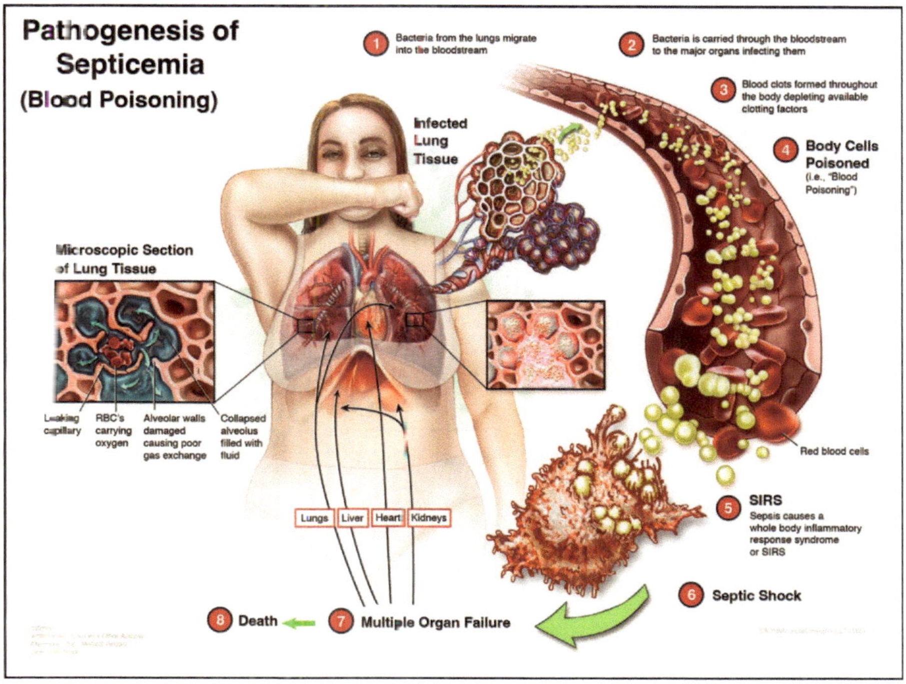

FIGURE 3.13 This illustration depicts the pathogenesis of septicemia. The infection began in the lungs, traveled through the blood, and eventually caused multiple organ failure.

The final illustration board for this case depicted the different ways to take blood oxygen saturation levels. In the decedent's case, her most alarming symptom was the critically low blood oxygen saturation level at 81%. The normal oxygen saturation range is between 95–100%. The physician insisted her acrylic nails were the reason behind her low oxygen reading and didn't try another method of taking it. The following illustration (Figure 3.14) shows the multiple ways to measure oxygen saturation levels in the clinic.

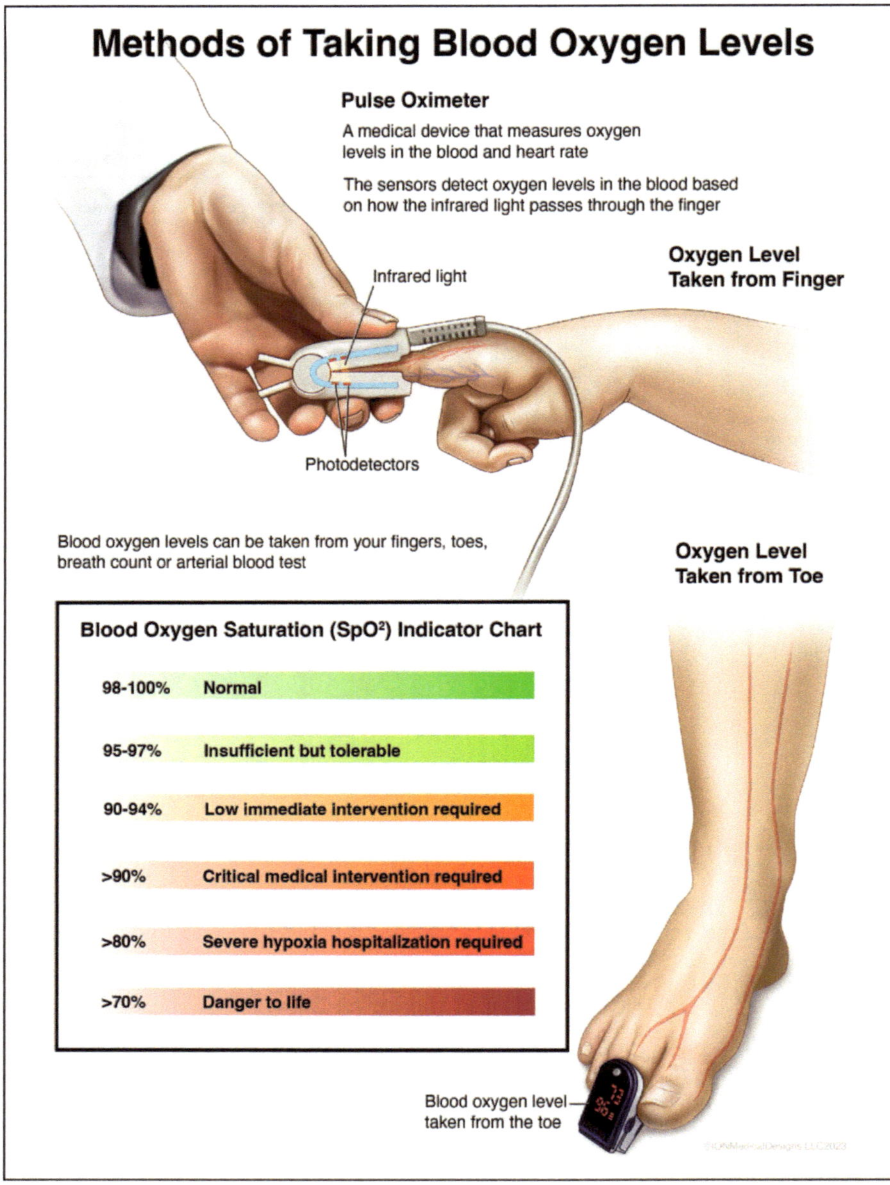

FIGURE 3.14 This illustration depicts the different ways to measure oxygen saturation levels. O^2 saturation levels can be taken by infrared light from the fingers and toes with pulse oximeters, by breath count, or by arterial blood test.

Attorney Howard Thigpen—interview questions and answers:

1) What is the process in which you use the illustrations for exchange, depositions, mediation, trial?

I use the illustrations in multiple ways. First, I use the illustrations in my settlement demand packages, to help explain the science either to the defendant directly or to insurance adjusters. Second, they are extremely helpful in mediation, to help the mediator understand the science at-issue. This better equips the mediator, when he/she goes back into the oppositions room and talks with opposing counsel and their client. Whether the mediation is on Zoom or in person, it is easy to show the illustrations to the mediator and explain what is happening. Sometimes they are shown to opposing counsel in mediation, to help combat their arguments. Third, I use the illustrations at trial, to explain the science in a very simplified, easy-to-remember way for the jury. The jury is more likely to remember our key points if provided to them not only in words but in images. I simply use the demonstrative with my expert, to provide the expert an opportunity to explain the science at-issue. In my experience, the testimony has more of an impact and has been remembered more when visuals are used.

2) How do you decide what cases you think would benefit from medical illustrations?

I believe that every case benefits from the use of medical illustrations. We are such a visual society. It is hard to do nothing more than listen to people talk all day throughout a trial. The jury appreciates it when visuals are used. It's just one more way to connect with the jurors, and I find that they retain the information longer after seeing the visuals. When we are allowed to talk with the jurors following a trial, typically they remember and discuss areas in which such visuals were used. Regardless of how complex the case may be, it is critical that we are able to simply the issues so that the jury understands our position. There is no better way to force yourself to simplify the issues than to create visuals.

3) How do you use the artwork in the courtroom?

The artwork is typically projected onto a screen by our IT tech, who is there to help with exhibits and visuals. I've used the visuals in my opening statements, closing statements, and with expert witnesses, to allow them an opportunity not only to explain in words our position but also to reinforce the argument with a visual impact. The jury perks up when visuals are used. They are more attentive and involved in the process.

4) What medical art service have you tried, for example, illustration, animation, interactive application, timeline?

I have used illustrations, animations, interactive applications, and timelines throughout various stages of my cases. Each of these forms of visual presentation provide unique value to each case. Timelines are great for mediations and trials, to give either the mediator or the jury a more concise, clear understanding of the events that are critical to the case. Illustrations help to involve the jurors, placing them back in time at the incident or with the doctors trying to sort out the medicine. I have not used the animations or interactive applications as much, but they are tools that get the jury involved and excited on an even higher level than the illustrations. I strongly encourage people to start utilizing all forms of the medical art services throughout the litigation process. Each form has a place and is beneficial to the process.

5) Is the artwork well received in the courtroom?

The artwork is well received in the courtroom. I find that both jurors and judges love having the artwork to look at and examine. I believe using the artwork not only impacts how well the jurors and judges retain the information but it also impacts their ability to understand your client's position and fight for that position during deliberation or for judges to rule in your client's favor. Lastly, I believe the artwork brings credibility to your arguments. If you are willing to put your arguments down in print, available for the opposing side to attack, I believe that a jury is more willing to give more weight to those arguments.

6) Do you find the artwork educational to the jury? In what ways are visuals helpful: visually displaying events or injuries, helping experts to educate them, or the whole presentation overall?

The artwork is educational. Whether it's in the automobile collision case or the medical malpractice case, the artwork takes very unfamiliar settings and brings them to life for the jury so that they feel like they are part of the process. It's hard to understand what parts of the body look like, or how they interact, until you see it displayed and can visualize it. It's easier for the jury to discuss the case and the testimony from the experts once they have a visual understanding. Simply telling the judge or jury in words just doesn't provide them with the same understanding.

7) How often do you utilize medical artwork with your cases?

I'm trying to use medical artwork in all my cases these days. The more I use it, the more I hear from jurors that they appreciated the visual presentation and the impact that it had on their ability to understand the case and discuss the case more in-depth during deliberations. I'm able to present a much better case with medical artwork.

8) What type of medical art demonstrative aids have you used?

I have used timelines, illustrations, animations, and interactive applications.

9) What is your level of comfort with more advanced applications? What factors determine what you decide to go with as demonstrative aids: technological capability/comfort level, price, ease of getting the illustration approved?

   I haven't had any trouble getting any of the more advanced applications approved as demonstrative aids. Typically, I only use the more advanced applications on higher-value cases due to the cost, but they are worth it.

10) Does opposing counsel have medical illustrations when you do? If so, how does that play out?

   Sometimes opposing counsel has their own medical illustrations, but not all the time. Often, I will use both my own illustrations as well as their illustrations with my experts, to point out why our illustrations are more accurate and reliable. Typically, the illustrations are used with our own experts, and then, during closing arguments, the illustrations are distinguished.

11) Please choose a case in which you used medical demonstrative aids, and describe how it was helpful. Did they help you to achieve a verdict higher than expected?

   I used a lot of demonstrative aids in a recent medical malpractice case, concerning a newborn girl who was born healthy but contracted sepsis. The nursing staff ignored the clear signs of sepsis, failing to notify the physicians, which delayed the administration of antibiotics, resulting in severe, lifelong developmental delays. Demonstrative aids were used throughout the case, including opening statements, direct and cross-examinations of the treating providers, as well as during the experts' testimony, and closing arguments. We used timelines, illustrations, and animations. The demonstrative aids simplified what could have been a very complex medical issue. The jury was very alert and interactive throughout the presentation, in large part to the frequent use of demonstrative aids. Opposing counsel did not use any medical demonstrative aids, which I believe had an impact on the jury and our credibility throughout the trial. I firmly believe that our use of demonstrative aids played a large role in getting the largest medical malpractice verdict in the State of Colorado's history.

3.4 CASE STUDY FOUR—MEDICAL MALPRACTICE

Attorney Andrew Sibbernsen, Sibbernsen Law Firm, P.C.

My family and I lived in Nebraska for about six years, and in that time frame our business sponsored NATA (Nebraska Trial Attorneys Association). Attorney Sibbernsen and I have associated with one another during those conferences, and after I gave a presentation of services and a recommendation from a colleague, we began to work with one another.

Attorney Sibbernsen and I spent more time getting to know one another as our relationship was new. I like to take the time to go over medical records and potential visual solutions with clients directly. Andy had a complicated medical malpractice case described in the text and images later.

In medical malpractice cases, the object is to prove that the injury or complication was a direct and proximate result of the alleged negligence.

The featured case is a medical malpractice case in which a 49-year-old woman passed away from a surgical complication sustained during her hysterectomy and salpingo-oophorectomy procedure (removal of uterus and ovaries). The plaintiff was unwell after her surgery and had a distended abdomen with fluid (Figure 3.19). The nursing staff noticed and annotated purulent drainage from one of her drains and were told, by the physician, that it was to be expected. Her condition continued to deteriorate over the course of five days. Post-operative day five, plaintiff was taken back to the operating room for an exploratory laparotomy (open abdominal exploration). The surgeons discovered a small bowel perforation. However, by that time it was too late, she was septic, and she was experiencing multiple organ failure. She passed away after a 100-day hospital stay from sepsis (blood poisoning).

Ultimately the jury came back with a defense verdict in favor of the defendants. In talking with the jurors after the trial, the illustrations were helpful with educating them about the operation and the plaintiff's injuries, although they were not a deciding factor in the verdict.

To prove injury, causation, and damages, Attorney Sibbernsen used a lot of demonstrative aids, including a medical timeline of events (Figure 3.15 and 3.16), medical illustrations, normal/standard bowel stock anatomy board (Figure 3.17), laparoscopic portal placement board (Figure 3.18), bowel perforation board, and a fatality (death) board (Figure 3.20). Please see the following illustrations for this case. (Figures 3.15–3.20)

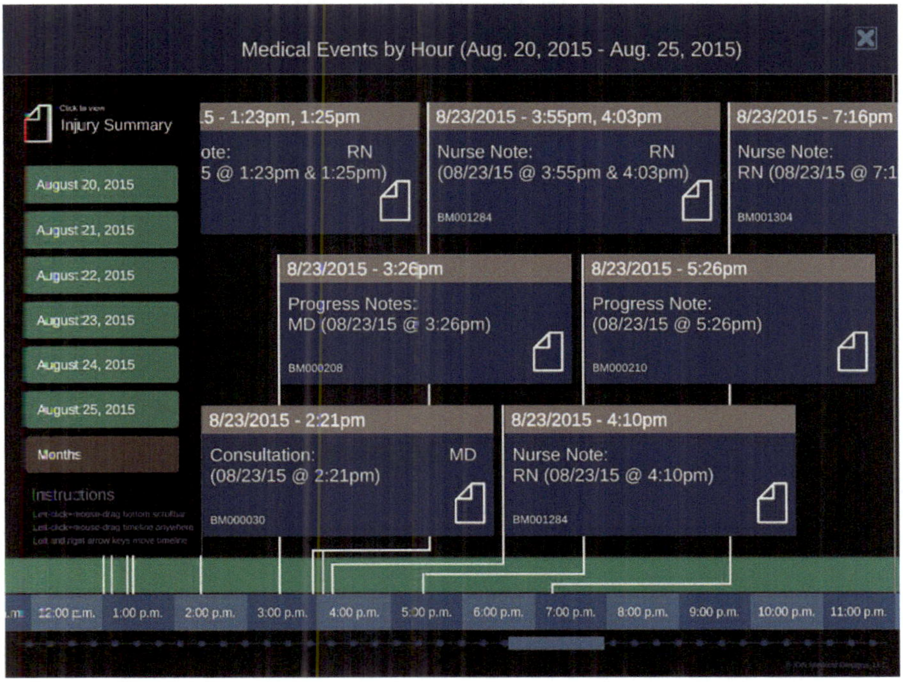

FIGURE 3.15 This is a screenshot of the plaintiff's timeline. The pertinent medical records were highlighted and can be blown up if needed. Blown up meaning clicked on, and records will open and close on touch. This is an interactive application for the iPad.

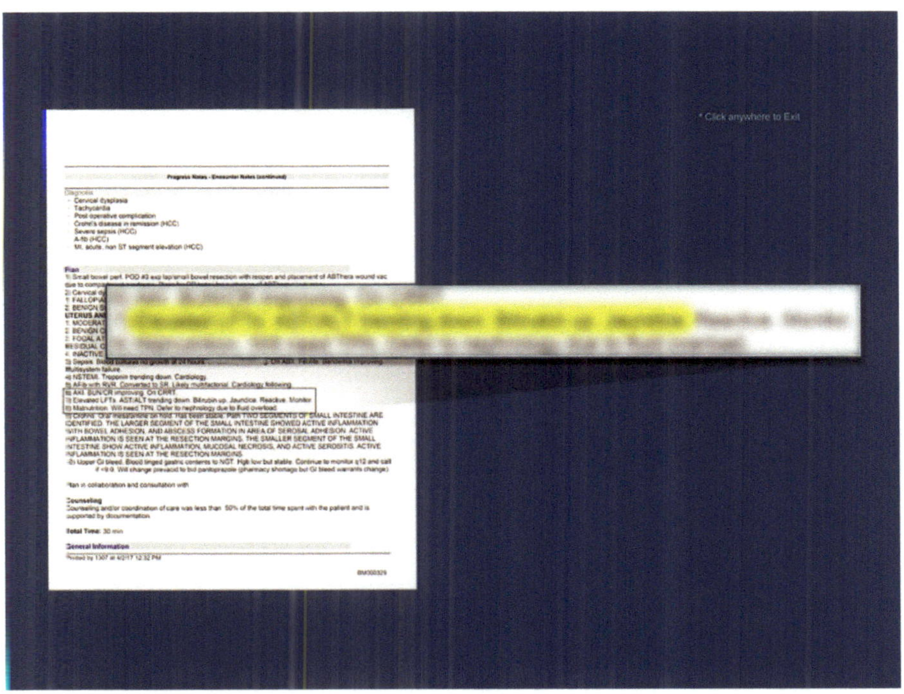

FIGURE 3.16 This is a screenshot of the decedent's timeline. The pertinent medical records were highlighted and can be blown up if needed. This is an interactive application for the iPad.

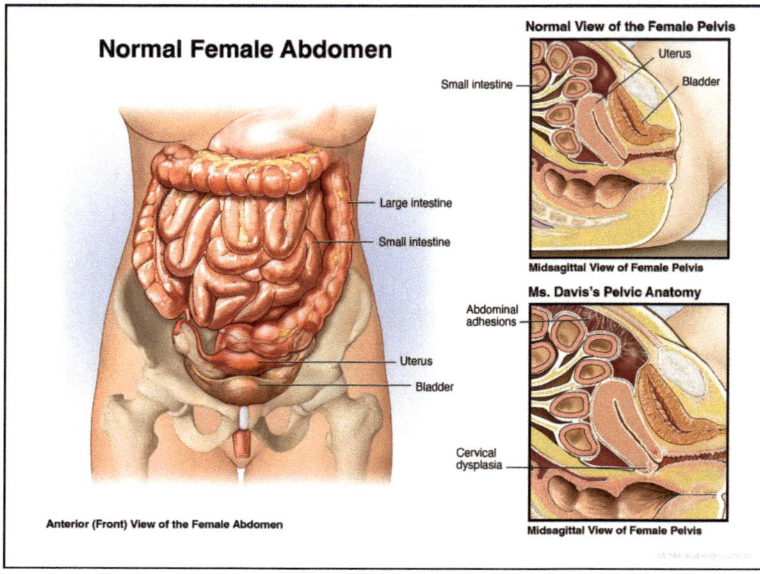

FIGURE 3.17 This illustration depicted the normal/standard anatomy of the abdomen and pelvis. The illustration on the left is an AP (anterior/posterior view) that shows the relationship of the bowels and reproductive organs (uterus, ovaries, fallopian tubes). The illustration on the top right is a normal/standard anatomy of the female pelvis (midsagittal view), and the bottom right is the decedent's anatomy prior to surgery, showing slight abdominal wall scarring and cervical dysplasia.

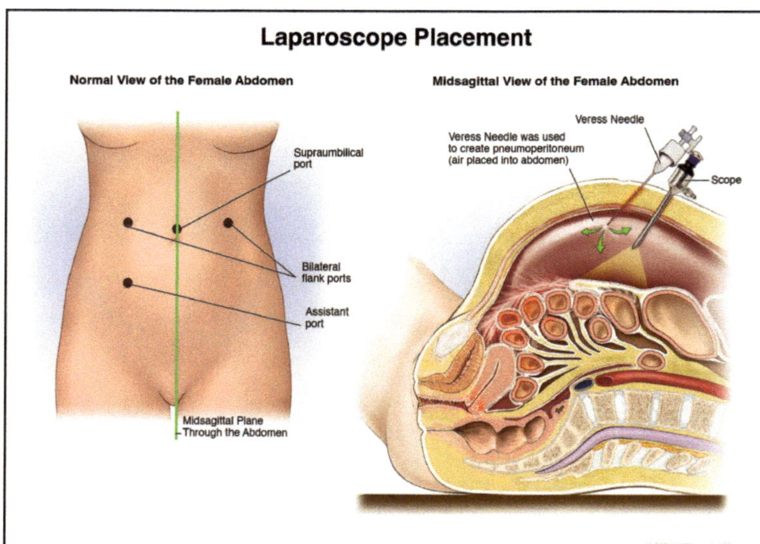

FIGURE 3.18 This illustration depicts the placement of the laparoscopic trocars for abdominal surgery. The illustration on the left shows where the surgeon placed the surgical instruments during surgery. The green line represents the decedent's midline (center line). The illustration on the right is a midsagittal cut through the abdomen and pelvis, showing the abdomen insufflated (filled with air) and the scope placed.

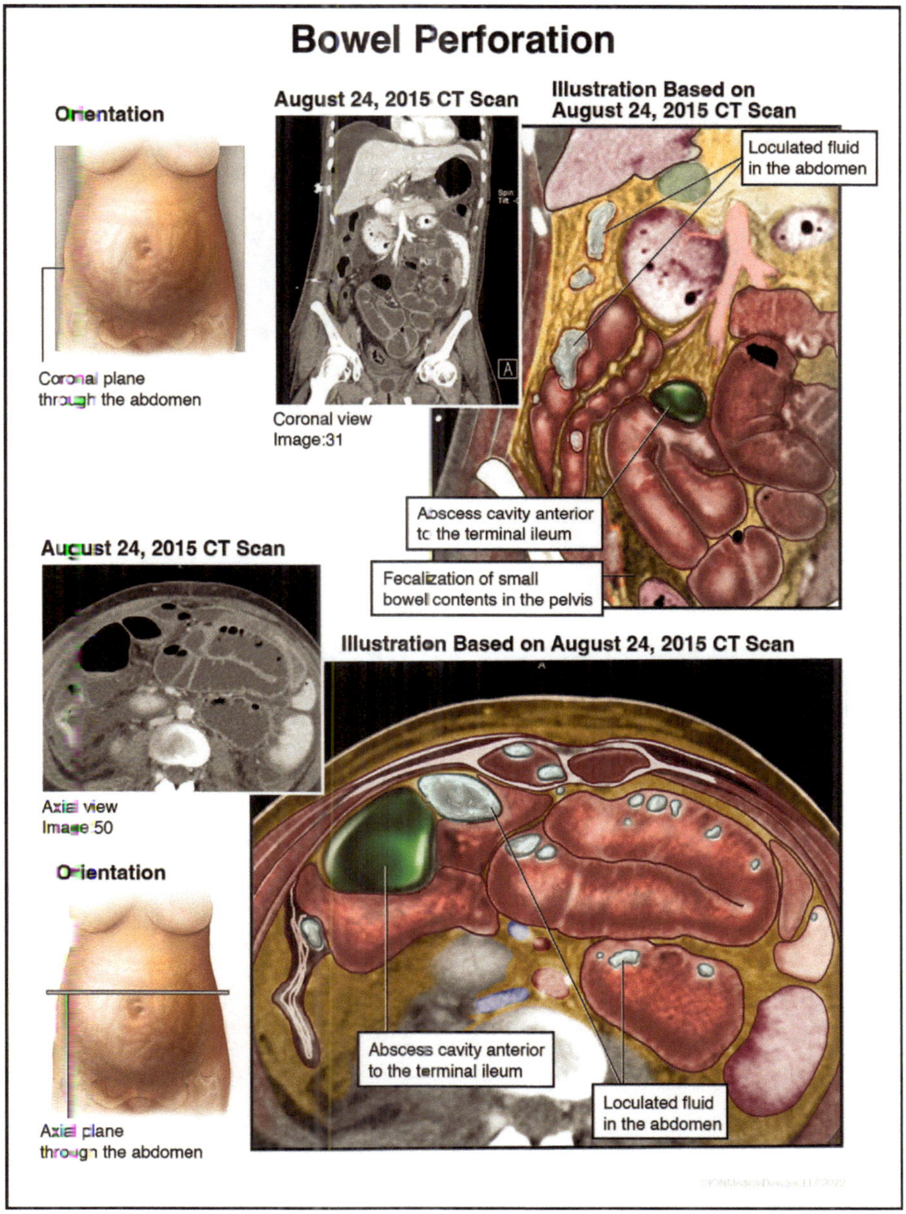

FIGURE 3.19 This illustration represents the condition of the decedent's abdomen after surgery. The illustrations are drawn from her CT scans taken after her health started to decline. These CT scans show an abscess and loculated fluid. The bowels are also swollen with a protruding abdomen.

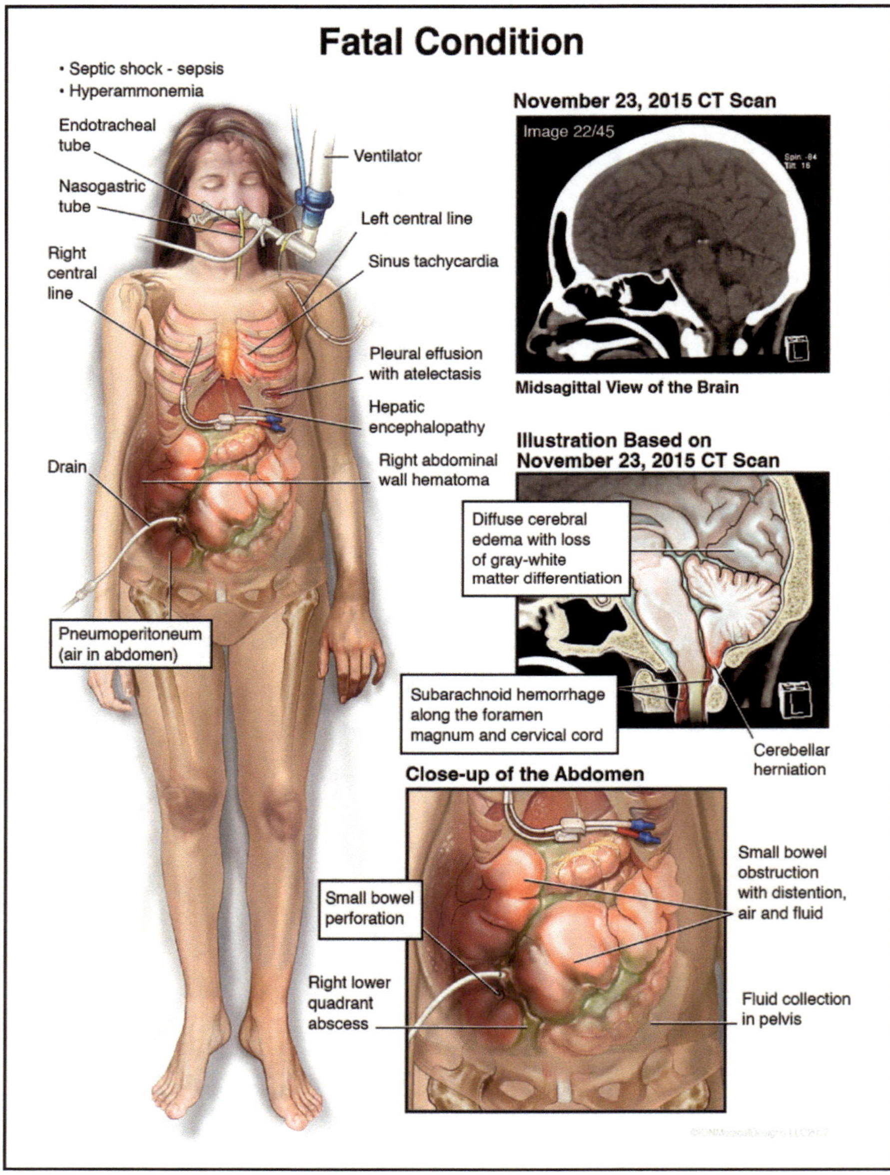

FIGURE 3.20 This illustration represents the condition of the descendent prior to her death.

Attorney Andrew Sibbersen—interview questions and answers:

1) What is the process in which you use the illustrations for exchange, depositions, mediation, trial?

In the past I have typically only used illustrations at trial. However, in certain cases, I can see the benefit of illustrations during depositions and mediations to better help explain the injuries sustained as a result of the alleged negligence.

2) How do you decide what cases you think would benefit from medical illustrations?

When I have a case going to trial that involves anatomy and think an illustration(s) will help me and my experts explain the anatomy, surgery, or damages to the jury, then using diagrams and illustrations is extremely helpful.

3) How do you use the artwork in the courtroom?

I use artwork to help educate and explain to the jury parts of the anatomy, the surgery at issue if applicable, and demonstrate the nature and extent of injuries and how they occur.

4) What medical art service have you tried, for example, illustration, animation, interactive application, timeline?

To date I have tried illustrations and timelines. And while both can be beneficial, I think it is important to read your jury and avoid overkill, give them the information, explain to the jury what you/your experts are talking about, and allow them to connect the dots.

5) Is the artwork well received in the courtroom?

Absolutely! But the illustrations and artwork better be accurate, as I have seen inaccurate illustrations backfire.

6) Do you find the artwork educational to the jury? In what ways: visual, helping the expert to educate, whole presentation?

Artwork allows the jury to better visualize and grasp the anatomy, operations at issue, and the injuries the experts are describing and talking about.

8) How often do you utilize medical artwork with your cases?

I mostly use the artwork with my own experts while discussing the anatomy, operations, and injuries. There have also been times when I have referred to the artwork in my closing argument.

9) What type of medical art demonstrative aids have you used?

To date I have only used illustrations of the anatomy, operations, and a few that depict injuries.

10) What is your level of comfort with more advanced applications? What factors determine what you decide to go with as demonstrative aids: technological capability/comfort level, price, ease of getting the illustration approved?

    With a little bit of guidance and practice, I'm generally quite comfortable with applications and devices. Like everything else, the more you do it/use it, the easier it becomes. With that said, you must also take into consideration technological capabilities of the courtroom and how easy it will be to show your aids to the jury.

11) Does opposing counsel have medical illustrations when you do? If so, how does that play out?

    Yes, opposing counsel typically has illustrations they use with their client(s) and/or their own expert(s).

12) Please choose a case in which you used medical demonstrative aids and describe how it was helpful. Did they help you to achieve a verdict higher than expected?

    My most memorable trial involving demonstrative aids was a laparoscopic cholecystectomy case where the defense had these nice, and presumably expensive, illustration boards with overlays that were very well done. The only problem was, these aids only showed three ports/trocars, and the surgery at issue had four. This made for an interesting cross-examination of the defendant.

CHAPTER 4

Medical Illustrations for Medical Malpractice Defense Cases

This chapter features actual cases and describes the work that was done to depict injuries, what was visualized, and how the artwork was utilized. In addition, an interview with the representative attorney, to coincide with each case, will also be provided. The chapter will focus on medical malpractice cases, specifically those in which attorneys are working on behalf of the defense.

4.1 CASE STUDY ONE

Medical Malpractice Defense, Attorney John Sly, Partner, Waranch & Brown, LLC

John was referred to me by an existing client and is a prominent attorney that represents prestigious hospitals and insurance companies on the east coast. He is familiar with utilizing medical artwork to enhance his presentations. He typically wants to visualize the alleged injury made by the surgeon if it is within the standard of care, meaning that it's a possible—and known—complication with the surgery. In some cases, when a patient has a lot of health problems that may include scar tissue or is overweight, such complications are more likely to occur. John also likes to note, and illustrate, such possible outcomes in such instances. That is what happened with the plaintiff in the case we will be discussing, where John represented a neurosurgeon who was being sued.

DOI: 10.4324/9781003336310-4

The featured case is a medical malpractice case where a neurosurgeon was sued for a complication that occurred during a revision anterior cervical discectomy and fusion. The revision surgery was to replace failed hardware. The left side incision was reopened to expose the anterior cervical plate that needed to be replaced. There was an abundance of scar tissue, and the plate was fused to the soft tissues of the neck (Figure 4.3), causing the surgeon to allegedly injure the esophagus during the surgery. This surgical complication is within the standard of care for the procedure. One of the key concepts in medical malpractice defense law is whether a complication falls within the standard of care for the patient, meaning is it possible to injure this anatomical part of the body during this surgery. In this case we needed to prove the surgeon operated within the standard of care.

The plaintiff had copious amounts of scar tissue that adhered the esophagus to the cervical spine plate. As a result, blunt and sharp dissection were performed in order to take down the failed hardware. The patient's tissue near the previous plate was very friable (delicate), thereby making the surgery even more difficult to perform (Figure 4.4).

Due to this surgical complication, many surgeries were performed to correct the hole in the esophagus. A myofascial flap (Figure 4.17) was what finally repaired the hole, and the plaintiff regained esophageal functioning and was able to swallow on her own. Legally and medically, they term it as being made "medically whole." Medically whole meaning that they are functioning as well as they can be physically. This is an important statement and distinction for the purposes of legal cases and arguments.

After this plaintiff regained the ability to swallow on her own, she said that she was unable to leave the house without a towel to cough into. Since she was asking for quite a large sum of money in the lawsuit, she was followed by a private investigator hired by defense Attorney Sly. She was followed for a while and was never once seen coughing into a towel. Due to this inconsistency, coupled with an unwillingness to settle with the hospital, there was a verdict in favor of the defense, and the plaintiff was awarded nothing.

Attorney Sly's strategy in this case was to show the pre-operative condition of the plaintiff's spine, the many surgical steps to fix the esophageal hole, the extubation, and the final surgery depicting the myofascial flap that repaired the esophageal hole. All the illustrations were to teach the jury the nature and challenges of the complicated surgery and all the steps it took to fix her esophagus. Attorney Sly wanted to show what her medical condition was before the surgery and how tough it was for the surgeon to navigate. He also wanted to depict how the complications could have happened during the delicate surgery. He wanted to express that this plaintiff was made whole medically. She had a myofascial graft that fixed the hole and, again, was able to eat, drink, and swallow on her own. This fact, in and of itself, constituted a huge success!

Illustrations from this case include the following:

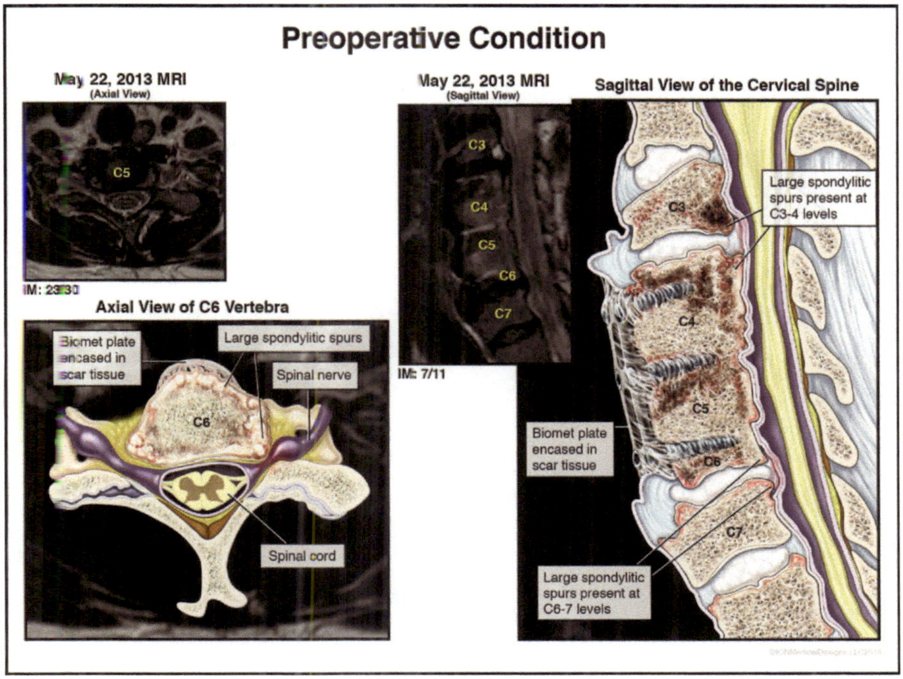

FIGURE 4.1 This colorized MRI features the condition of the plaintiff's spine prior to her revision ACDF (anterior cervical discectomy and fusion). It shows all the scar tissue, which is an important factor in this case. It is extra difficult to operate on a person with an abundance of scar tissue.

The series of illustrations collectively outlined the many steps of the surgery—including the complexity of the procedure and complicating factors (e.g., scar tissue). This served as a successful tactic in proving that the surgery was successful and that standard of care was clearly met.

Interview questions:

1) What is the process in which you use the illustrations: for exchange, depositions, mediation, trial?

   My specialty is the defense of complicated civil matters. To assist jurors in understanding what can sometimes be esoteric issues of science and medicine, illustrations can be critically important. I often integrate them into PowerPoint presentations or as stand-alone slides.

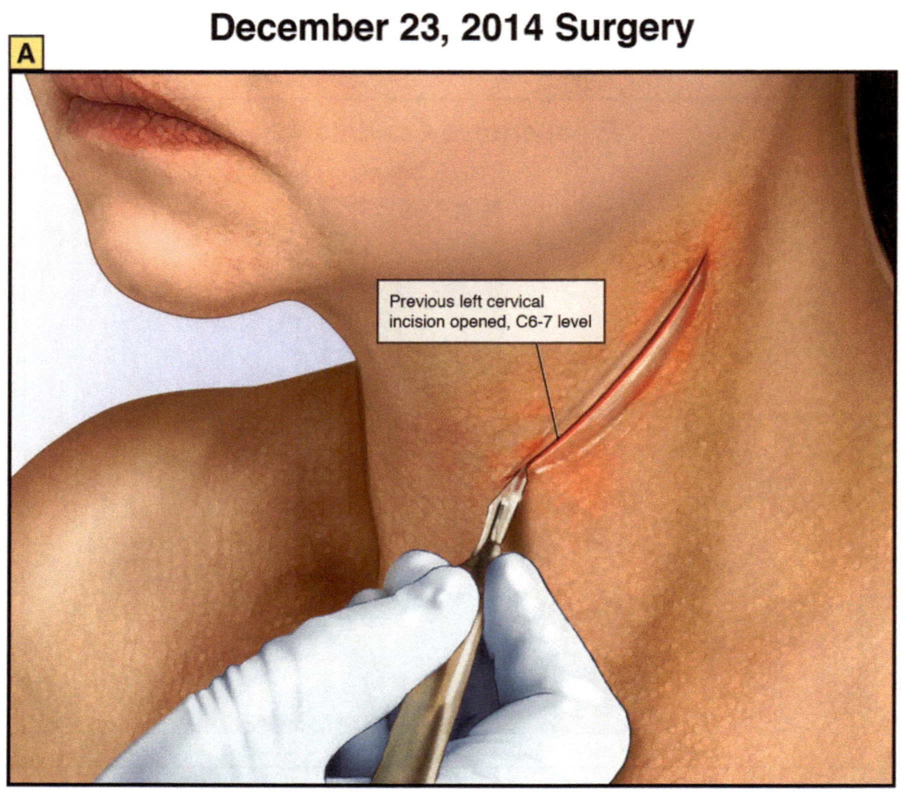

FIGURE 4.2 This illustration is #1 of 14 that were separated into individual illustration boards for clarity. The illustration shows the incision over the C6–7 cervical spinal level.

These are five ways I have used illustrations in depositions and trial:

1. *To explain complex or technical information*: Illustrations can be a great way to help jurors understand complex or technical information. For example, I have used an illustration to explain a surgery, how a multi-vehicle accident happened, or how a product malfunctioned.

2. *To highlight key points*: Illustrations can also be used to highlight key points in a case. For example, I've used illustrations to show the jury the location of a surgical procedure, or to depict the sequence of events leading up to a surgical complication.

3. *To create a visual record of testimony*: Illustrations can be used to preview coming testimony and then to create a visual record of testimony. This can be helpful for jurors who may have difficulty remembering what they heard during a long trial.

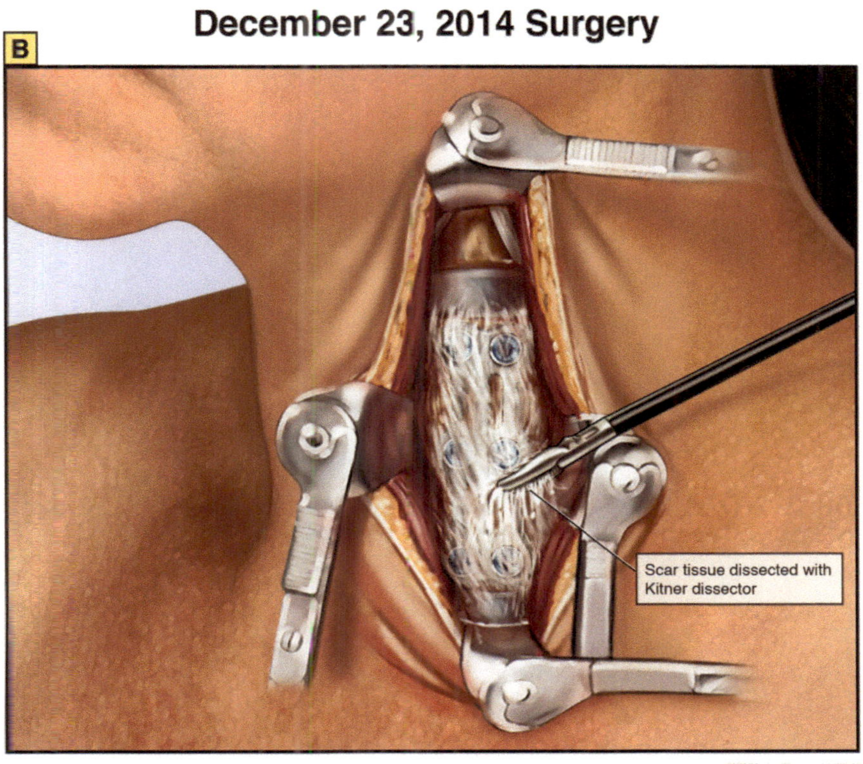

FIGURE 4.3 This illustration is #2 of 14. This one shows the abundance of scar tissue that covered the anterior surface of the cervical plate. The plate was adhered to the soft tissues of the neck, including the esophagus. Again, this illustration visually depicts the scar tissue and the added difficulty it presents to a surgeon operating on a person with an abundance of scar tissue.

4. *To engage the jury*: Illustrations can be a great way to engage the jury and keep their attention. For example, I try to use illustrations to create a story out of what might appear to be disparate facts. Done right, a lawyer can create a sense of suspense which helps to hold jurors' attention.

5. *To persuade the jury*: Illustrations can be a powerful tool for persuasion. For example, I've used illustrations to make a point that is difficult to argue against.

When used effectively, illustrations can be a valuable asset to any lawyer. They can help to explain complex information, highlight key points, create a visual record of testimony, engage the jury, and persuade the jury.

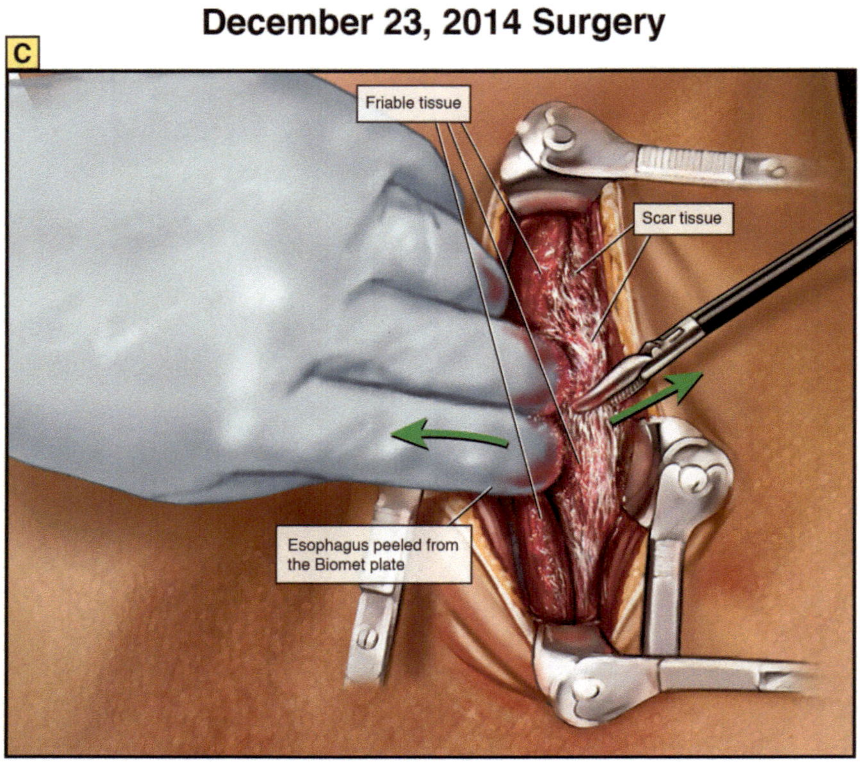

FIGURE 4.4 This illustration is #3 of 14. This one shows the blunt dissection performed by the surgeon to separate the tissues from the cervical plate. This illustration helps to show the care the surgeon took in order to not injure the tissues of the neck. Figure 4.5 illustration is #4 of 14 that shows the original plate and screws being removed.

Here are some additional tips I've picked up over the years using illustrations in depositions and trial:

- Make sure the illustrations are clear and easy to understand.
- Use illustrations that are relevant to the case.
- Keep the illustrations simple and uncluttered.
- Use illustrations to supplement testimony, not replace it.
- Practice using the illustrations before the deposition or trial.

2) How do you decide what cases you think would benefit from medical illustrations?

   The vast majority of matters I'm involved with involve complicated facts and medicine. I decide what cases would benefit from medical illustrations based on a number of factors, including the following:

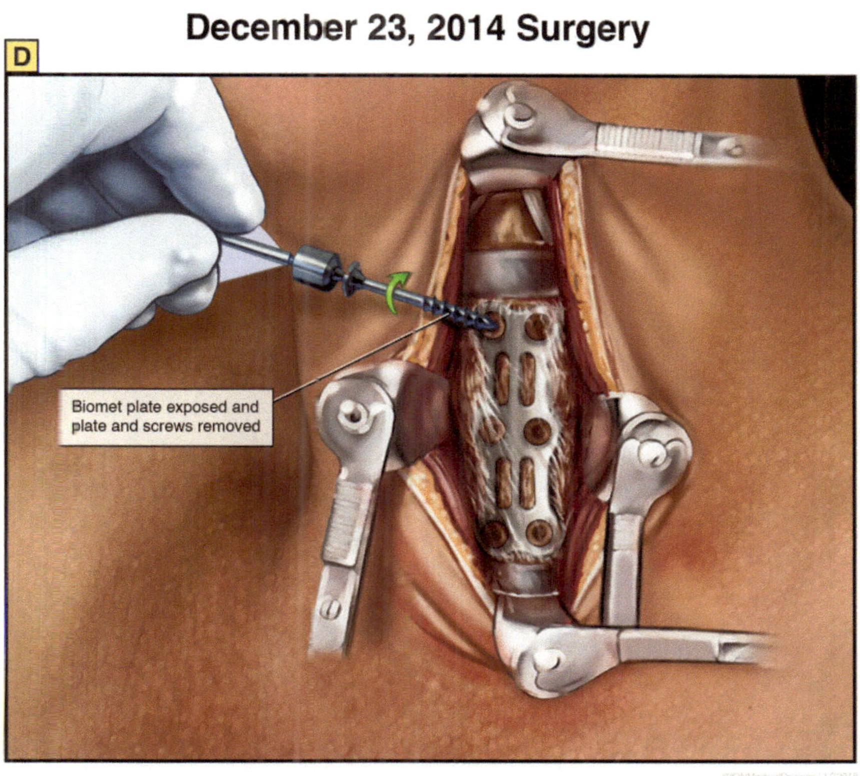

FIGURE 4.5 This illustration is #5 of 14, which shows the bony arthritis removed with a high-speed bur.

- The complexity of the issues involved in the case
- The need to educate the judge or jury about the issues
- The need to help the judge or jury understand the plaintiff's alleged injuries
- The need to rebut the plaintiff's expert testimony
- The need to make the case more visually appealing

Frankly, in some cases, medical illustrations, in particular, may be the only way to effectively communicate the issues involved in a case to the judge or jury. For example, in a medical malpractice case, a medical illustration can be used to show the jury how a complication may have occurred without medical negligence.

Medical illustrations can also be used to help the judge or jury understand the testimony of expert witnesses. For example, if an expert witness is testifying about the cause of a plaintiff's alleged injuries, a medical illustration can be used to show the jury how the injuries occurred without medical negligence.

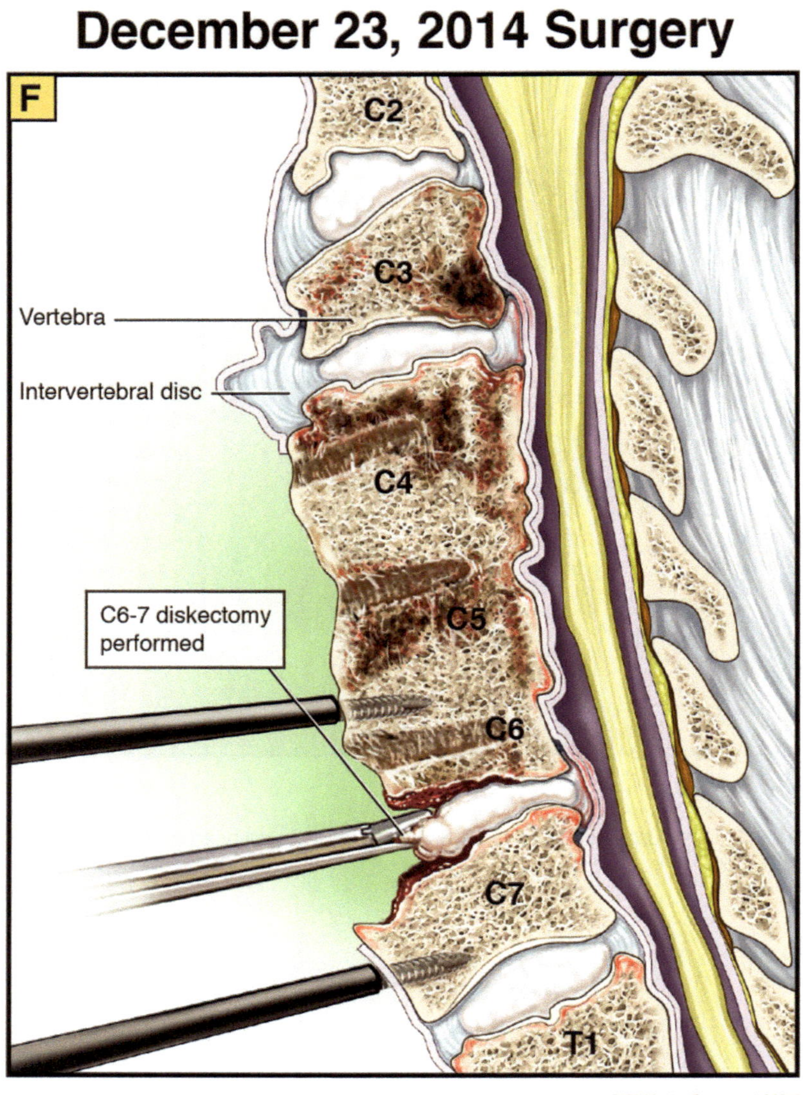

FIGURE 4.6 This illustration is #6 of 14, which shows a C6–7 discectomy (i.e., the removal of the intervertebral disc).

Finally, medical illustrations can be used to make a case more visually appealing. This can be helpful in cases where the judge or jury may be more likely to remember a case if it is presented in a visually appealing way—this holds true in nearly all cases.

Overall, medical illustrations can be a valuable tool for lawyers in a variety of cases. They can be used to educate the judge or jury about the medical issues involved in the case, help the case be more visually appealing.

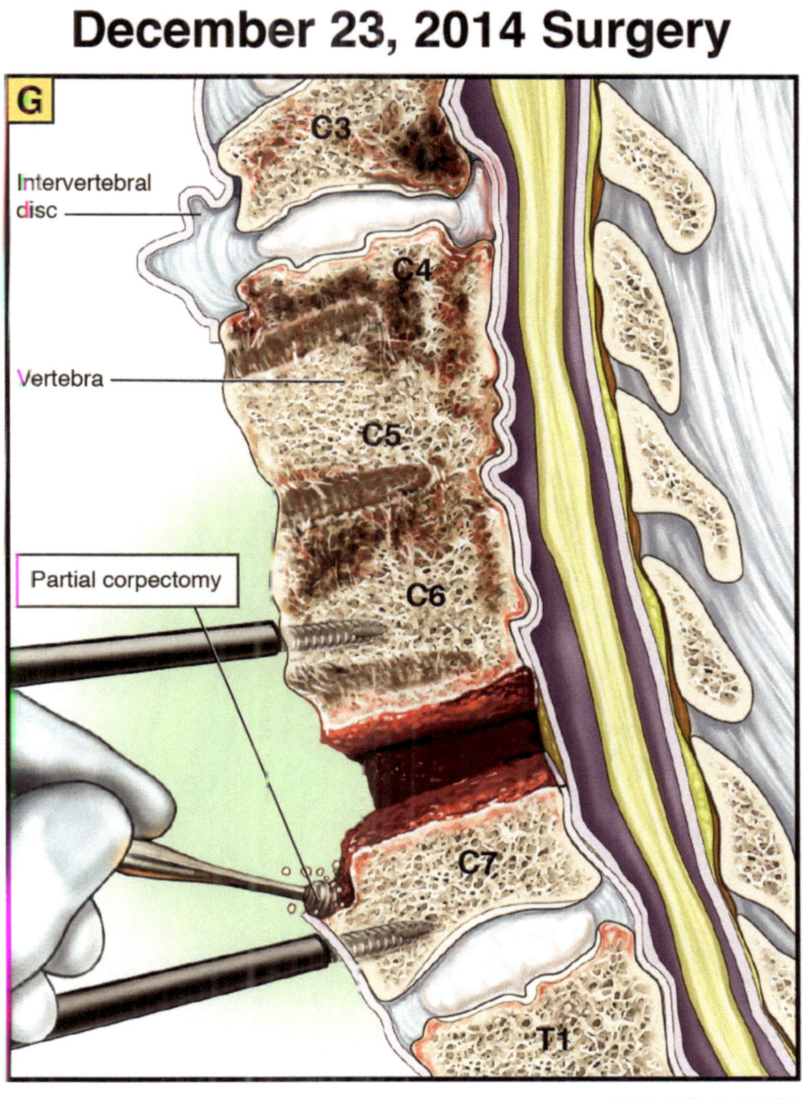

FIGURE 4.7 This illustration is #7 of 14, which shows the bony arthritis being removed from the anterior C7 vertebra.

3) How do you use the artwork in the courtroom?

I like to present illustrations during opening using PowerPoint, as I'm describing the science and/or medicine. Then I use those illustrations with relevant witnesses during the trial. Finally, I show the illustrations again in closing. The repetition of the presentation of illustrations helps jurors understand difficult concepts and lends credibility to them.

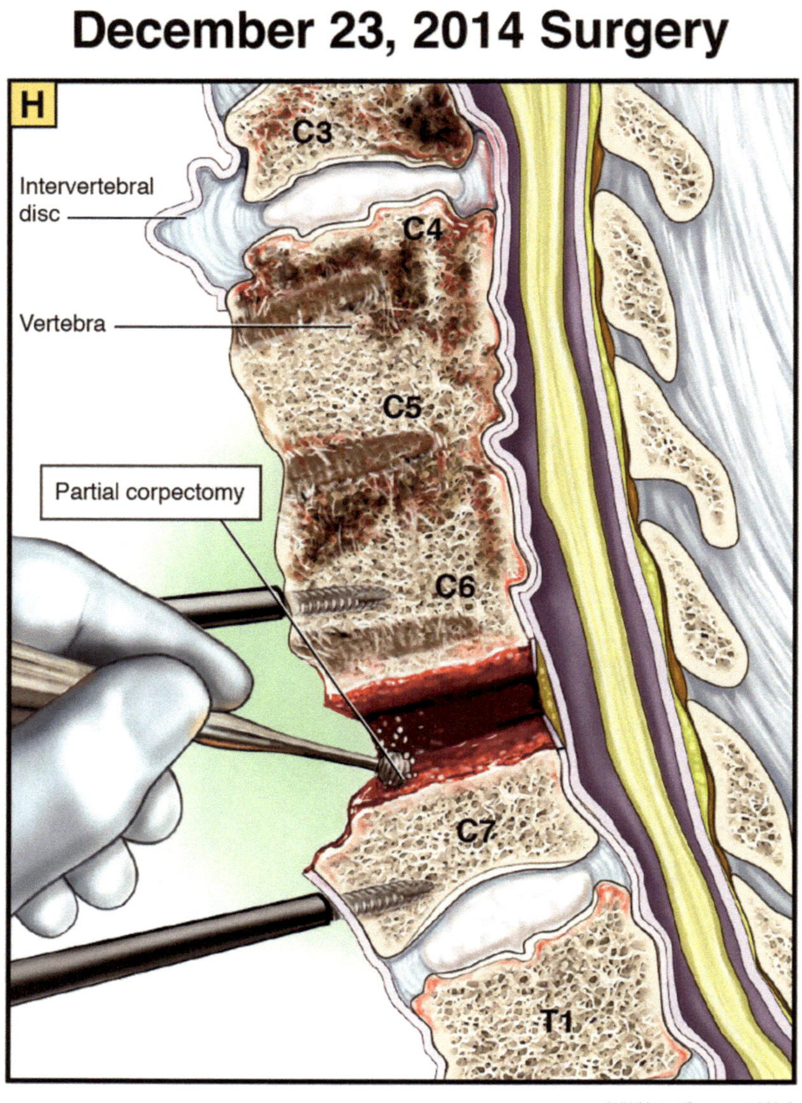

FIGURE 4.8 This illustration is #8 of 14, which shows the end plates being prepared for fusion.

Medical malpractice attorneys can effectively use artwork in a trial in several ways. Artwork can be used to do the following:

- Explain complex medical concepts: Medical malpractice cases often involve complex medical concepts that can be difficult for jurors to understand. Artwork can be used to help jurors visualize these concepts and better understand the facts of the case. For example, an

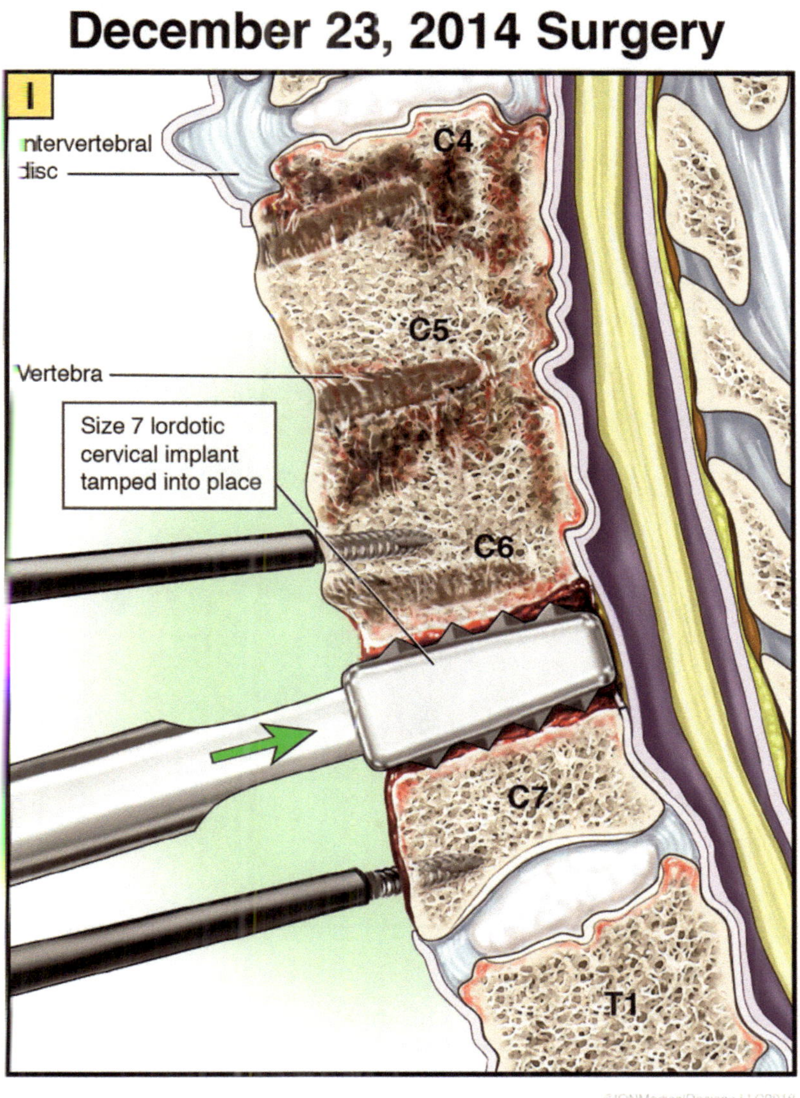

FIGURE 4.9 This illustration is #9 of 14, which shows the lordotic cervical implant being inserted.

attorney might use an illustration to show the anatomy of a particular organ or to explain the steps involved in a medical procedure.

- Demonstrate the standard of care: In order to prove that a doctor was negligent, the plaintiff must show that the doctor failed to meet the standard of care. Artwork can be used to demonstrate the standard of care by showing what a reasonable doctor needed, or would be

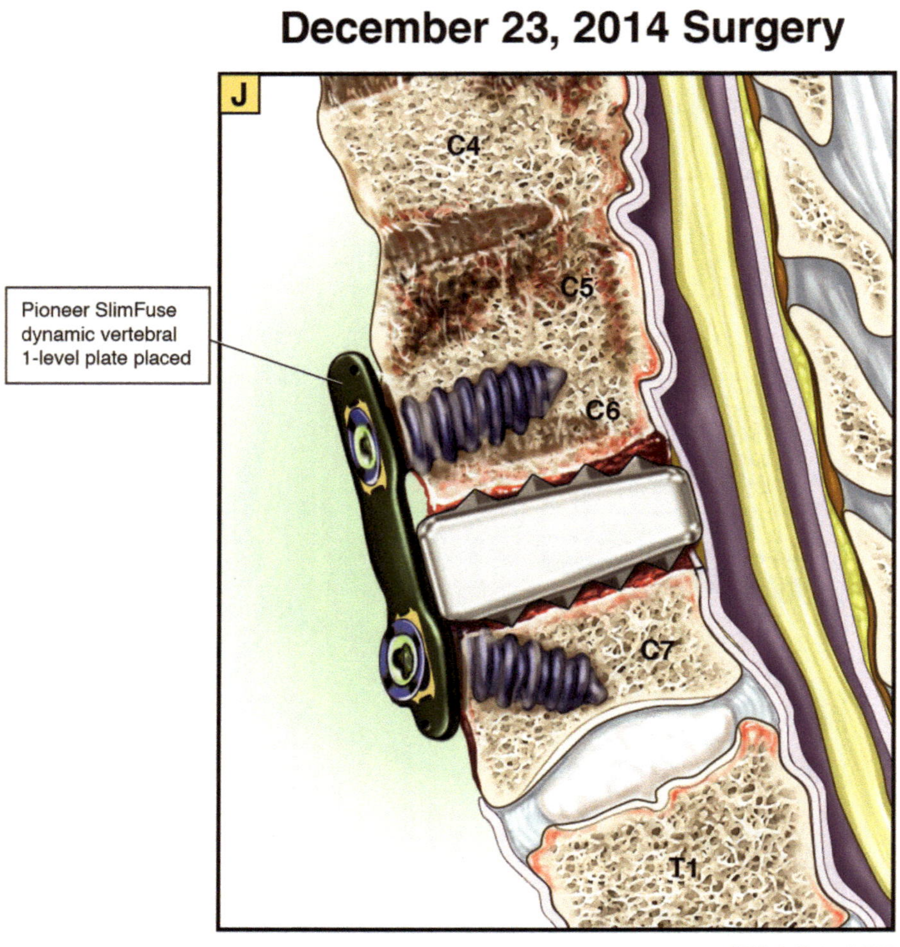

FIGURE 4.10 This illustration is one of #10, which shows the Pioneer SlimFuse® plate placed over the cervical implant to secure the fusion.

reasonably expected, to do. The use of artwork can be used by counsel on both sides to illustrate their points.

4) What medical art services have you utilized and tried out in court, for example, illustration, animation, interactive application, timeline?

   I have used illustrations, animations, and timelines. I also use illustrations and then include animations with them using PowerPoint. From a legal perspective, there are often limitations on the use of true animations. This is because some jurisdictions require disclosure of the animation long before one may be prepared and ready for trial. Instead, I've found it possible to

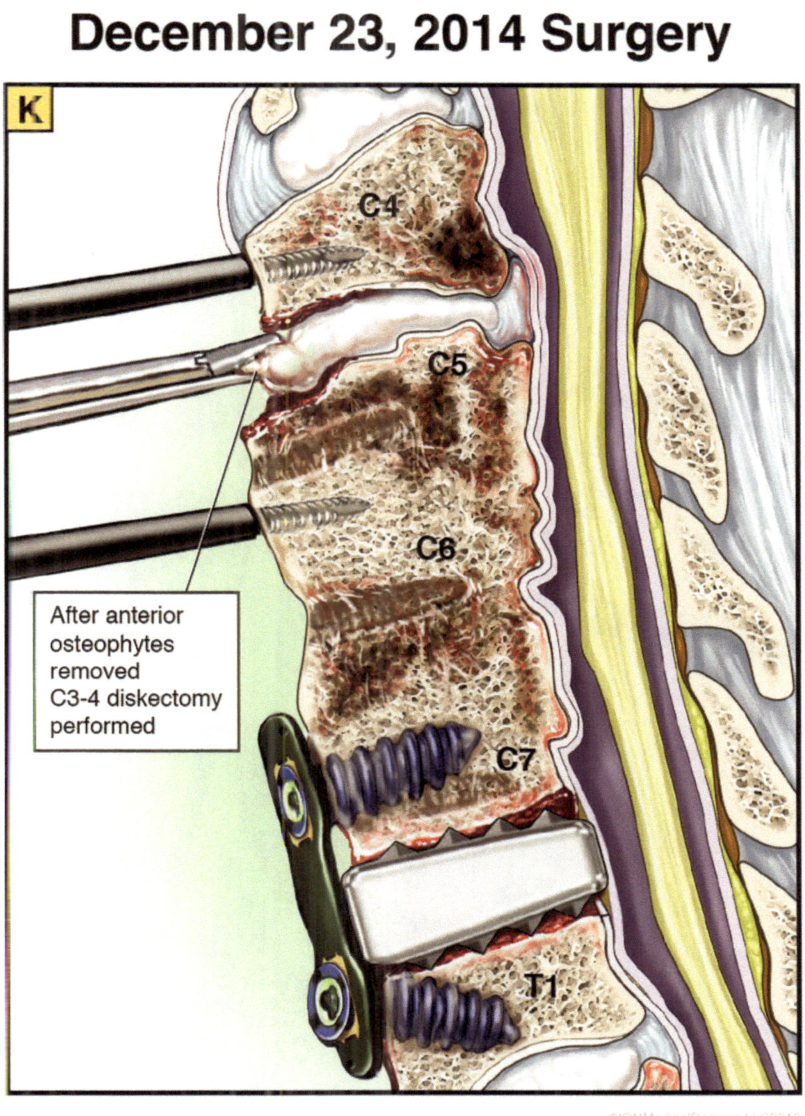

FIGURE 4.11 This illustration is #11 of 14, which shows the removal of the C4–5 intervertebral disc.

effectively use illustrations embedded into timelines to depict the same points.

5) Is the artwork well received in the courtroom?

My impression, based on responses I've received from focus groups and jurors, is that quality artwork is critically important for laypeople in understanding complex scientific/medical issues.

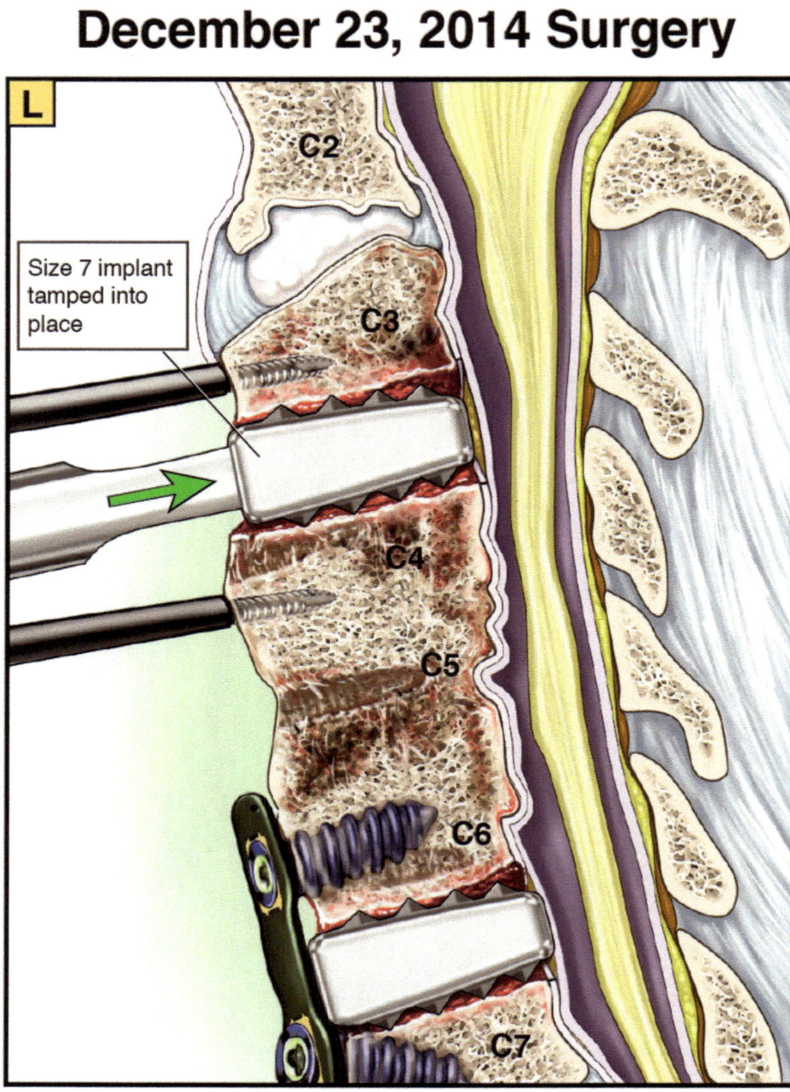

FIGURE 4.12 This illustration is #12 of 14, which shows the placement of the C3–4 lordotic implant.

As lawyers, we must remember that jurors are in a very difficult position when serving in a complicated case involving issues beyond their personal experiences. Artwork can be critical in helping them do their job by informing them of the key issues in the case and by visually displaying relevant anatomy and scientific concepts.

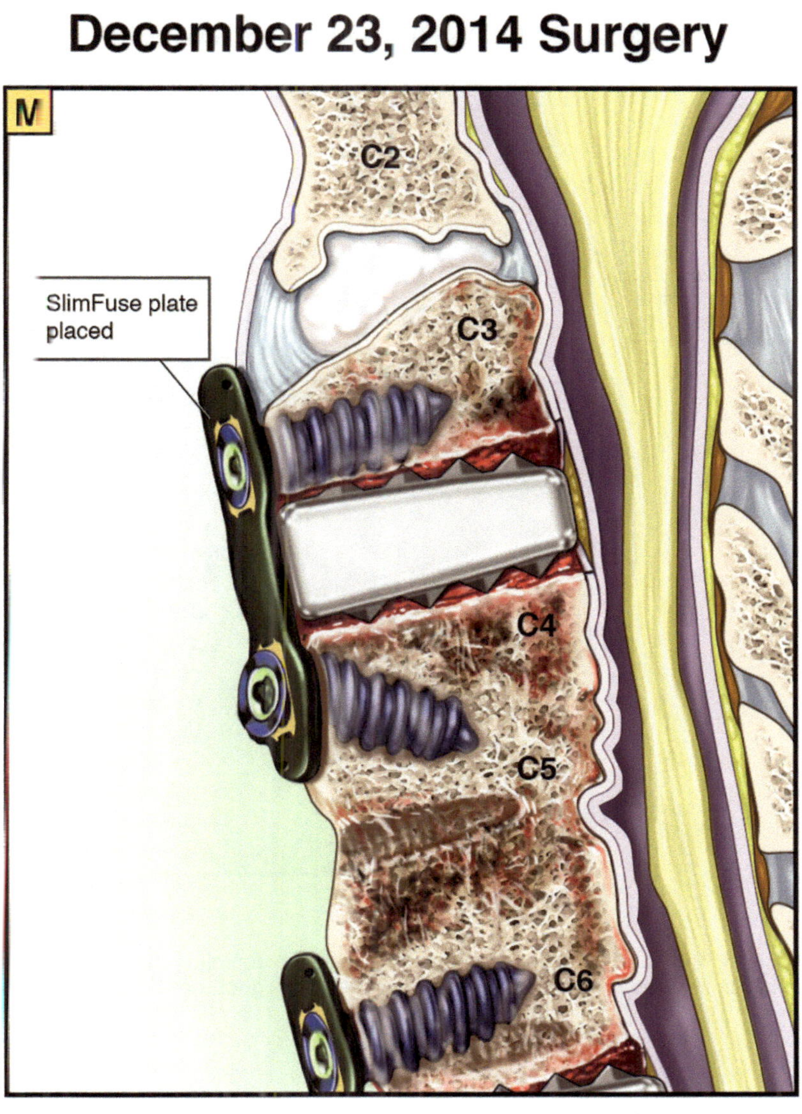

FIGURE 4.13 This illustration is #13 of 14, which shows the Pioneer SlimFuse® plate placed over the cervical implant to secure the C3–4 lordotic implant.

This is particularly true with younger jurors. In my experience, younger jurors—used to YouTube and similar platforms—are very adept at learning through visual media but are quickly bored and/or confused if testimony is provided without the anchor of visual aids.

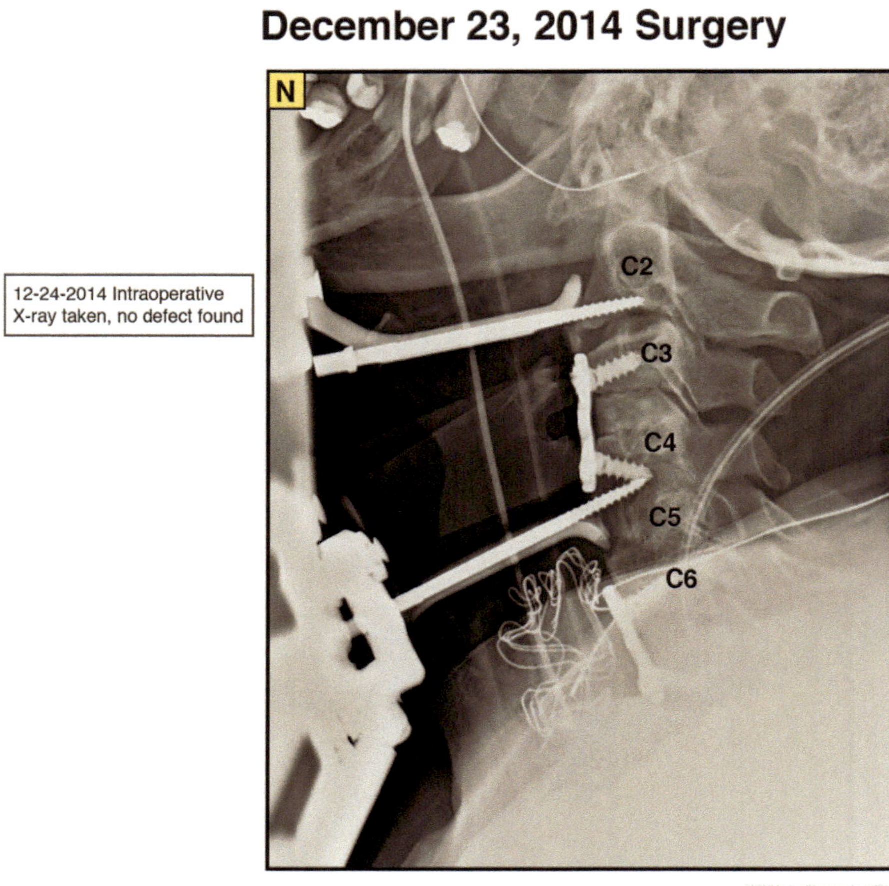

FIGURE 4.14 This is an intraoperative x-ray reproduction depicting the placement of the cervical spine plates, to make sure the placement is in good position, before closure.

6) Do you find the artwork educational to the jury? In what ways: visual, helping the expert to educate, whole presentation?

   Artwork is an integral part of my entire presentation process during trial. It can educate a jury during a medical malpractice case in a number of ways. For example, it can help to illustrate complex medical concepts in a way that is easy for jurors to understand. In cases involving radiology, I have had artwork created that overlays the original image and more clearly depicts the relevant organs and other structures.

   In addition to these general benefits, artwork can also be used to educate a jury about specific aspects of a medical malpractice case. For example, if the case involves a surgical procedure, artwork can be used to show the

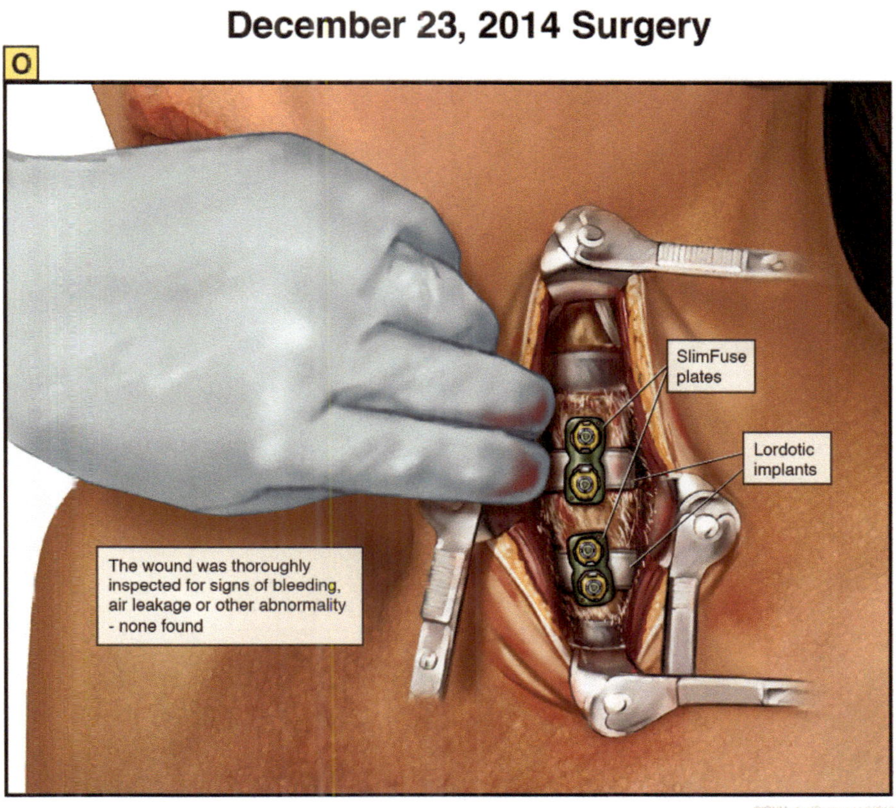

FIGURE 4.15 This illustration is #14 of 14, which shows the two cervical plates in position over the lordotic implants, and the surgeon inspecting the surgical site for signs of bleeding.

steps of the procedure and how it is supposed to be performed. This can help jurors to understand whether the doctor deviated from the standard of care and whether this deviation caused the patient's injury.

Here are two examples of how I have used artwork to educate juries in medical malpractice cases:

- In a case involving a patient who was paralyzed after surgery, I used a depiction of a spinal cord and the surgical process to illustrate the alleged injury and alternative causes. The illustration helped the jury to understand the complex anatomy of the spinal cord and why the surgical technique of the physician did not damage it.
- In a case involving a patient who died after an alleged medication error, I used a photograph of the patient's medication bottles, and illustrations relating to the rate of absorption, to show the jury how the patient had misused the medication.

Extubation

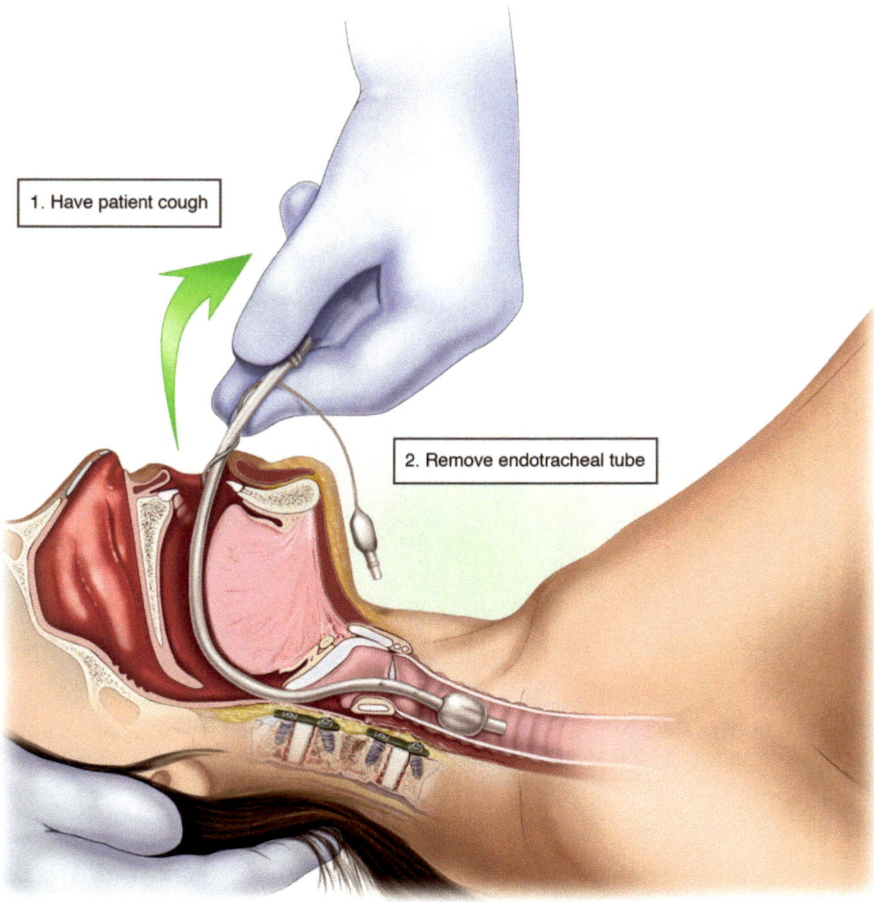

FIGURE 4.16 This illustration shows how to remove an endotracheal tube: have the patient cough and then remove.

7) How often do you utilize medical artwork with your cases?

   I use medical artwork in every medically related case because even basic anatomy can be very difficult to verbally explain to a lay jury.

8) What type of medical art demonstrative aids have you used?

   I have used artwork to demonstrate anatomy, surgical approaches, and complications. Medical art demonstrative aids can be used by a medical

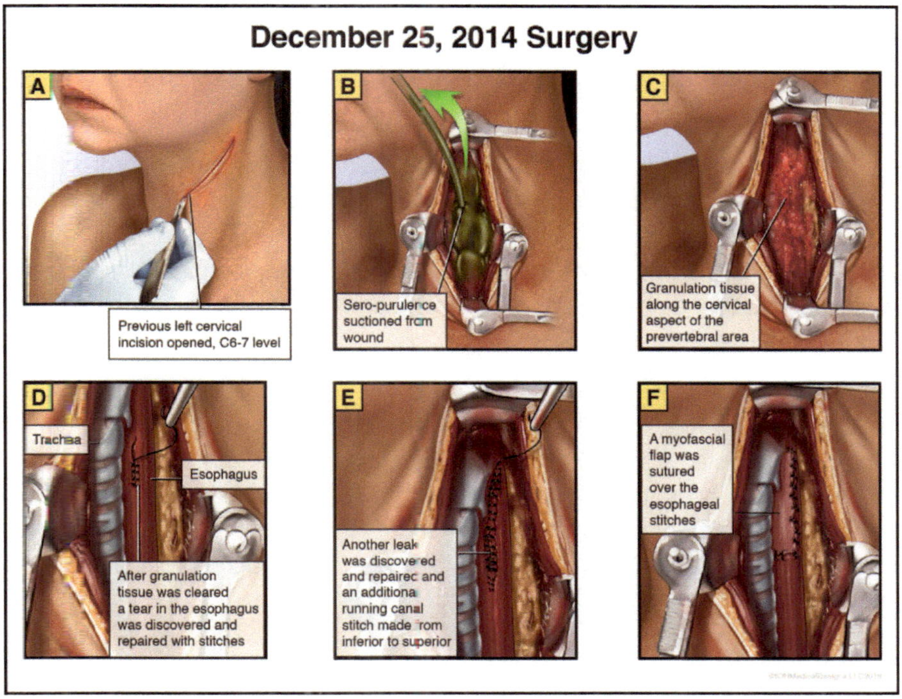

FIGURE 4.17 This illustration was the last illustration board showing how the esophagus was patched with a myofascial flap. This surgery was successful, and the plaintiff was able to swallow on her own!

malpractice attorney to help explain complex medical concepts to a jury. These aids can be in the form of drawings, photographs, or even 3D models. They can be used to illustrate the anatomy of the human body, the steps involved in a medical procedure, or the injuries that were sustained as a result of medical malpractice.

Some examples of medical art demonstrative aids that I have used include the following:

- Diagrams of the human body, showing the location of organs and tissues.
- Photographs of medical procedures, taken during or after the procedure and then enhanced by artist renderings.
- 3D models of the human body, which can be used to demonstrate how injuries occurred.
- Animation, which can be used to show how a medical procedure is done. This can either be done through true animation/computer-generated visuals or by using PowerPoint to overlay visuals in temporal order by using the “animation” tool.

9) What is your level of comfort with more advanced applications? What factors determine what you decide to go with as demonstrative aids: technological capability/comfort level, price, ease of getting the illustration approved?

   I am very comfortable integrating new technologies and applications into depositions and trials.

Jurors come to the courtroom with their own learning approaches. Nevertheless, we are increasingly a visual-learning society, so any lawyer who wishes to persuade jurors must engage them with effective visuals.

In my experience, jurors expect that lawyers will present their points in clear and interesting ways. They have all watched television shows and movies where entire trials are completed visually in mere minutes. My impression is that if a lawyer is not able to demonstrate their points efficiently and clearly, the jurors are left with the impression that the points themselves are not well-thought-out. In other words, being able to seamlessly use a multitude of aids to present complex ideas creates in the minds of the jurors a sense of credibility.

10) Is there a demand for visual aids (CSI) effect?

    Yes, there is evidence that jurors expect visual aids in trial because of the CSI effect. The CSI effect is a phenomenon in which people's expectations about forensic science are influenced by their exposure to crime dramas like CSI: Crime Scene Investigation. These shows often depict forensic scientists using cutting-edge technology to solve crimes, and this can lead jurors to believe that forensic evidence is always available and reliable. As a result, jurors may be more likely to find a defendant guilty if the prosecution does not present visual aids that demonstrate the forensic evidence.

    But it goes further than simply the CSI effect. Remember that jurors are almost constantly exposed to visual depictions of litigation in television shows, on the internet, and in movies. What they see on these platforms is what they expect to see in the courtroom when they serve as jurors.

11) Do opposing counsel have medical illustrations when you do? If so, how does that play out?

    The use of visual aids by opposing counsel has been hit-and-miss over my career. The effective use of those aids has also varied widely.

    They key is both having effective visual aids and seamlessly integrating them into attorney argument and witness testimony. This takes practice. So, for example, it is not enough to have great visuals in an opening statement that otherwise lacks theme and cohesion. Likewise, without embedding the visuals into expert testimony, otherwise effective testimony can be overshadowed, and/or the visuals can be distracting. My experience is that lawyers, in particular, are slow to adopt new technologies. Where I have quality visuals and have worked them into my arguments and witness outlines, they can help to overwhelm an opponent who does not have them or has failed to effectively use them.

12. Please choose a case in which you used medical demonstrative aids and describe how it was helpful. Did they help you to achieve a verdict higher than expected?

Take this case of mine that you featured here to start the chapter. I represented a spine surgeon who revised a cervical spine fusion. Other surgeons had refused to perform the revision surgery because the esophagus had fused to the plate that had been previously placed. My client, a world-renowned surgeon, successfully completed the revision, but a perforation of the esophagus occurred that necessitated multiple subsequent procedures and left the patient with an impaired ability to speak.

The neck is a surprisingly complicated area of anatomy. Without the use of demonstrative aids, there was no way a lay jury would be able to fully appreciate the relevant anatomy in this case.

In the trial presentation, starting with my opening statement and running through testimony and closing argument, we integrated artwork to educate the jurors on general anatomy. Then individualized artwork was used to show how the plaintiff's anatomy was divergent.

The entire surgical procedure was depicted throughout the trial, and we used the actual radiology of the patient, enhanced by artist renderings, to explain how the complication happened without medical negligence. In the end, we were successful in defending the surgeon, and the jurors afterward explained that the illustrations were very helpful to them in reaching their collective decision.

4.2 CASE STUDY TWO

Medical Malpractice Defense, Attorney Christina Billiet, Partner, Waranch & Brown, LLC

Attorney Billiet was also referred to me by a client of mine. She works at the same law firm as Attorney Sly. She is also a prominent east coast defense attorney. She is familiar with medical illustration and uses art with most of her cases. Attorney Billiet is very talented in researching medical theories and working with medical experts for her cases and puts in the time effort to defend her clients in medical malpractice claims. The case we will be discussing is a medical malpractice case with a very interesting medical theory proved correct.

The featured case is a medical malpractice case where an obstetrician was sued due to a complicated delivery where the fetus contracted a chorioamnionitis infection from a preterm rupture of membranes. The baby was preterm and was in breech position. The membranes had ruptured, and the amniotic fluid was diminished. When membranes are ruptured, and delivery is delayed, there is a larger window and higher probability for infection to occur.

In this case, the mother contracted a chorioamnionitis infection during delivery. Once the infection occurs in the mother's bloodstream, the fetus will contract it even if antibiotics are administered (Figure 4.20). Chorioamnionitis is a serious condition that can occur during pregnancy where the membranes surrounding the fetus are infected with bacteria. The chorioamnionitis can cause a fetal inflammatory response where the body releases cytokines that can cross the blood-brain barrier (Figure 4.31) and cause fetal brain damage. Thus, it is categorized as an autoimmune disease wherein the body is attacking itself.

The strategy in this case was to establish and prove that the fetus didn't have a hypoxic brain injury, but that the baby contracted chorioamnionitis at birth and had an inflammatory response. Thus, it would be shown that the baby ended up with brain damage due to the infection. The defense theory was to show that with inflammation happening in the body, an autoimmune (body attacking itself) disease can be triggered. Cytokines (inflammatory cells) can cross the blood-brain barrier with the help of our own immune cells ingesting them and subsequently carrying them over (Figure 4.31). Most cells, bacteria, and viruses cannot cross the blood-brain barrier. Once the cytokines are in the brain, they cause inflammation, damage neurons (Figure 4.33), and fluid pockets within the brain tissue form (Figure 4.34). This causes a lot of damage to the brain and medical impairments to the fetus, causing lifelong impairment.

The defense's argument is that the brain damage was caused by inflammation of the brain caused by the infection (chorioamnionitis), not an anoxic brain injury (lack of oxygen to the brain). An anoxic brain injury was the prosecution's argument.

This case resulted in a successful verdict for the defense!

Attorney Billiet decided on using illustration boards, a 2D animation, a fetal monitoring strip, and a timeline to help defend her case.

The following are the demonstrative aids that were created.

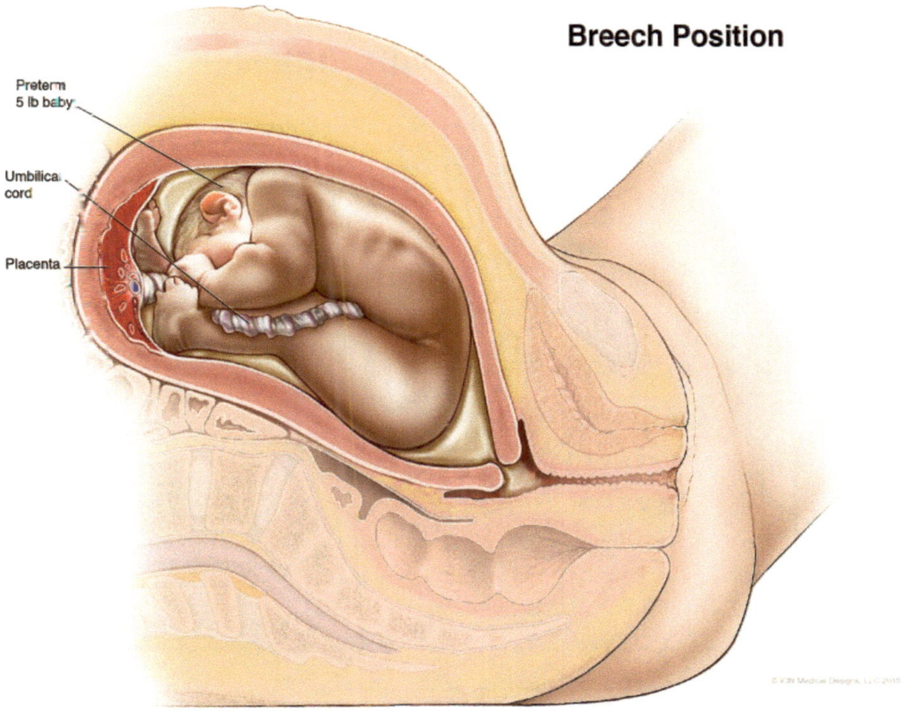

FIGURE 4.18 This illustration depicts a preterm (early) baby in breech (upside down) position with diminished amniotic fluid (fluid in utero). Breech position and low amniotic fluid is abnormal during childbirth. Anatomical abnormalities are something defense attorneys look for in their cases. Any such complications or otherwise extenuating circumstances possible for causing the medical issues claimed. The illustration is used to show anyone who is not medically trained on what the medical terminology means.

Infections can occur during childbirth. Unfortunately, once the mother has contracted a chorioamnionitis infection, the fetus will contract it too. Attorney Billiet and her team of experts scientifically proved that inflammation of the brain that results can have similar damage to the brain as a hypoxic brain injury. However, hypoxia occurs when there is lack of oxygen to the brain, which did not occur in this case.

It was proven that the baby contracted a chorioamnionitis infection that caused inflammation to the brain tissue. As a result, though a tragedy, the obstetrician was not at fault for the unfortunate outcome of the birth and the baby's related injuries.

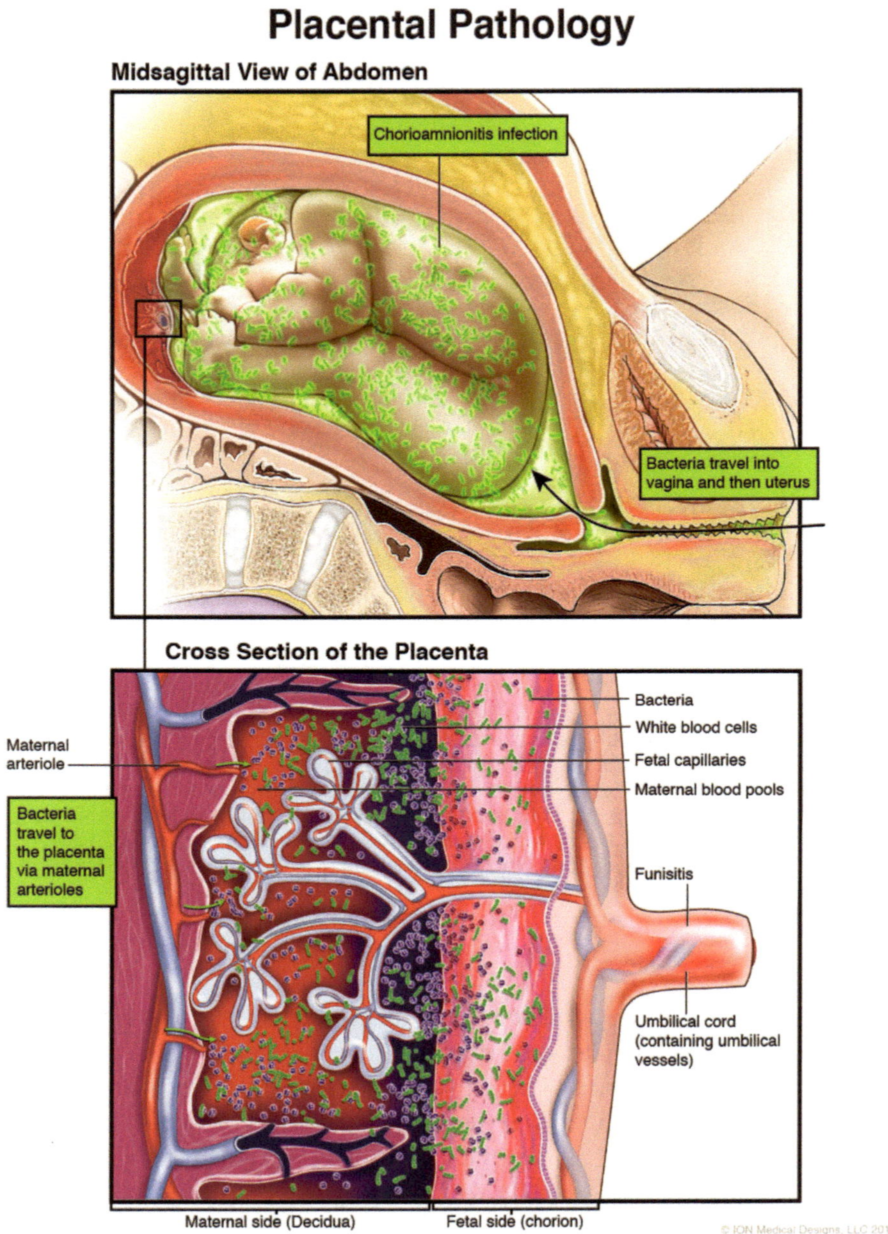

FIGURE 4.19 This illustration depicts the pathology (disease) of the placenta after the rupture of membranes (water breaks). The mother contracted a chorioamnionitis infection which was passed through the blood to the fetus. The illustration on the bottom is a close-up section of the placenta and depicts how the infection travels through the mother's bloodstream and mixes with the fetus' blood. Once a mother gets an infection, the fetus will also contract it through the bloodstream.

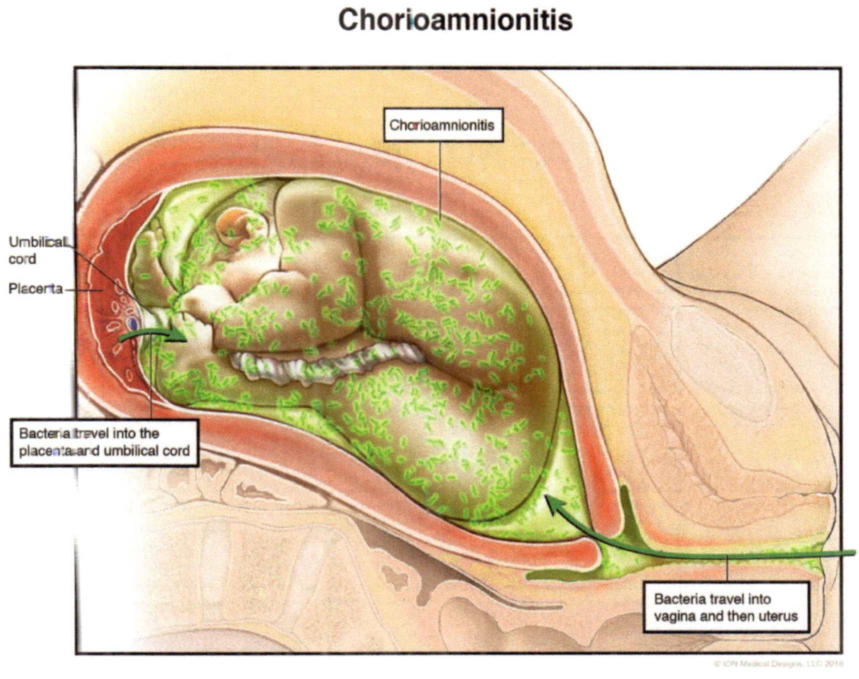

FIGURE 4.20 This illustration depicts a preterm baby in breech position after the ruptured membranes (water breaks). The chorioamnionitis has entered the vagina and is in the uterus. The infection has traveled to the placenta and umbilical cord, infecting the fetus.

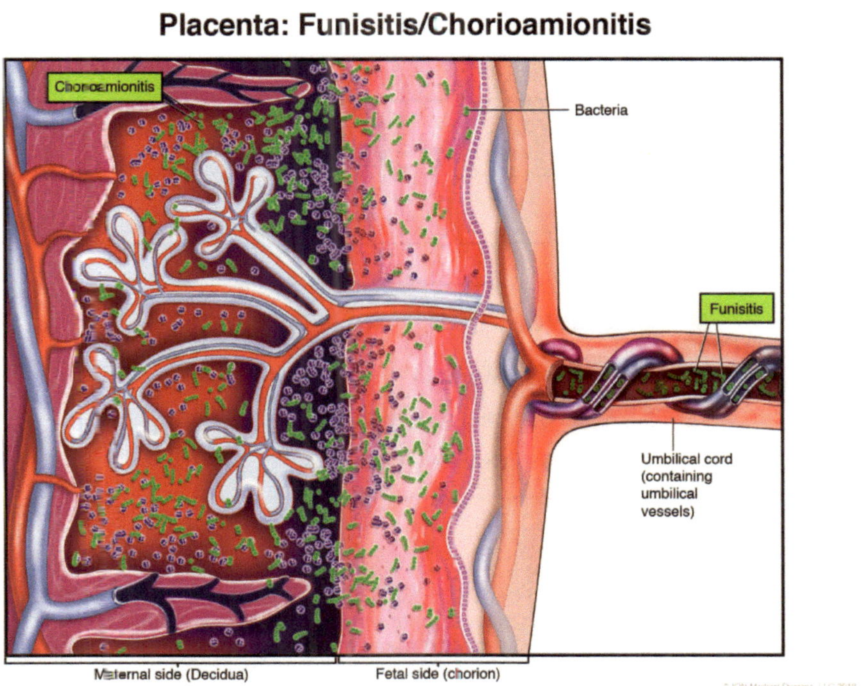

FIGURE 4.21 This illustration is a close-up section of the placenta with a chorioamnionitis infection and funisitis (inflammation of the umbilical cord). The maternal and fetal side of the placenta are represented in this illustration.

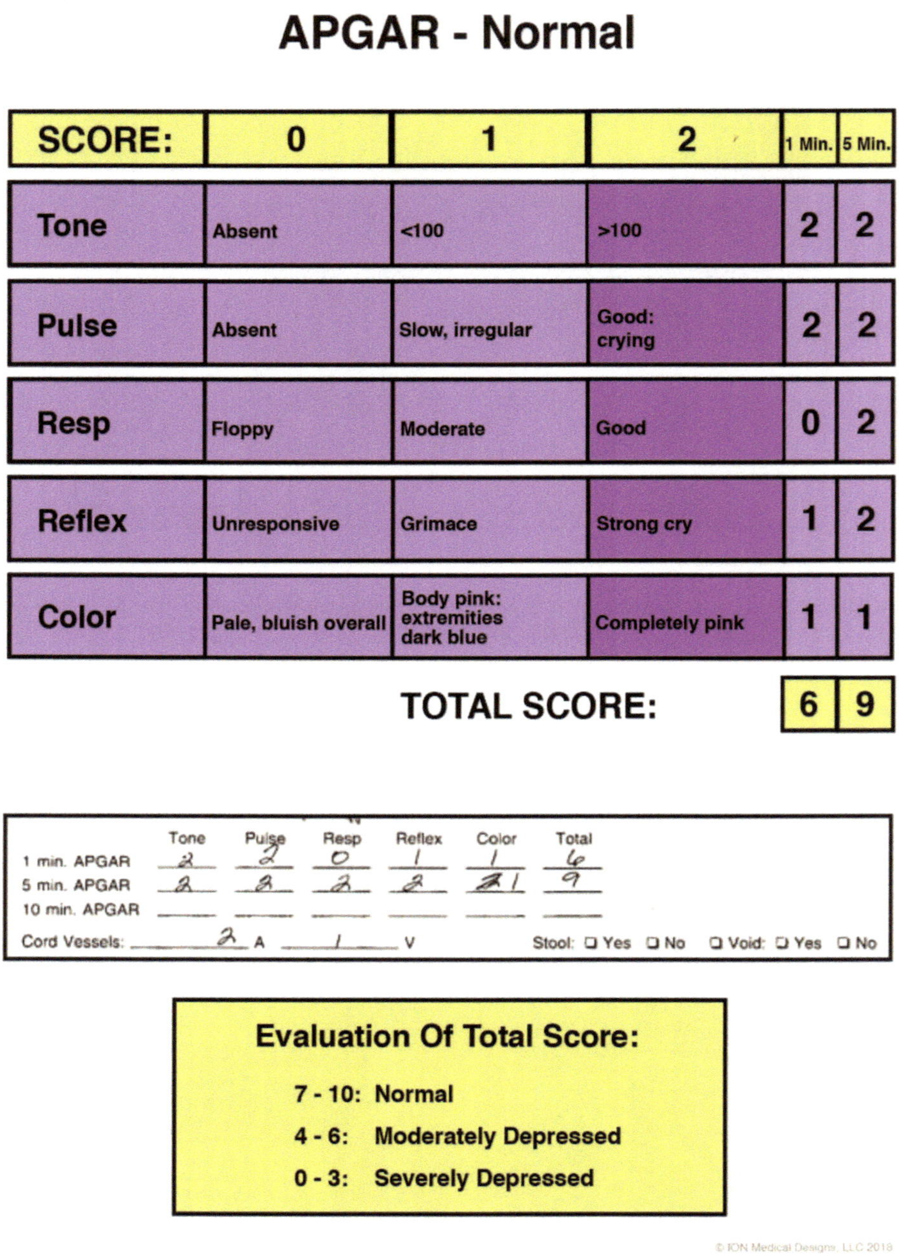

FIGURE 4.22 This is a chart of the baby's APGAR score at birth and at several time increments after birth. APGAR stands for appearance, pulse, grimace, activity, and respiration. An APGAR chart is a rapid means to measures the health attributes of the baby immediately after they are born and in response to resuscitation.

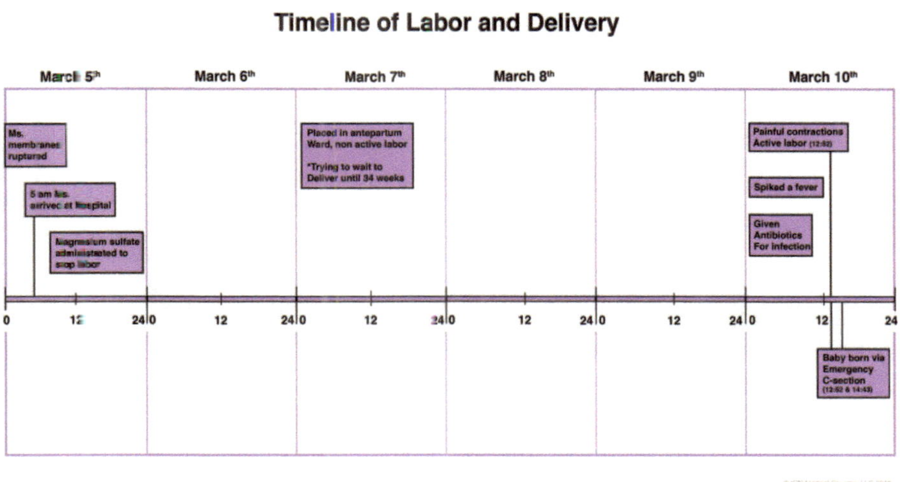

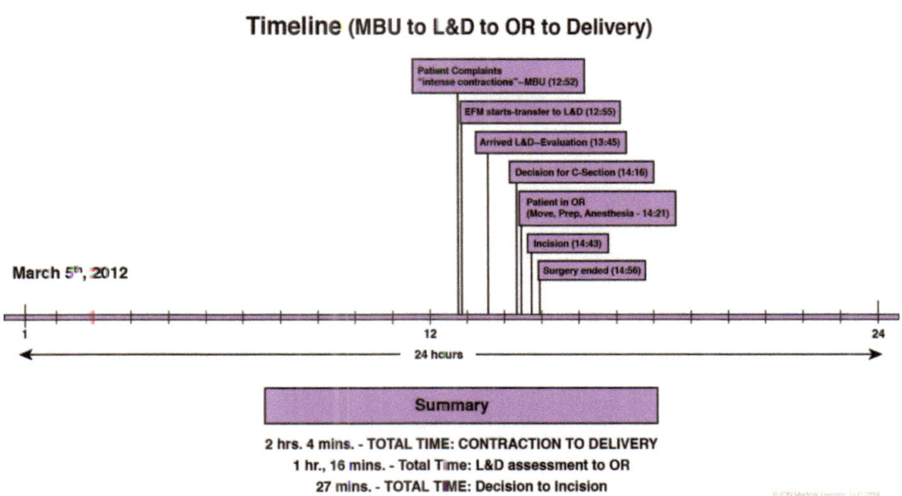

FIGURE 4.23 This chart represents the timeline of events during labor and delivery. Attorney Billiet used this chart to explain what happened during childbirth to the jury. Timelines are used to highlight specific events that can be critical to determine what happened and for legal arguments. The timing of the events can also be very important and relevant to circumstances and outcomes.

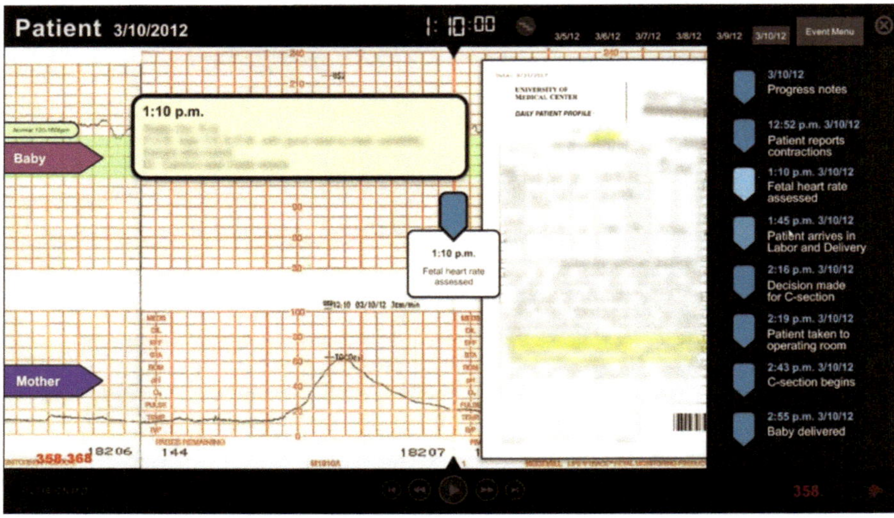

FIGURE 4.24 This is a screenshot of an interactive (user controls presentation) fetal monitor strip from the delivery of the baby. Fetal monitor strips measure the heartrates of both mother and child and can include time, medical records, and images. Attorney Billiet used the fetal monitor strip to explain to the jury what happened during childbirth.

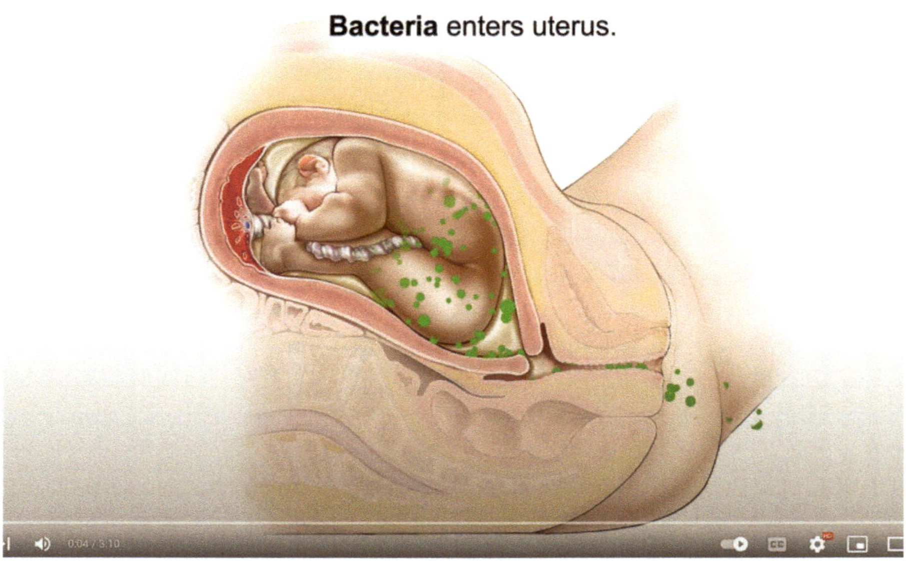

FIGURE 4.25 This is a screenshot of the animation created to depict fetal inflammatory response due to a chorioamnionitis. This screenshot shows the infection traveling into the uterus via the vagina. The following screenshots are of the 2D animation created to show how the infection was contracted, ended up in the bloodstream, transferred to the fetus and then caused the resultant swelling in the fetal brain. Attorney Billiet, along with the medical expert, used the animation to help explain this process to the jury.

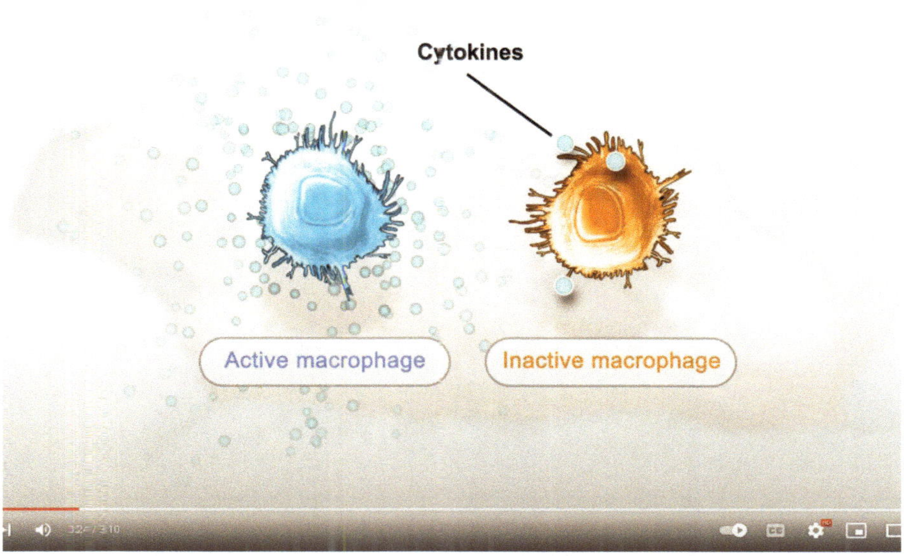

FIGURE 4.26 This is a screenshot of the animation created for a fetal inflammatory response due to a chorioamnionitic infection. This image depicts an inactive and then cytokine-activated macrophage. Cytokines are signaling proteins that control inflammation in your body. Too many cytokines can lead to excess inflammation and conditions like autoimmune diseases. A macrophage is a white blood cell activated by an immune response to an infection.

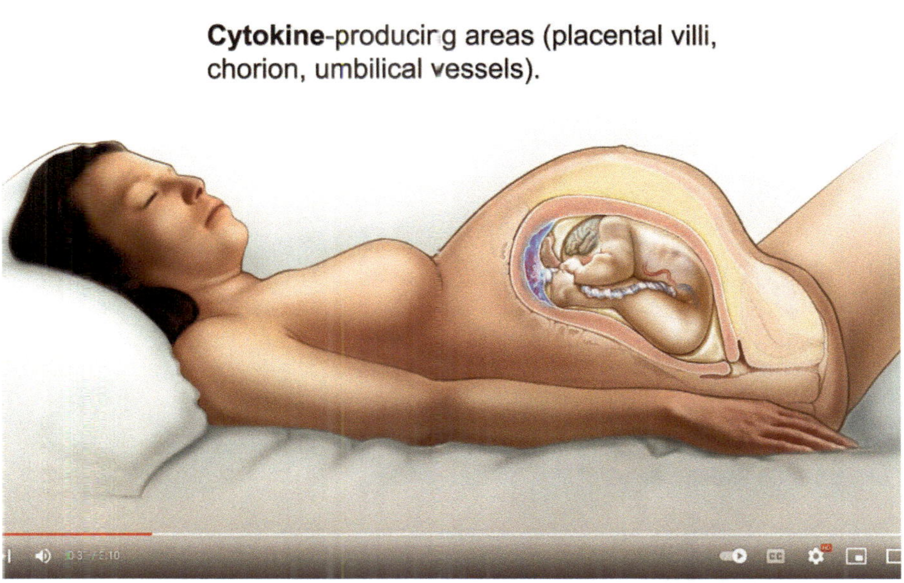

FIGURE 4.27 This is a screenshot of an animation created for a fetal inflammatory response due to a chorioamnionitic infection. This image is of the active cytokines that are produced by the body in the placenta traveling through the umbilical cord and to the fetus' brain. They are shown in blue to represent activation.

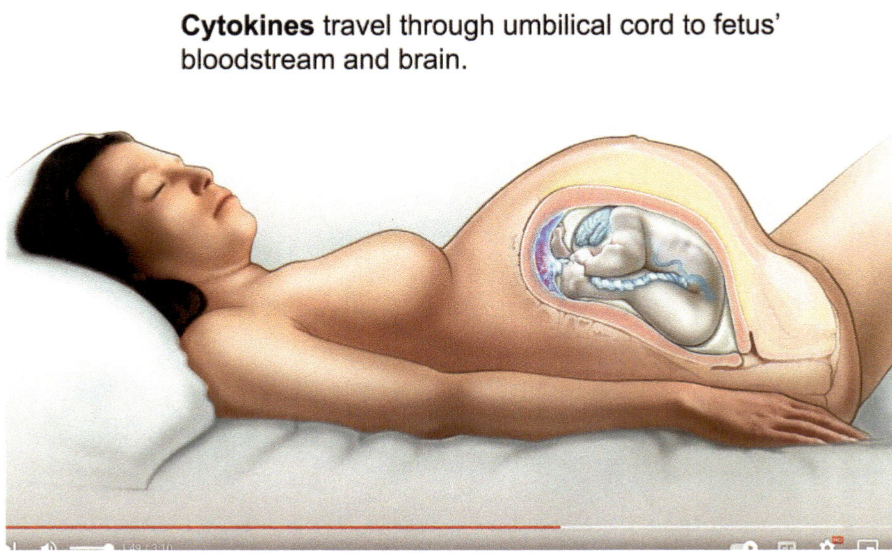

FIGURE 4.28 This is a screenshot of the animation created for a fetal inflammatory response due to a chorioamnionitic (bacterial) infection. In this illustration the cytokines (naturally occurring proteins that can cause inflammation) are active throughout the womb in the fetus' umbilical cord, bloodstream, and brain.

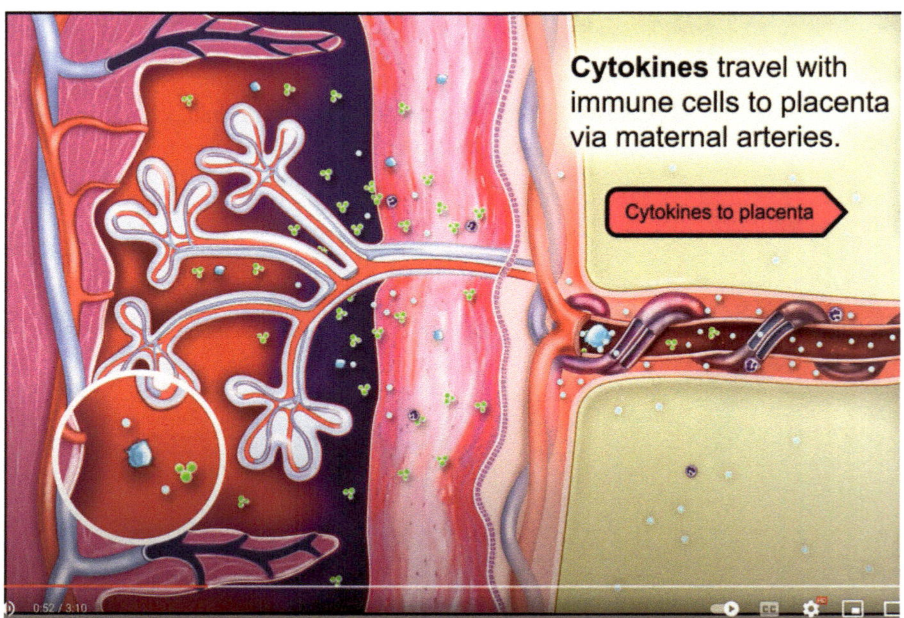

FIGURE 4.29 This is a screenshot of the 2D animation created for a fetal inflammatory response due to a chorioamnionitic infection. In this illustration, the cytokines are traveling with the immune cells (macrophages) to the placenta via maternal arteries.

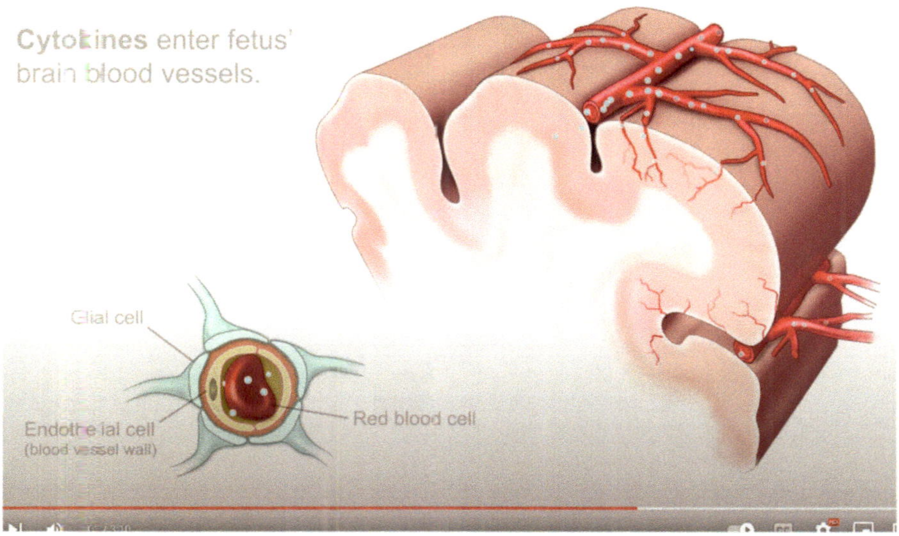

FIGURE 4.30 This is a screenshot of the 2D animation created for a fetal inflammatory response due to a chorioamnionitic infection. In this illustration, the cytokines have reached the blood vessels in the brain and are traveling through the bloodstream.

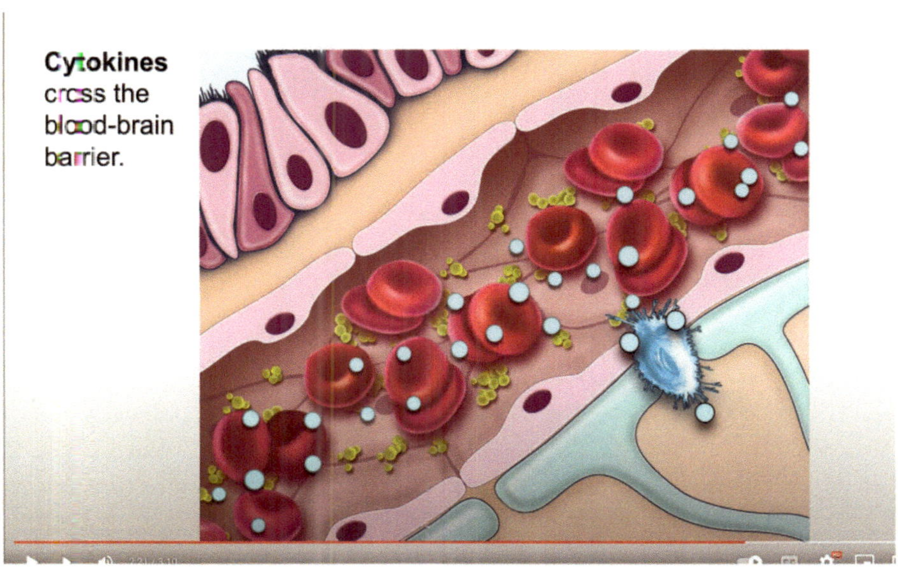

FIGURE 4.31 This is a screenshot of the 2D animation created for a fetal inflammatory response due to a chorioamnionitic infection. This image is of the cytokines that were engulfed by macrophages that can cross the blood-brain barrier and reach the parenchyma of the brain, thus causing inflammation to occur.

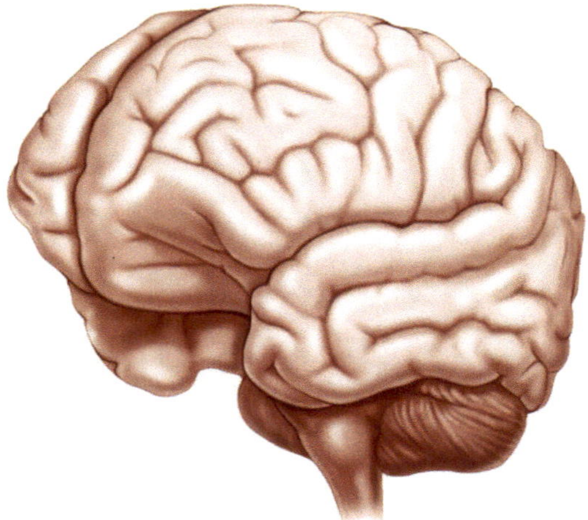

FIGURE 4.32 This is a screenshot of the 2D animation created for a fetal inflammatory response due to a chorioamnionitic infection. This image is one of a series of brain images used to orient the viewer to change views to an axial (horizontal) cut section of the brain illustrating inflammation of the brain. These types of gross anatomical images are good to show the viewers what part of the body we are looking at, especially if we are zooming in on a microscopic level.

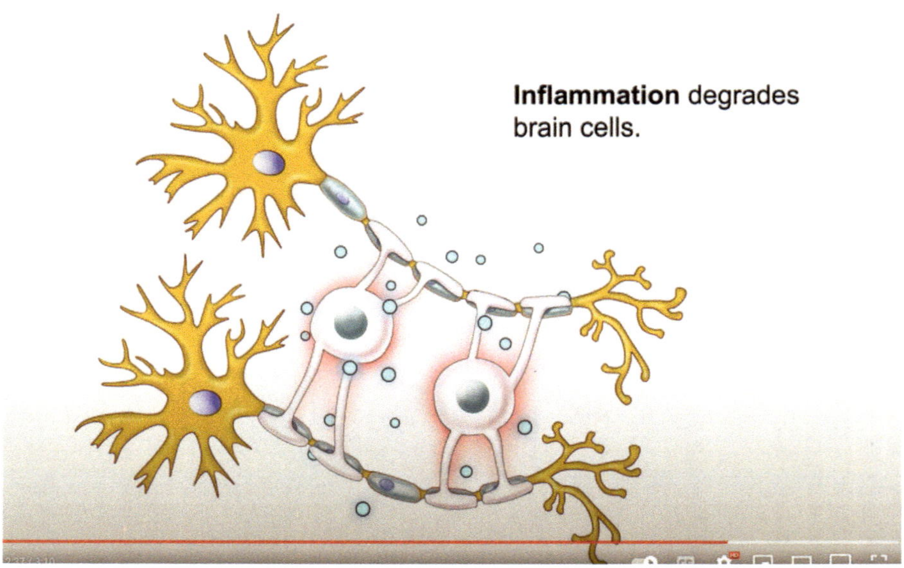

FIGURE 4.33 This is a screenshot of the 2D animation created for a fetal inflammatory response due to a chorioamnionitic infection. This image depicts axons and the glial cells degrading from the cytokines. Axons and glial cells are brain cells. Axons send electrical impulses from one neuron to another. A glial cell is a type of nerve cell that provides chemical and physical support to the neurons and maintains their environment. Cytokines can degrade these cells within the brain tissue.

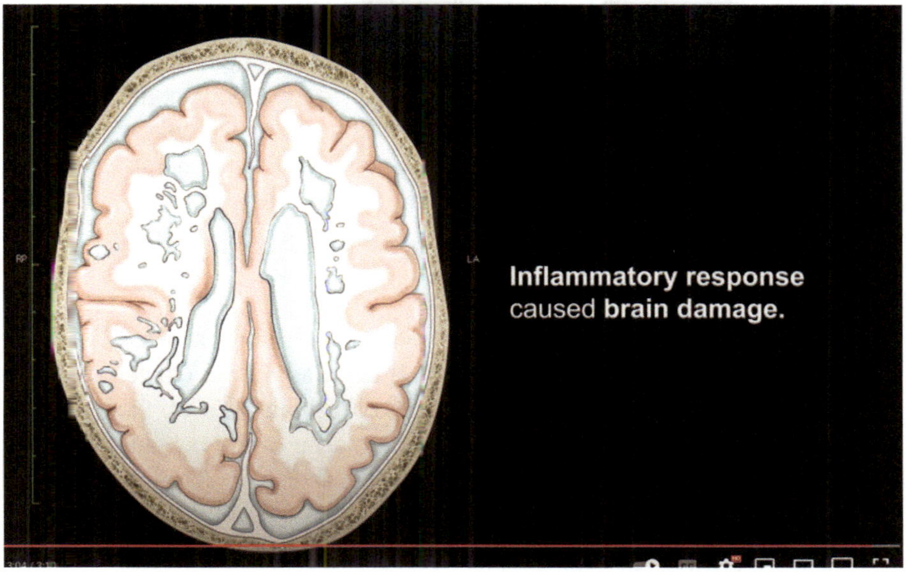

FIGURE 4.34 This is a screenshot of the 2D animation created for a fetal inflammatory response due to a chorioamnionitic infection. This image depicts the inflammation of the brain that occurred due to cytokines (inflammatory cells) in the brain tissue.

The 2D animation, along with her medical expert, assisted attorney Billiet to explain to the jury how the chorioamnionitis infection traveled from the vagina to the placenta, then the maternal/fetal bloodstream to the fetal brain, causing inflammation and damage to the fetal brain tissue.

Attorney Christina Billiet—interview questions and answers:

1) What is the process in which you use the illustrations for exchange, depositions, mediation, trial?

   I almost always use illustrations for trial. We use them to educate the jury on concepts that may otherwise be challenging for non-medical experts, and to reinforce our defense themes throughout.

2) How do you decide what cases you think would benefit from medical illustrations?

   I use them in almost every trial, either to explain a challenging medical concept or to illustrate a key defense point. I find the most important illustrations to be in radiology cases, where the radiology imaging is difficult to interpret with an untrained eye; colorized images can truly enable a jury to "see" something that otherwise would have been invisible to them in black-and-white.

3) How do you use the artwork in the courtroom?

   I always use illustrations during opening and closing. I also like to have artwork printed on boards (the old-fashioned way!) and get my witnesses up out of the witness box, and close to the jury, so that they can make a connection with them, using artwork/graphics. Great illustrations should educate the jury but also reinforce my defense themes.

4) What medical art service have you tried, for example, illustration, animation, interactive application, timeline?

   I have used many medical illustrations as well as animations. One of the more exciting concepts we've done is using artwork to create interactive electronic fetal heartrate monitoring. We did an animation of the electronic fetal heartrate running over time, with images of the contemporaneous medical findings interspersed. This allowed the jury to follow the patient's condition in "real time."

5) Is the artwork well received in the courtroom?

   Always. We find that the jury really leans in and begins to pay attention when they are shown a visual image. I was always taught to appeal to all different types of learners—oral, visual, etc., and the use of artwork is integral to that.

6) Do you find the artwork educational to the jury? In what ways: visual, helping the expert to educate, whole presentation?

   Artwork is helpful to the whole presentation. The use of meaningful and appropriate artwork that is well put together gives the defense case a polish that is important. Even when we have an uphill battle on the defense of a certain case, quality artwork gives our team credibility with the jury.

7) How often do you utilize medical artwork with your cases?

   In almost every case I try (or prepare to try), so I'm developing it five or six times a year.

8) What type of medical art demonstrative aids have you used?

   I have used colorized radiology imaging, fetal illustrations, infection animations, etc.

9) What is your level of comfort with more advanced applications? What factors determine what you decide to go with as demonstrative aids: technological capability/comfort level, price, ease of getting the illustration approved?

   In high-value cases, there is no issue getting advanced applications approved, if I believe it will be helpful to the jury and to our defense.

10) Does opposing counsel have medical illustrations when you do? If so, how does that play out?

    Yes, opposing counsel almost always has artwork. Our defense artwork is usually better, and I usually present it first (opposing counsel doesn't do as good of a job using theirs during opening). When that happens, the jury looks to our defense artwork as the baseline.

11) Please choose a case that you used medical demonstrative aids and describe how it was helpful. Did they help you to achieve a verdict higher than expected?

    We used medical demonstratives in a case which involved a patient with a traumatic injury to their leg, reconstruction, and then the development of an MRSA infection over time. We obtained a defense verdict in that case, in part thanks to quality medical illustrations.

4.3 CASE STUDY THREE

Medical Malpractice Defense, Kiely Keane—Crowley Fleck Attorneys, Kevin J. Kuhn—Wheeler Trigg O'Donnell LLP

I met Attorney Kuhn at a conference for defense attorneys which many attended to obtain their required CEUs. I was sponsoring/exhibiting at the conference. Attorney Khun then introduced me to Attorney Keane. We all worked together to create illustrations for this case that I am detailing here. They have worked with medical illustrators before and so are familiar with the process.

The featured case was a medical malpractice case in which an obstetrician was represented in a complicated delivery. The fetus experienced meconium aspiration syndrome. Meconium is the first feces, or stool, of a fetus. Meconium aspiration syndrome is when a fetus breathes a mixture of feces and amniotic fluid at the time of delivery (Figure 4.37). While meconium aspiration syndrome is a rare condition occurring in roughly 5–10% of births, it can cause severe injury or death. It typically occurs when the fetus is stressed during labor or is being delivered past the due date.

In this case, the uterus had lower amniotic fluid, and the fetus breathed in meconium in utero for a significant amount of time due to fetal stress; it is suspected for two days prior to delivery. In fact, the fetus breathed in so much meconium that there was a tracheal blockage. The bronchiole tubes and alveolar sacs also had meconium in them. Because of all the meconium, the fetus' lungs wouldn't inflate.

The infant appeared dead upon delivery, with a pale appearance and no respiration (Figure 4.38).

The attorneys decided on using illustration boards to help defend their case. The following are the demonstrative aids that were created. They included an illustration of a healthy placenta to show what the anatomy generally looks like (Figure 4.35), a diseased placenta (Figure 4.36), based on the fetus' medical records, an illustration on meconium (Figure 4.37), a healthy baby vs a baby with meconium aspiration syndrome (Figure 4.38), and sizes of placentas ranked by percentiles (Figure 4.39).

Please see the following illustrations.

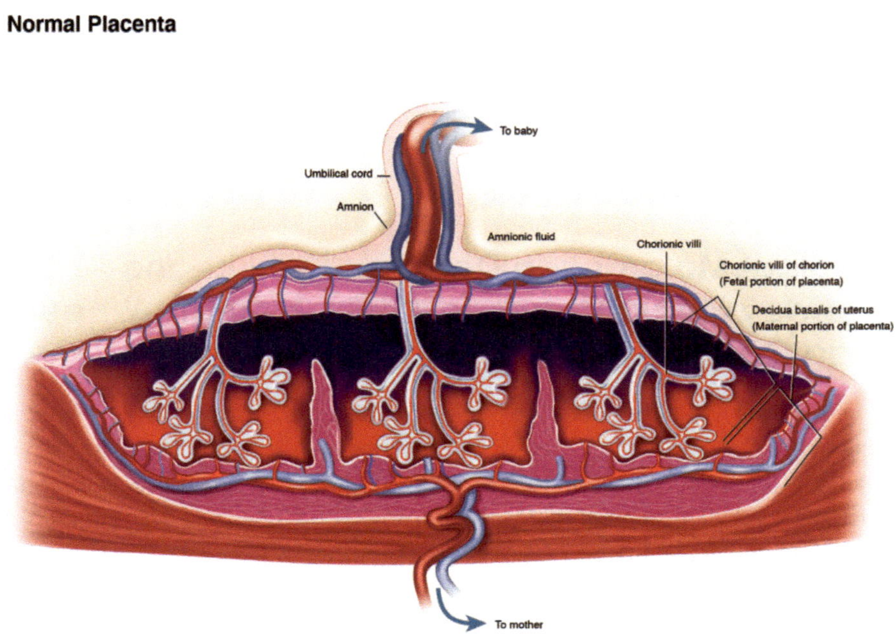

FIGURE 4.35 This is an illustration of a cross section of a normal placenta. Both maternal and fetal blood supply are depicted. The vessels going to the mother and fetus are illustrated. The attorneys wanted to show the jury what the normal/healthy anatomy looks like since most jurors don't have a medical background. The illustration gives them a starting point and baseline—something to compare the unhealthy/injured anatomy to.

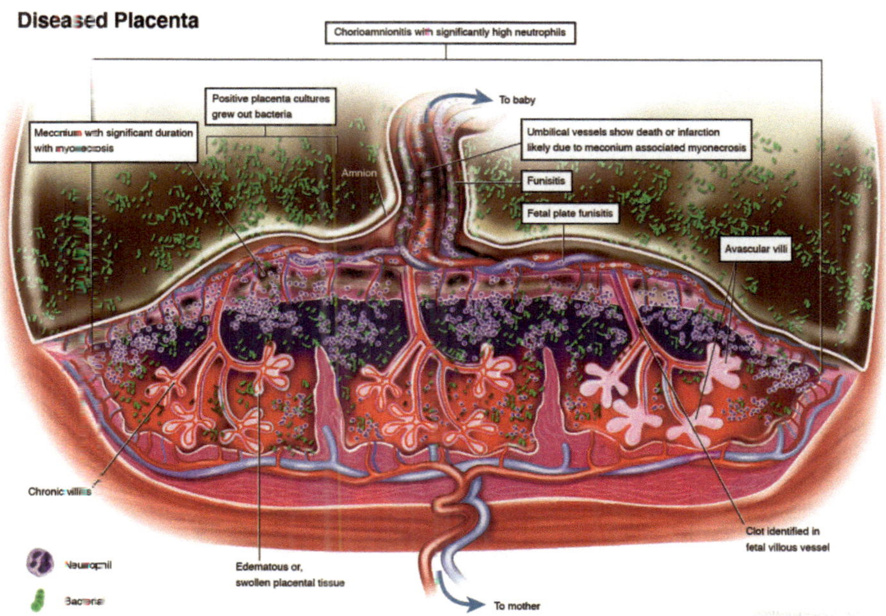

FIGURE 4.36 This is an illustration of a cross section of an abnormal placenta. Both the maternal and fetal blood supplies are depicted. The vessels going to the mother and fetus are illustrated. This is a demonstrative aid showing how the fetus' placenta looked at the time of delivery. The illustration shows acute chorioamnionitis, stage 2 (moderate), acute funisitis, stage 3 (severe), and acute villitis, moderate.

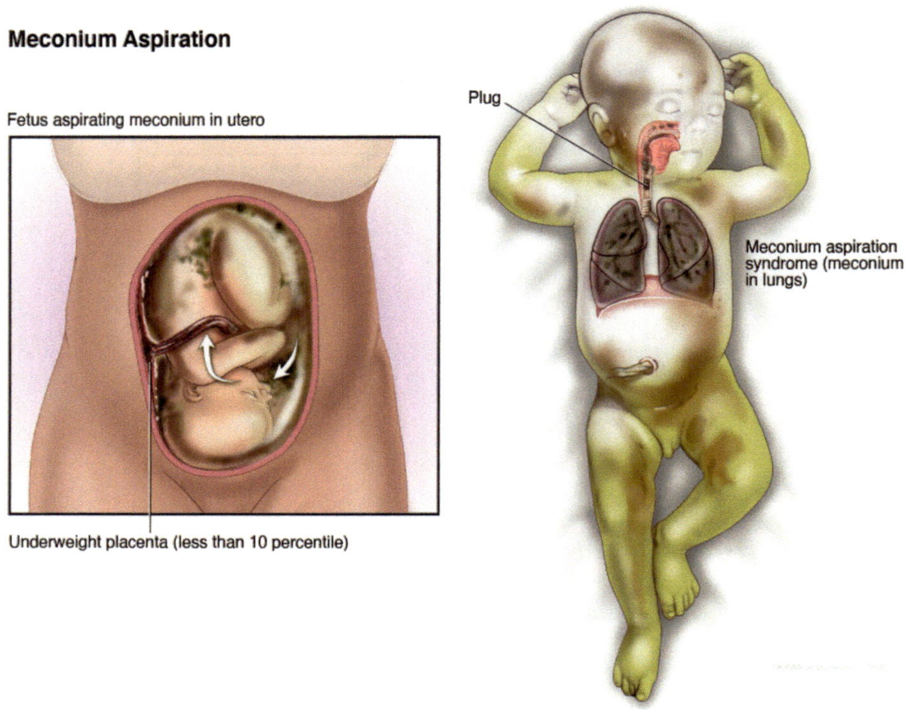

FIGURE 4.37 This is an illustration that depicts the process of meconium (fetal feces) aspiration syndrome (breathing stool in utero). The baby was greenish/brown and white in color due to lack of oxygen from a mucous plug lodged in his throat, which is depicted in the baby on the right. The illustration on the left shows how the meconium circulates in utero. The illustration will help the attorneys to explain what meconium aspiration syndrome is and what the condition of the baby was at birth.

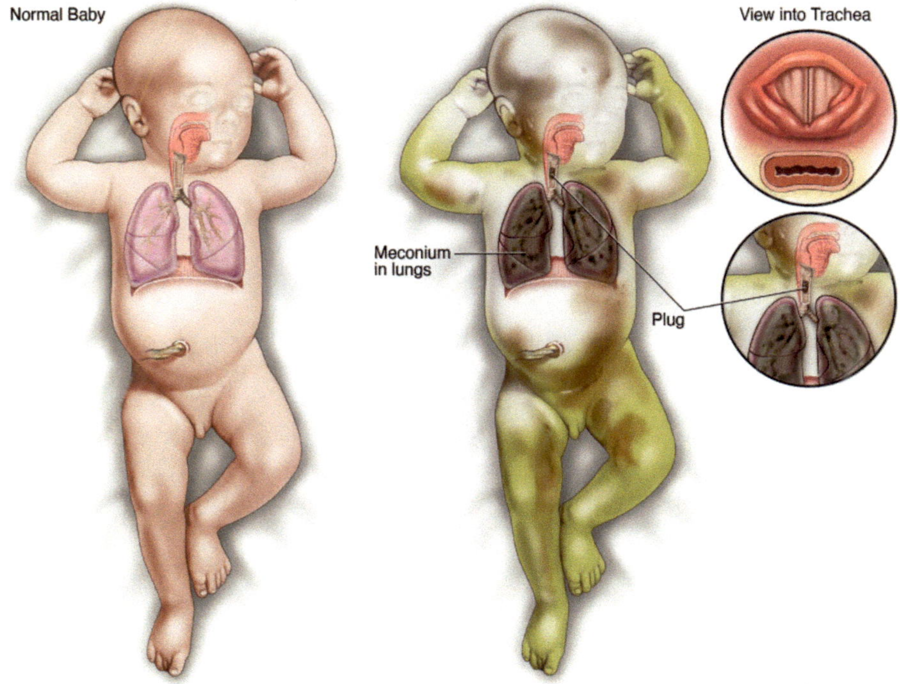

FIGURE 4.38 This is an illustration that depicts a normal healthy baby, for reference, versus a baby that aspirated meconium. The baby on the right breathed in meconium and had a mucous plug stuck in his trachea, which is represented on the circular inset.

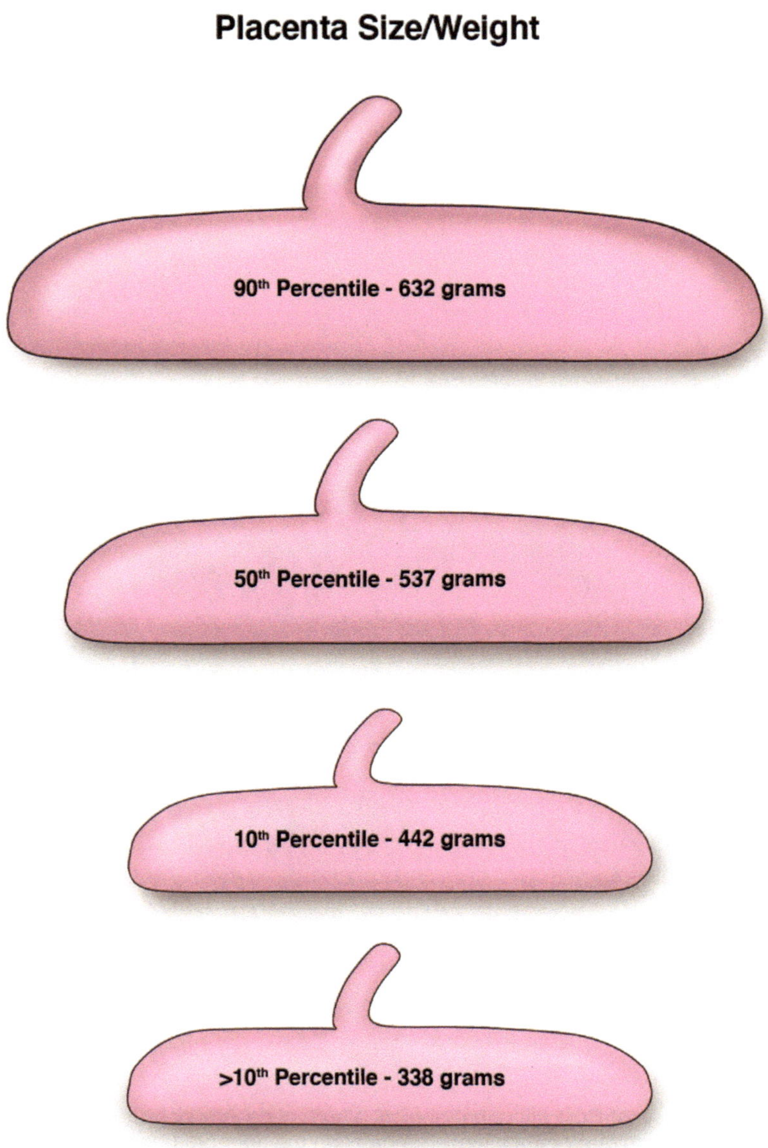

FIGURE 4.39 This is a diagram that shows the different weights and sizes of the placenta. It also shows what percentile each placenta is in based on weight. The size of the plaintiff's placenta was in the 10th percentile, and there was also low amniotic fluid in the uterus. These two factors make a fetus more susceptible to disease and complications.

Summary of interview with Attorneys Keane and Khun.

The attorneys on this case noted that they always use illustrations in all phases including exchange, depositions, mediation, and at trial—and that they are generally quite well received.

CHAPTER 5

Medical Illustration—Interpersonal Violence

This chapter features cases involving interpersonal violence. When my article about medical illustration was published for *Inform Magazine*, I was contacted by the Academy of Forensic Nursing (AFN). They read the article and were interested in having standard anatomy packages created. The standard anatomy packages, created for distribution through the Academy of Forensic Nursing, were developed for healthcare professionals, law enforcement, and criminal justice professionals to support standardized documentation of injuries sustained in cases of trauma, violence and criminal activity. The diagrams can be incorporated into electronic medical records and handwritten documents used by forensic nurses and used in the courtroom as demonstration to a jury of injury or trauma that may have been sustained by a victim of crime.

5.1 FORENSIC NURSING

Forensic nurses provide trauma-informed care and evidentiary examinations for adults, adolescents, children, and the elderly who have been affected by interpersonal violence and crime. Forensic nurses are specially educated and trained to provide trauma care in cases of physical and sexual assault, intimate partner violence child maltreatment, elder abuse, and human trafficking. Forensic nurses practice in a wide variety of facilities and organizations and often provide expert testimony in criminal and civil proceedings.

DOI: 10.4324/9781003336310-5

5.2 DIAGRAMS FOR DOCUMENTATION

In addition to artistic and specialized illustrations, anatomic diagrams supporting in-court casework can be used by associations or standardizing bodies looking to support professional and accurate documentation to help improve best practices—including findings observed during a medical forensic examination. The Academy of Forensic Nursing recognized the need to have standardized diagrams that can be used to document typical/average/healthy anatomy, as well as injury findings in a variety of patients with forensic healthcare needs.

Subtle, as well as significant, injury is often observed in patients seen after intimate partner violence, sexual assault, strangulation, elder abuse, and child maltreatment. The opportunity to utilize standardized, realistic, black-and-white diagrams to accurately document findings in patients affected by interpersonal violence will support best practice forensic documentation in multiple arenas. Examples of the diagrams are found subsequently (Figures 5.1–5.13) and can be utilized as part of an electronic medical record or handwritten documents in healthcare facilities, clinics, child advocacy centers, independent practices, or medical examiner offices. These standardized diagrams can also be utilized in the courtroom to educate the jury in a criminal or civil trial about injuries that may be difficult to appreciate with color photos.

5.3 DIAGRAMS FOR DOCUMENTATION—VALERIE SIEVERS, MSN, RN, CNS, AFN-C, SANE-A, DF-AFN

Accurate, thorough, and consistent documentation is an essential competency for healthcare professionals who provide care to patients who have been affected by violence and crime. Poor or absent documentation, in cases requiring a forensic healthcare response, can adversely affect legal outcomes. Standardized body diagrams are typically used in addition to photography for documentation in cases of sexual assault, domestic violence, strangulation, child maltreatment, elder abuse, and human trafficking.

Diagrams and body maps (Figures 5.9 and 5.10) allow for visual placement of injuries, so that anyone reviewing a medical record can see the locations of injuries, wounds, or findings. Forensic diagrams should include the size, shape, and color of the findings next to the drawing (Figures 5.2, 5.4, 5.6, 5.8, 5.13). Expertly curated diagrams can also be used in criminal and civil trial proceedings, to effectively educate the jury about normal (healthy) anatomy or injury.

The saying "if it wasn't documented, then it wasn't done" applies even more to forensic nursing practice and supports the standard for comprehensive documentation as part of the medical forensic examination.

The Academy of Forensic Nursing recognized the need to have standardized diagrams useful for documentation in forensic practice and worked with the author's company, ION, to develop a variety of anatomic images that can be incorporated into medical records, used for education purposes, or admitted as evidence during legal proceedings.

Please see the following illustrations created for forensic documentation.

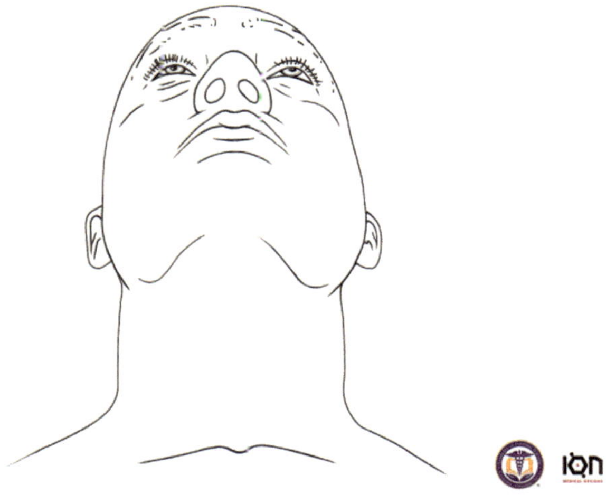

FIGURE 5.1 This illustration is one of a series of illustrations created for accurate forensic documentation.

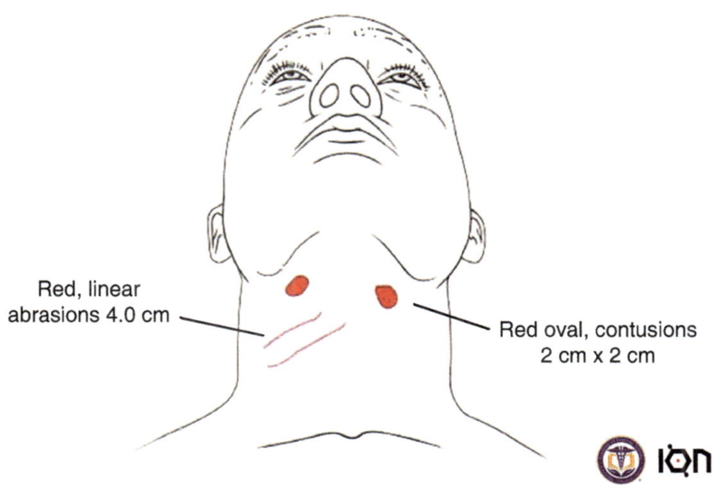

FIGURE 5.2 This illustration is one of a series of illustrations created for accurate forensic documentation. The abrasions and contusions represent the injuries sustained by a victim of strangulation.

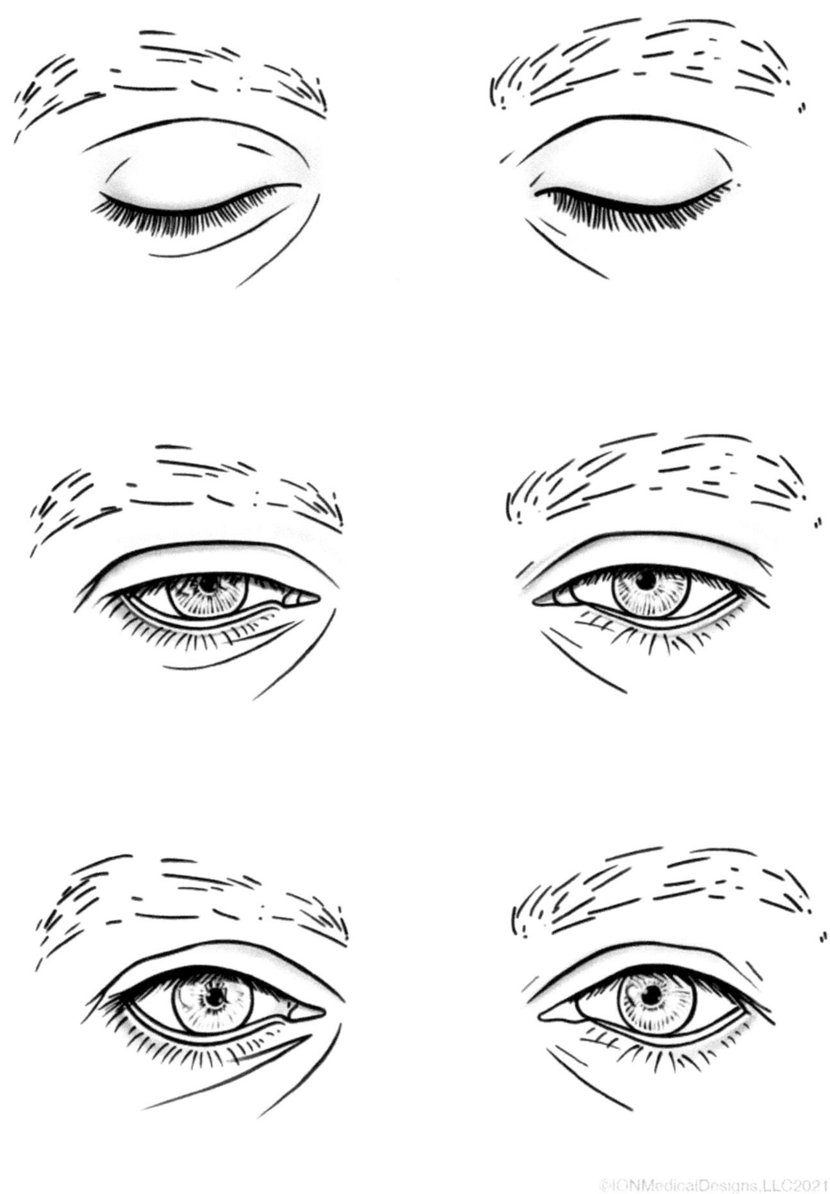

FIGURE 5.3 This illustration is one of a series of illustrations created for documentation of injuries as part of a medical record, diagram, or for use in the courtroom. The anatomical drawings of the eyes are used to mark a variety of injuries including bruising, swelling, and petechiae (pinpoint hemorrhages of the sclera or periorbital tissues).

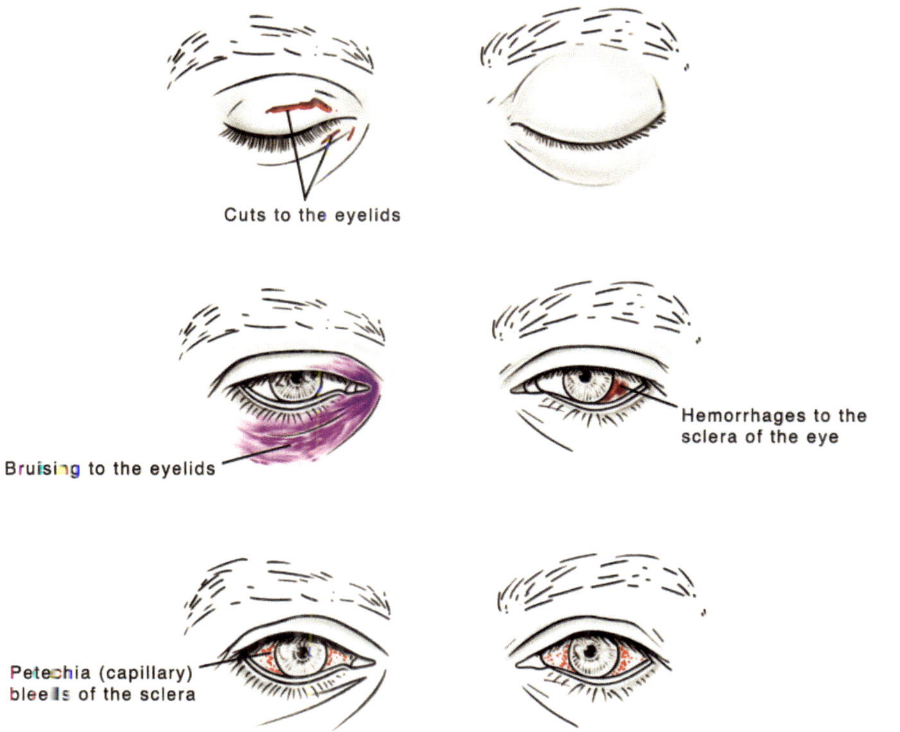

FIGURE 5.4 This illustration is one of a series of illustrations created for documentation of injuries as part of a medical record, diagram, or for use in the courtroom. The anatomical drawings of the eyes are used to mark a variety of injuries including bruising, swelling, abrasions, and petechiae (pinpoint hemorrhages of the sclera or periorbital tissues). I have marked up this example with the injuries mentioned. Not dilation specifically but used more for injury seen in the tissue which can be from strangulation or blunt trauma.

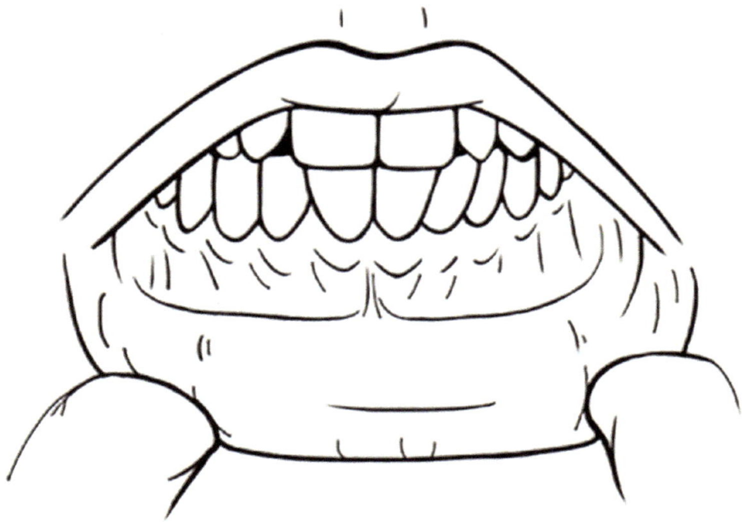

FIGURE 5.5 This illustration is one of a series of illustrations created for documentation of injuries as part of a medical record, diagram, or for use in the courtroom. Contusions, tears, injury to teeth, and areas of petechiae might be documented to the mouth, tongue, gum tissue, or lips. Anecdotal reports from forensic professionals have suggested that tattooed numbers or names may be found on the inner lip as branding associated with victims of trafficking.

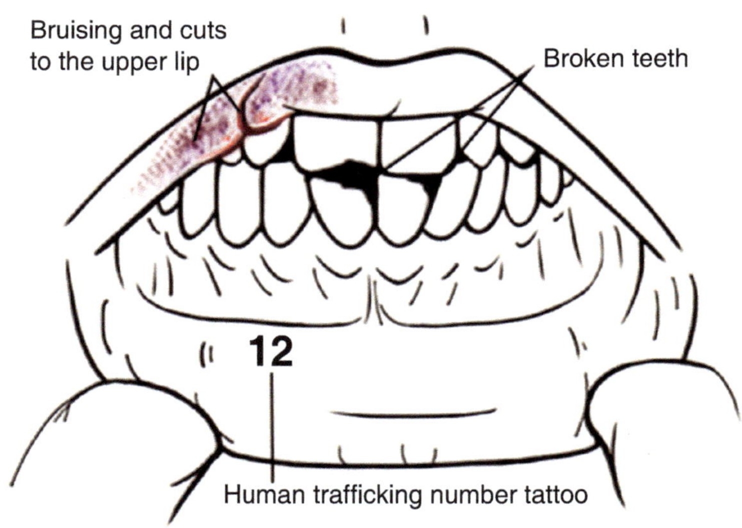

FIGURE 5.6 This illustration is one of a series of illustrations created for documentation of injuries as part of a medical record, diagram, or for use in the courtroom. Contusions, tears, injury to teeth, and areas of petechiae might be documented to the mouth, tongue, gum tissue, or lips. Anecdotal reports from forensic professionals have suggested that tattooed numbers or names may be found on the inner lip as branding associated with victims of trafficking. Marked up.

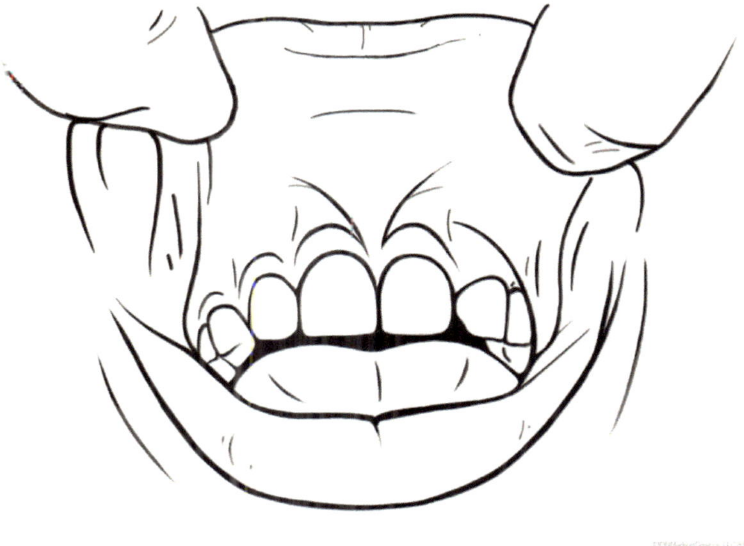

FIGURE 5.7 This illustration is one of a series of illustrations created for documentation of injuries as part of a medical record, diagram, or for use in the courtroom. Contusions tears, injury to teeth, and areas of petechiae might be documented to the mouth, tongue, gum tissue, or lips.

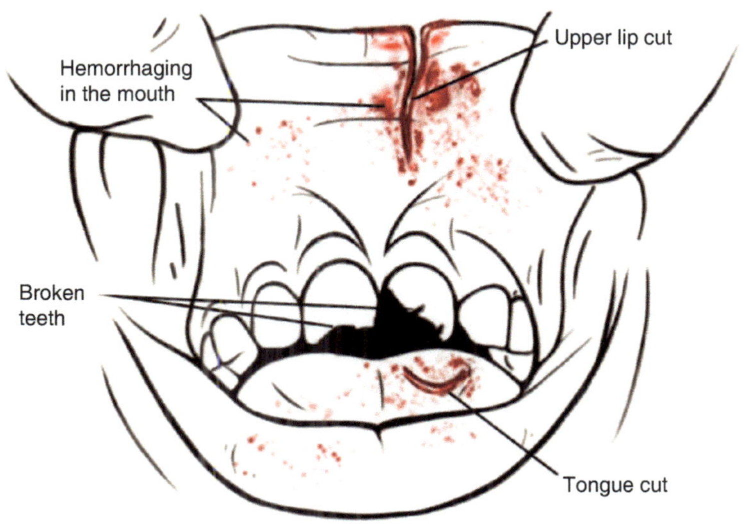

FIGURE 5.8 This illustration is one of a series of illustrations created for documentation of injuries as part of a medical record, diagram, or for use in the courtroom. Contusions, tears, injury to teeth, and areas of petechiae might be documented to the mouth, tongue, gum tissue, or lips.

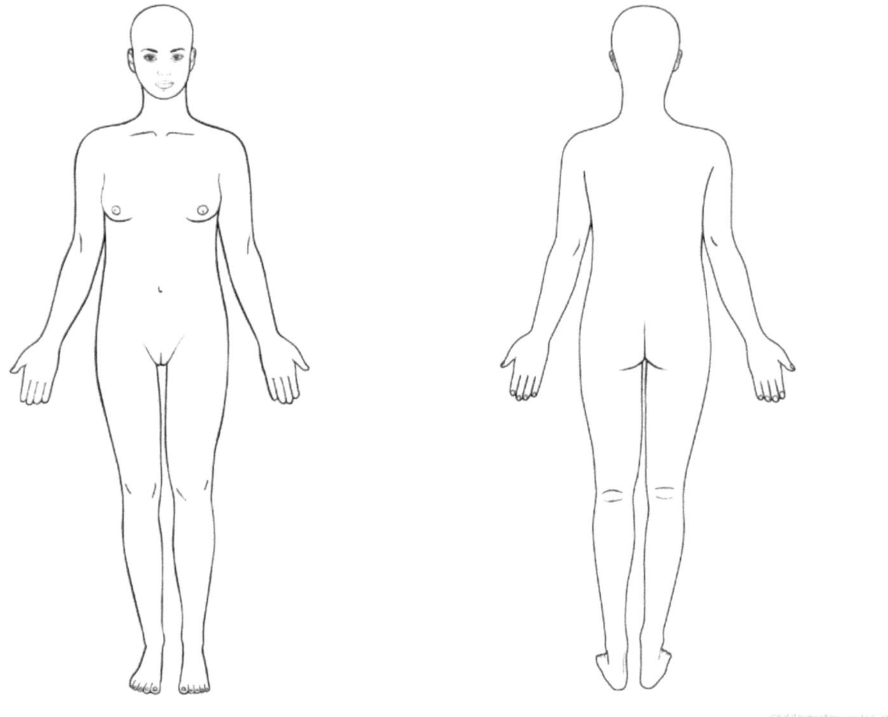

FIGURE 5.9 This illustration or "Body Map" is one of a series of illustrations created for documentation of injuries as part of a medical record, diagram, or for use in the courtroom.

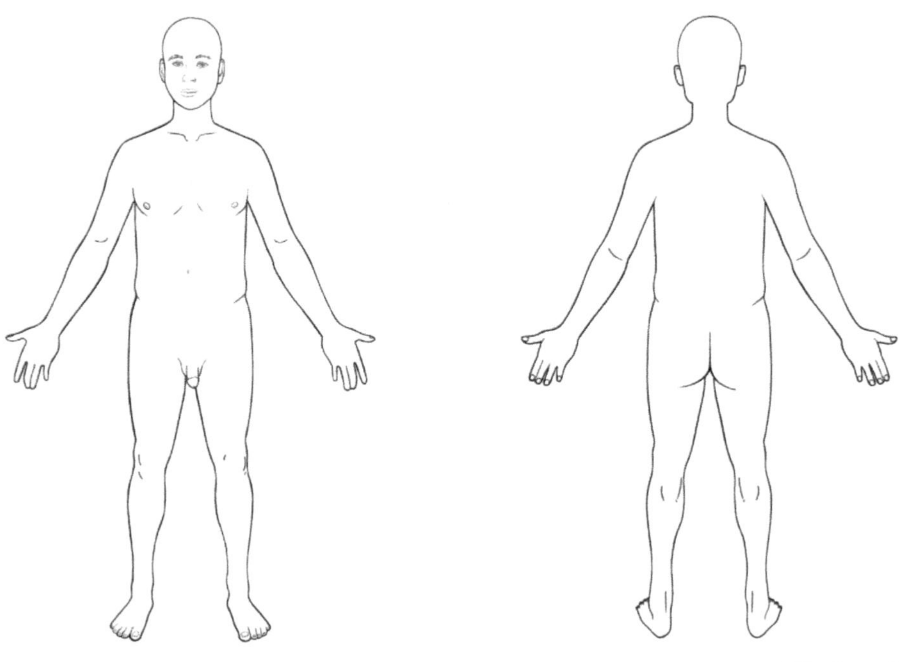

FIGURE 5.10 This illustration or "Body Map" is one of a series of illustrations created for documentation of injuries as part of a medical record, diagram, or for use in the courtroom.

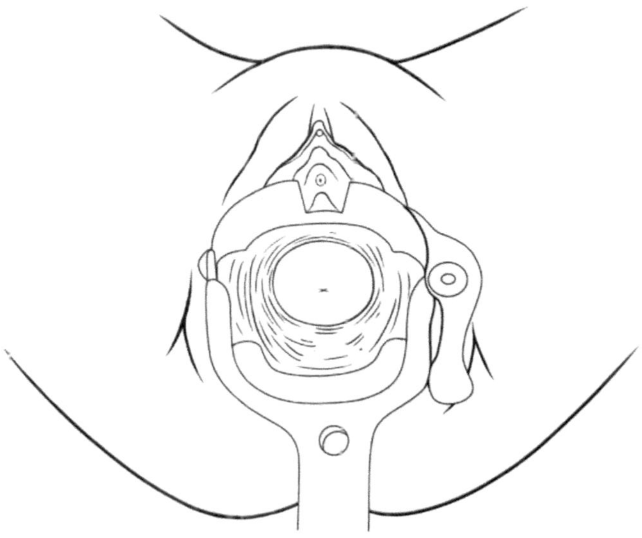

FIGURE 5.11 This illustration is one of a series of illustrations created for documentation of genital injuries as part of a medical record, diagram, or for use in the courtroom. The speculum exam with visualization of the vaginal vault and cervix is used to document a variety of findings that may be seen on a pelvic exam.

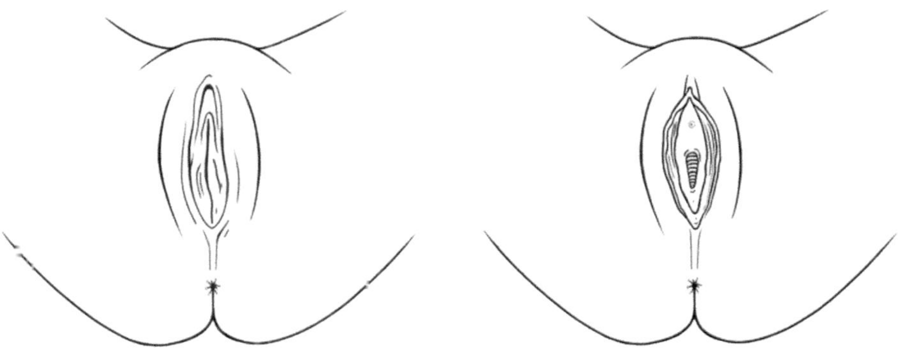

FIGURE 5.12 This illustration is one of a series of illustrations created for documentation of genital injuries as part of a medical record, diagram, or for use in the courtroom.

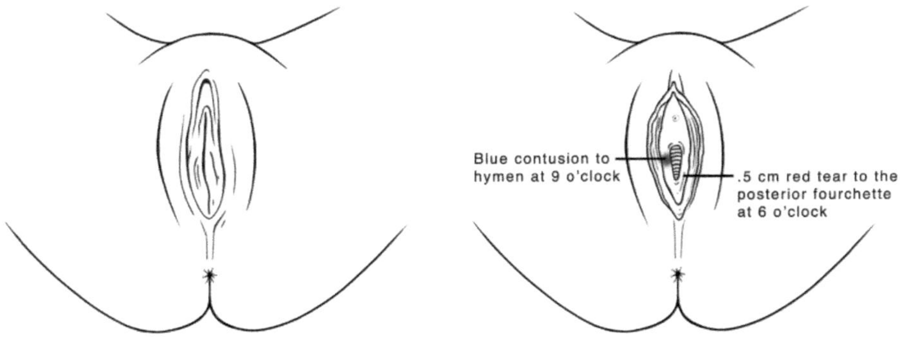

FIGURE 5.13 This illustration is one of a series of illustrations created for documentation of genital injuries as part of a medical record, diagram, or for use in the courtroom. Documentation of normal anatomy or injury findings to the vulva is an important step in the ano-genital assessment and pelvic examination.

There are many types of injuries and/or signs of abuse that can be seen across this spectrum of cases. Such injuries can include the following:

Tears or lacerations

Abrasions

Contusions (bruising)

Incised wounds or cuts

Burns

Bleeding

CHAPTER 6

Illustrating Gunshot Wounds

Guns, the truth behind the violence. This chapter will review ballistics, real cases involving gunshot wounds, wound trajectories, variations in tissue damage, organs traversed, and residual shrapnel.

Several cases are featured from a high-profile mass shooting that took place in Sutherland Springs, TX, on November 5, 2017. In addition, a separate case from an apartment shooting in Dallas, TX, is presented. The latter was a civil case with no criminal trial.

Mass shootings have become so prevalent throughout the world, but especially in the United States. They take place in schools, malls, churches, concerts, neighborhoods, households, and birthday parties. To say it was a societal epidemic would be a gross understatement. As a result, gun rights, gun legislation, as well as gun violence in general have all become a political hot topic issue. Statistically, the estimated number of firearm-related deaths, excluding suicides, in 2022 was 20,138. Hopefully, this chapter will bring to light the destruction that firearm projectiles inflict on the human body physically. In this, it has been shown to be a physically and mentally life-altering hardship for both the surviving victims and their families, not to mention the deceased and the community impact.

DOI: 10.4324/9781003336310-6

6.1 OVERVIEW OF BALLISTICS

Since this chapter is about gunshot violence, I would like to talk a little bit on ballistics. Ballistics is a term referring to the science of a bullet in flight. It refers to the path of a bullet that includes traveling down the barrel, air travel, and path through the target.

6.2 INTERNAL BALLISTICS

Ballistics is a term referring to the science of a projectile in flight. The path of a bullet includes traveling down the barrel, air travel, and path through the target.

From the inside out, internal ballistics refers to the path of a bullet. For instance, a rifle has more energy than a bullet from a handgun. More powder can be used in rifle cartridges due to the design of the chamber and being able to withstand more pressure. The higher pressure requires a bigger gun with more recoil to slow that pressure to slow the load and generate more heat. The force is a hard parameter to measure; however, velocity (where the bullet exits the barrel—muzzle) can be measured more easily (Klatt, n.d.).

The expansion of the gases from the burning gunpowder generates pressure. The energy transmitted to a bullet will depend upon mass x force x the time interval from the force applied. The last factor is the function of the gun barrel length. The bullets travel through the gun barrel by increased acceleration. The gases push on the bullet, and the pressure decreases in the barrel as the gas expands. The longer the barrel, the greater acceleration of the bullet (Klatt, n.d.).

6.3 EXTERNAL BALLISTICS

The external ballistics are the bullets path to the target and can be determined by several formulae. The formulas measure velocity, bullets energy, drag, and degree at which the bullet travels. Bullets don't follow a straight line to the target; rotational forces affect their flight paths.

6.4 TERMINAL BALLISTICS

Terminal ballistics is when the bullet hits the target. A short high-velocity bullet rotates severely upon entering, causing displacement. A longer, heavier bullet may have more kinetic energy at a longer range when it hits the target, then penetrate and exits the tissue with a lot of the kinetic energy remaining. If a bullet has low kinetic energy—for instance one from a handgun— it can cause significant injury to tissue if it is designed to give up its kinetic energy into the target at short range.

6.5 BULLETS CAUSE TISSUE DAMAGE

Projectiles produce injury patterns when they traverse human tissue and intermediate targets. As well as how the morphology and etiology of the wounds created by the projectiles present to the pathologist, that is, entry and exit wounds.

It depends on how exactly the bullet exits through the gyroscope, as it may tumble in an erratic fashion and may enter the target backwards, side on, or in oblique fashion. This results in the irregularity of the entrance wound. Because of this, the wound may look different than expected. It may have an ovoid, irregular, or irregular abrasion ring. Secondary wounds may be caused by bullet fragments or fragments of foreign materials such as wood, glass, or jacketing.

The projectile may fragment, causing a pseudo tattooing pattern. The human body can be an intermediary target, meaning a projectile may pass through one person and hit another.

6.6 ATYPICAL ENTRY WOUNDS

Atypical entry wounds are comprised of graze and tangential wounds. A graze wound is a surface wound that doesn't cause tissue penetration. This is a gutter wound that doesn't involve fat or fascia. There may be small splits in the skin, or one part of the wound may be deeper than the other.

A tangential wound impacts the skin at a shallow angle or tangent, and they are deeper than graze wounds. These wounds lose their symmetry and often have blunted entry wounds and torn exits. The orientation and splitting of the wounds and their orientation can often indicate the direction of the projectile's entry and exit.

High-velocity tangential wounds may cause extensive tissue loss.

6.7 RICOCHET

A ricochet is when a projectile deflects from a surface before hitting its target indirectly. This is a rare occurrence because the bullet must impact the surface at an acute angle for this to happen. The surface may be solid, irregular, or even water for this to occur. The jacket may deform or separate from its core.

The wound itself is ambiguous and can resemble any pattern described for intermediate targets. The ricochet may produce both graze and tangential wounds (Klatt, n.d.).

In the following cases, there are detailed illustrations of injuries caused by bullet projectiles. They include injuries to organs, bones, and human tissue.

6.8 CASE STUDY ONE—MASS SHOOTING

Sutherland Springs Church Massacre Victims vs the United States Government Department of Justice

Law Firms—Justin Demerath of O'Hanlon, Demerath & Castillo, April Strahan of The Ammons Law Firm, Brett Reynolds & Associates, Thomas J. Henry Law, Jamal K. Alsaffar National Trial Law, Tom Jacob National Trial Law, Marion M. Reilly of Hillard Martinez Gonzales LLP

In November of 2017 Devin Patrick Kelley, dressed in black tactical gear and armed with a Ruger AR-556 semi-automatic rifle, open fired outside the First Baptist Church in Sutherland Springs, Texas, killing two people outside of the church. He then entered through the right-side door of the church where the worshippers were attending their regular Sunday service. He yelled "everybody dies, motherfuckers" as he walked up and down the aisle methodically shooting. It was another instance of a high-profile mas casualty event, a massacre that left 26 people dead and 20 injured. Many of the victims were children. Texas Governor Greg Abbott stated that this was the worst mass shooting in the state's history.

Kelley was confronted by and traded fire with citizen Stephen Willeford (Figure 6.4), a local resident and former firearms instructor who was armed with an AR-15 semi-automatic rifle. Willeford took cover behind a truck across the street from the church and fired at Kelley twice, hitting him once in the leg and once in the upper left torso. Kelley fled the scene in his Ford Explorer, speeding north on FM 539. Willeford and another citizen, Johnnie Langendorff, pursued Kelley in Johnnie Langendorff's pickup truck in a high-speed chase reaching speeds of up to 95 mph. While chasing Kelley, the citizens called the police to report the route and direction of the chase. Kelley, bleeding from his wounds, eventually lost control of his vehicle and ended up in a ditch. He died of a self-inflicted gunshot wound to the head.

Kelley was a former U.S. Air Force member who served from 2010 to 2014. Kelley previously served in logistics readiness at Holloman Air Force Base in New Mexico until his discharge in 2014. He was responsible for moving passengers, cargo, and personal property in military transportation and had received several awards during his time with the Air Force.

However, Kelley had also been charged with multiple accounts of domestic violence assaults on his first wife and her child. Kelley physically assaulted his stepson by pushing him down, shaking him, and fracturing his skull, causing a severe hematoma.

Kelley pleaded guilty to assaulting his ex-wife and son and received a bad conduct discharge and reduction in rank as well as 12 months of confinement from the United States Air Force.

The United States Air Force Stated that the domestic violence case was a general court martial, the most serious level of military trial proceedings, reserved for more serious crimes such as felonies in civilian jurisdictions.

Thus, Kelley received a bad conduct discharge and not a dishonorable discharge, which would have prohibited him from purchasing a firearm.

Federal law in Texas prohibits those convicted of a domestic violence to purchase firearms. The military is responsible for reporting those charges to the FBI, in hopes that those abusers don't purchase firearms and can carry sentences of more than a year in confinement. The lawsuit was regarding this issue of not reporting Kelley to the FBI, and thus not banned from buying a gun. While the argument could be made that he could've purchased a gun in the black market, required protocols and the law were not adhered to, and thus Kelley had legally purchased several weapons, including the one involved in the assault.

It was reported at the time that Kelley's friends and family had noticed him getting dark, and that he had depressing and disturbing social media posts leading up to the massacre. He posted a picture of his AR -15 with the caption "She's a Bad Bitch" underneath. His motive for the shooting was over a dispute with his mother-in-law. Ironically, she was not at the church on that day.

The following are pictures of the scene, and a picture of the victims.

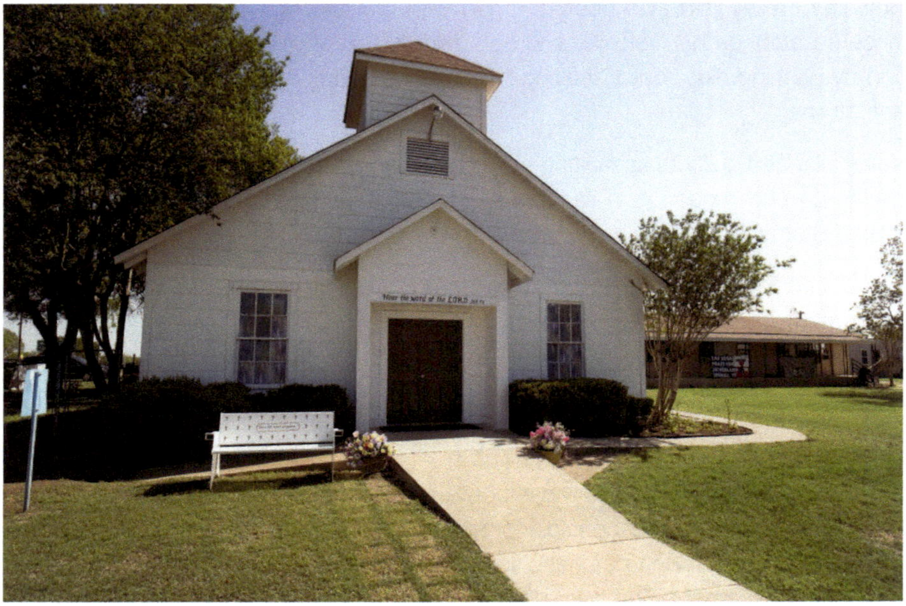

FIGURE 6.1 This is a photograph of the First Baptist Church of Sutherland Springs, Texas (Source: Used with permission from Alamy Stock Photo/Bob Daemmrich).

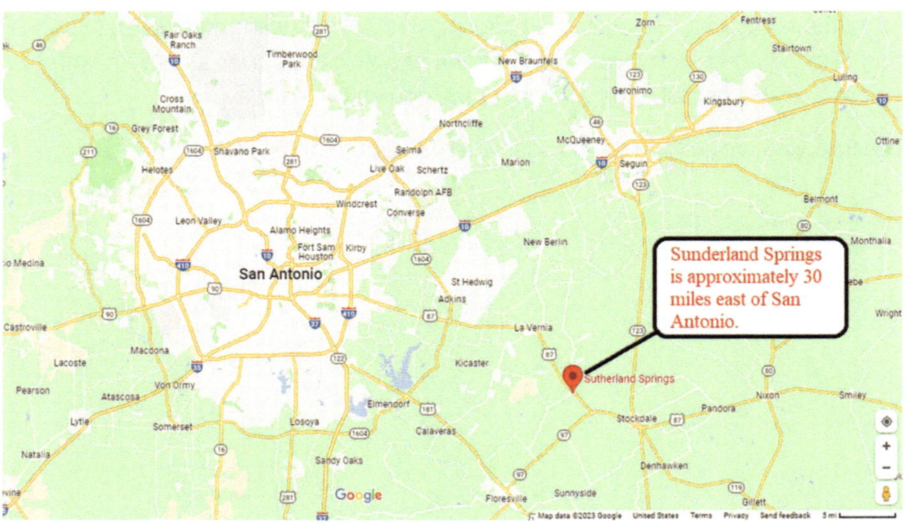

FIGURE 6.2 This is a photograph of a map of the scene of the First Baptist Church of Sutherland Springs, Texas, massacre. (Image source: Google Maps).

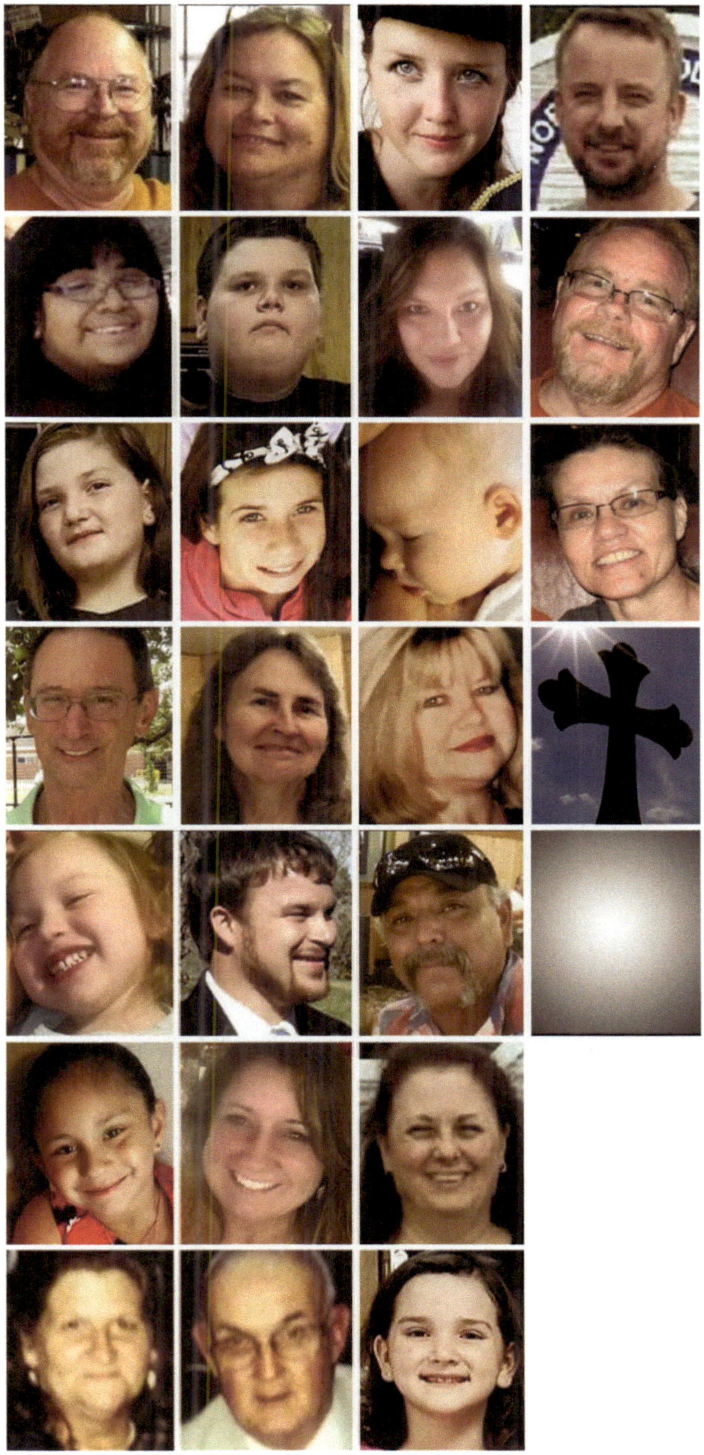

FIGURE 6.3 This is a photograph of the massacre victims that were killed at the First Baptist Church of Sutherland Springs, Texas. The picture represents the individuals that were killed at the time and/or immediately after the incident. Several other victims have passed away since the day of the shooting.

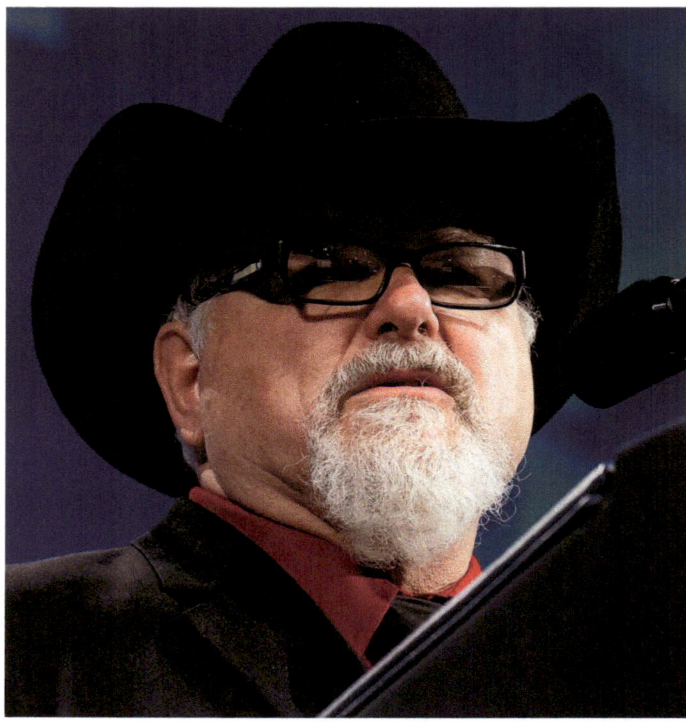

FIGURE 6.4 This is a photograph of Stephen Willeford, the hero who stopped Devin Kelley. (Source: White House Photograph, Tia Dufour).

6.8.1 MEDICAL ILLUSTRATIONS AS DEMONSTRATIVE AIDS

All Illustrations Used Are with the Permission of the Victims and/or Families

Nine separate law firms worked with the survivors and the families of the deceased in this case. The photographs of the victims and the crime scene could not be used in the trial because they were under a protective order from the United States government. As an alternative, the attorneys chose to represent the victims/survivors by hiring a medical illustrator (me) to create illustrations based on the photographs, medical records, and autopsy reports.

The attorneys wanted to depict an overview of ballistics, multiple traumatic injury, or fatal injury illustration boards showcasing how many bullet wounds each victim sustained, what organs were traversed, and the directionality that each bullet took. The illustrations were reviewed by a medical doctor and a medical examiner for accuracy.

The illustrations were utilized on the cover of a notebook for each of the victims to present their individual cases to the judge. The doctors used the illustrations to explain what happened to each plaintiff, and they were set up in the war room (room where strategic decisions are made) on the white board to determine damages.

Twenty-six people were killed and 20 injured in the attack. They are not all represented in the book. Please see several illustration boards that were created for the case.

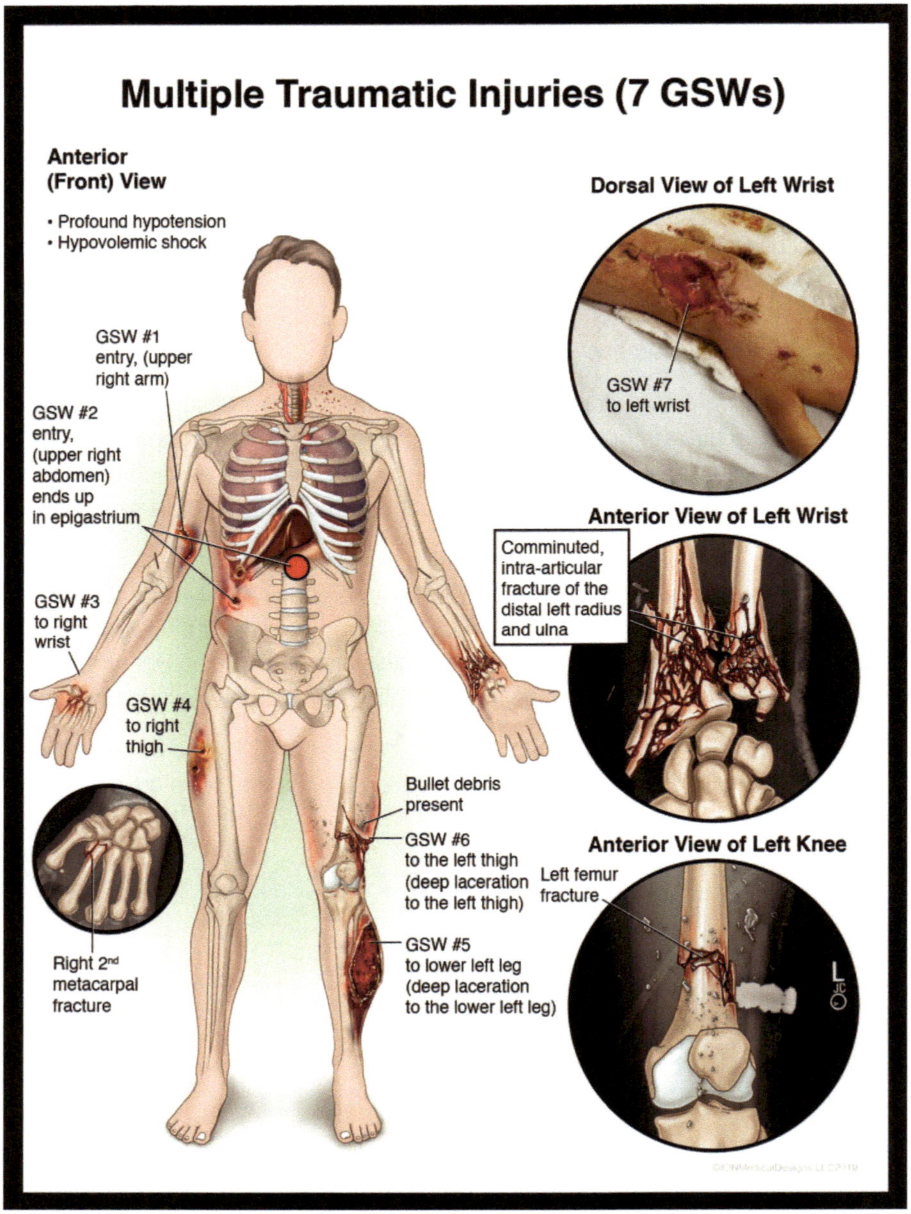

FIGURE 6.5 This is an illustration board depicting all the bullet wounds and trajectories sustained by this surviving plaintiff. As you can see, there is a lot of shrapnel left in his body, and the bullets shattered his bones. There is a photograph of a bullet would he sustained on the upper left side of the page.

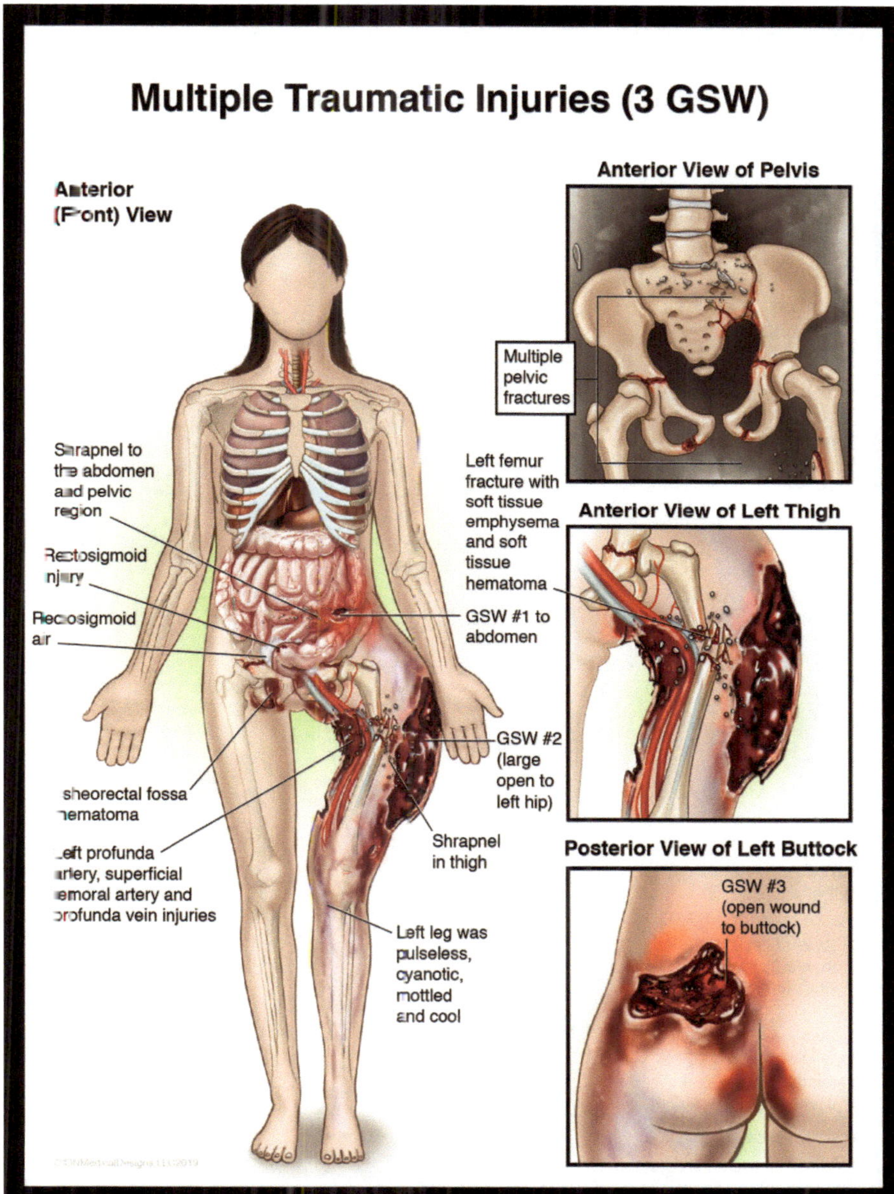

FIGURE 6.6 This is an illustration board depicting all the bullet wounds and trajectories sustained by the surviving plaintiff. As you can see, her left leg was nearly blown off entirely by the bullet. That was the shape of her leg at the time and was based off her medical imaging. The bullet wounded her femoral artery and fractured her femur, as well as many bones in her pelvis. A survivor, much of the shrapnel remains in her body.

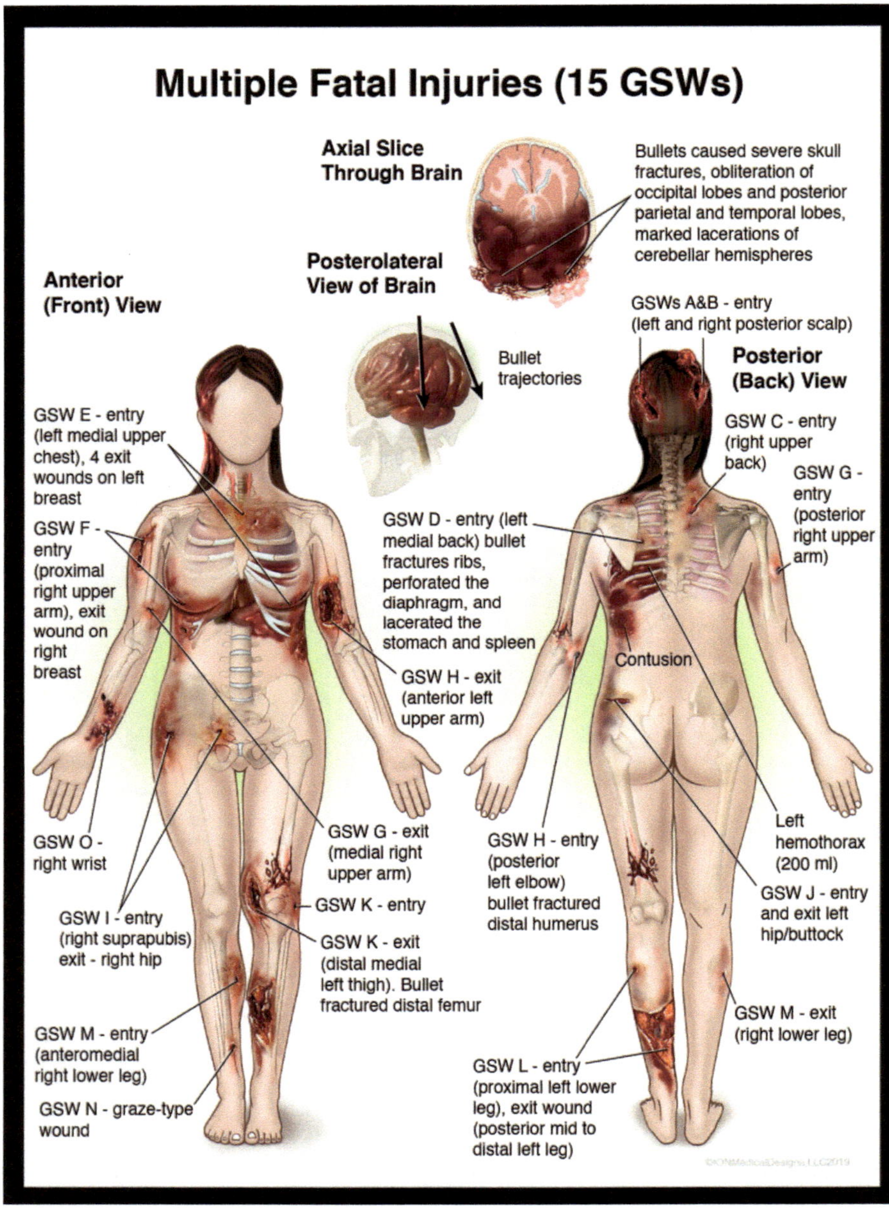

FIGURE 6.7 This is an illustration board depicting all the bullet wounds and trajectories of the bullets sustained by the victim. The insets are illustrations showing the bullet trajectory and the brain injury. Tragically, she passed away due to her multiple injuries.

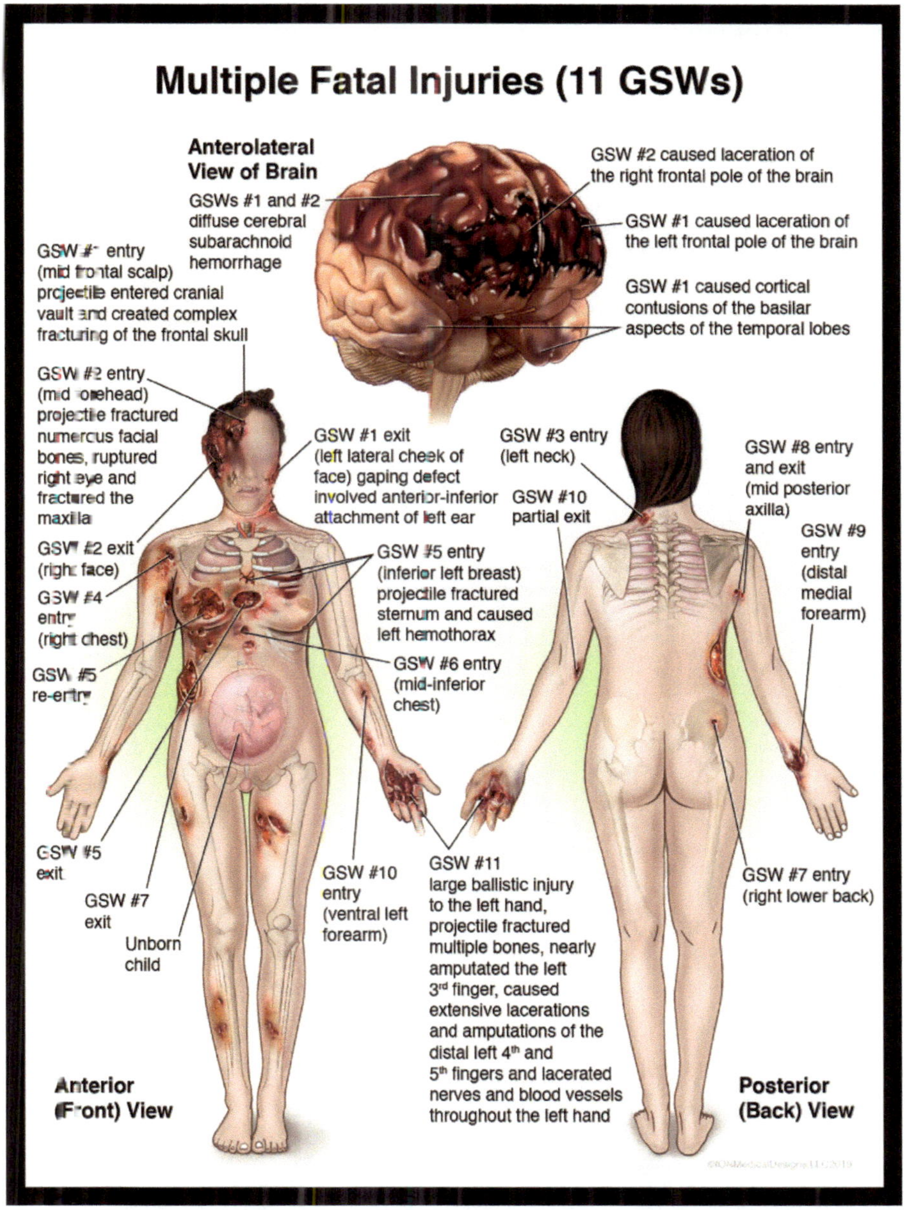

FIGURE 6.8 This is an illustration board depicting all the bullet wounds and trajectories of the bullets sustained by the victim. The large inset illustration of the brain shows the hemorrhages due to the gunshot wound to the head. She passed away from the injuries. She was pregnant at the time of the massacre, and, tragically, both she and her unborn child passed away.

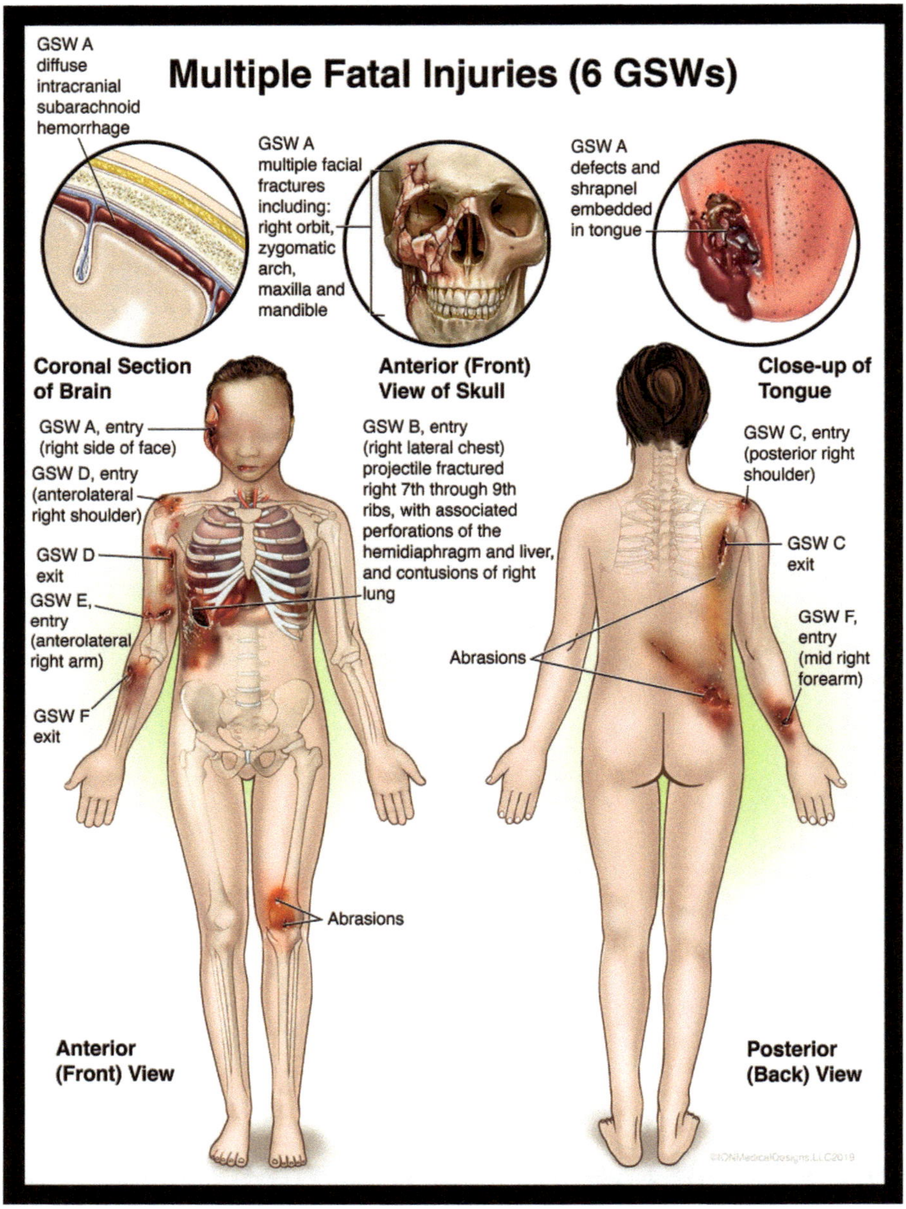

FIGURE 6.9 This is an illustration board depicting all the bullet wounds and trajectories of the bullets sustained by the victim. The large inset illustrations are of the brain hemorrhages, skull fractures, and shrapnel lodged in her tongue. Tragically, she passed away due to her multiple injuries.

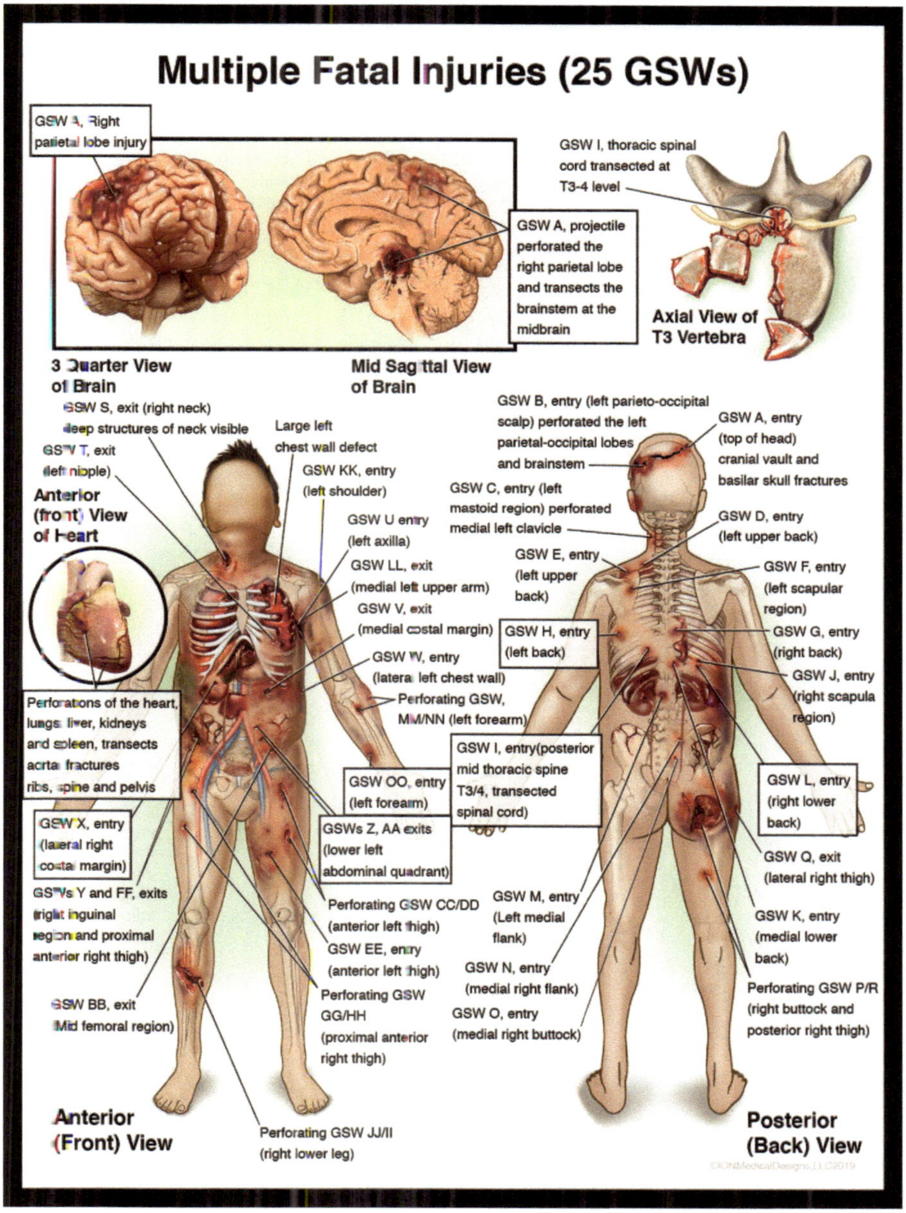

FIGURE 6.10 This is an illustration board depicting all the bullet wounds and trajectories of the bullets sustained by the victim. The large inset illustrations are of the brain hemorrhages, a heart perforation, and the thoracic vertebra that was penetrated by a bullet that was lodged in the spinal cord. Tragically, he passed away due to his multiple injuries.

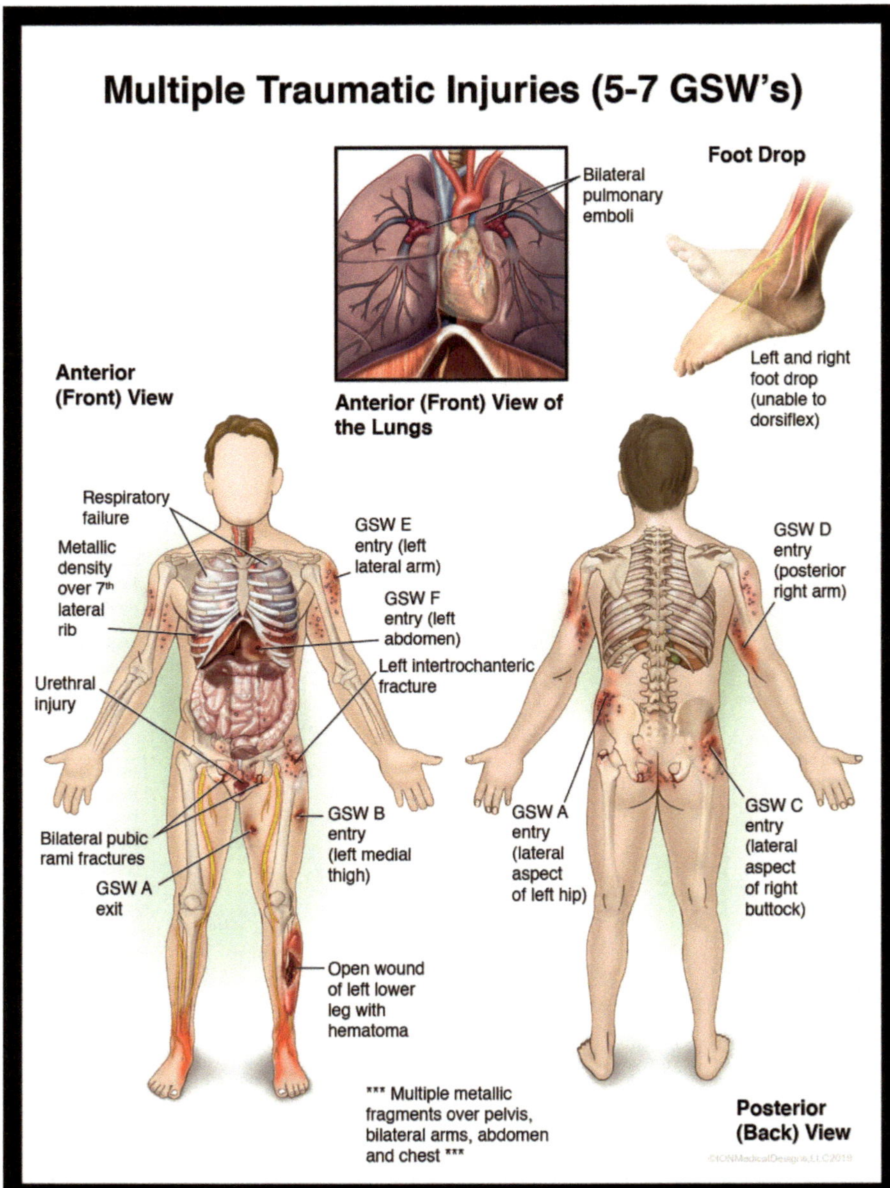

FIGURE 6.11 This is an illustration board depicting all the bullet wounds and trajectories of the bullets sustained by the surviving plaintiff. The large inset illustrations are of the blood clots in the lungs and foot drop, a nervous system condition where you can't dorsiflex your foot.

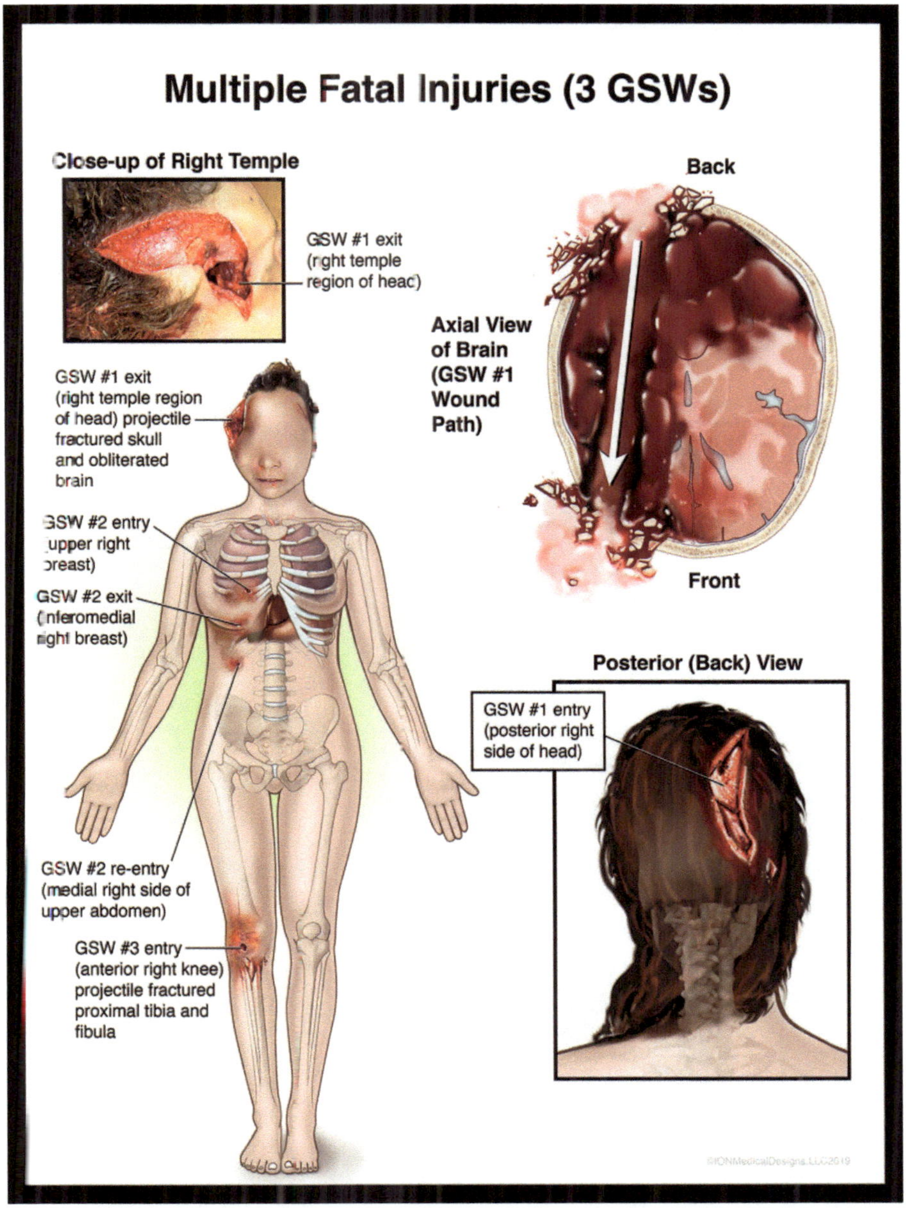

FIGURE 6.12 This is an illustration board depicting all the bullet wounds and trajectories of the bullets sustained by the victim. The large inset illustration depicts brain injuries to do the gunshot wound to the head. There is a close-up of her posterior skull fractures and a picture of her bullet wound to the head in the upper left corner. Tragically, she passed away from her fatal injuries.

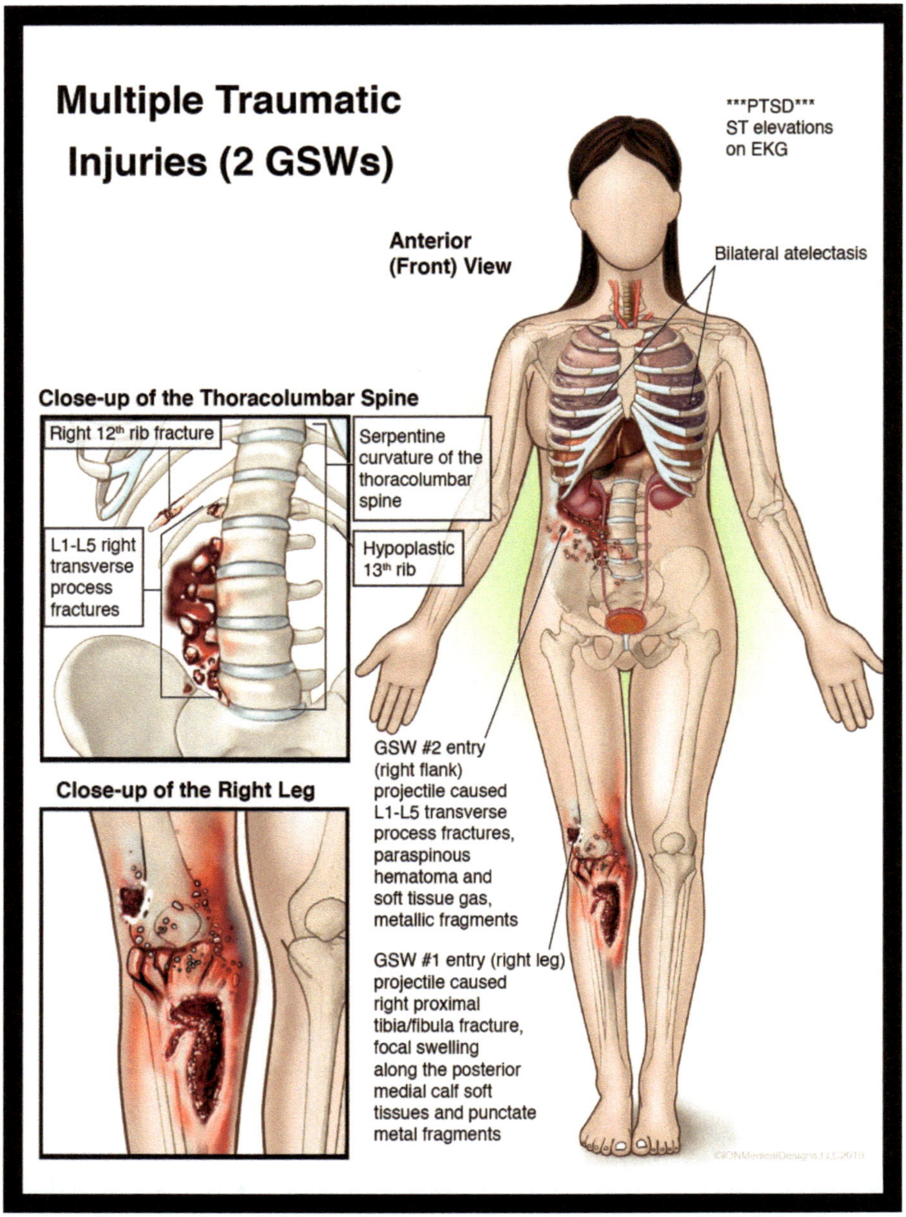

FIGURE 6.13 This is an illustration board depicting all the bullet wounds and trajectories of the bullets sustained by the surviving plaintiff. The large inset illustrations are of the plaintiff's spine and rib injuries and likewise show the large flesh wound of the right calf that includes shrapnel fragments.

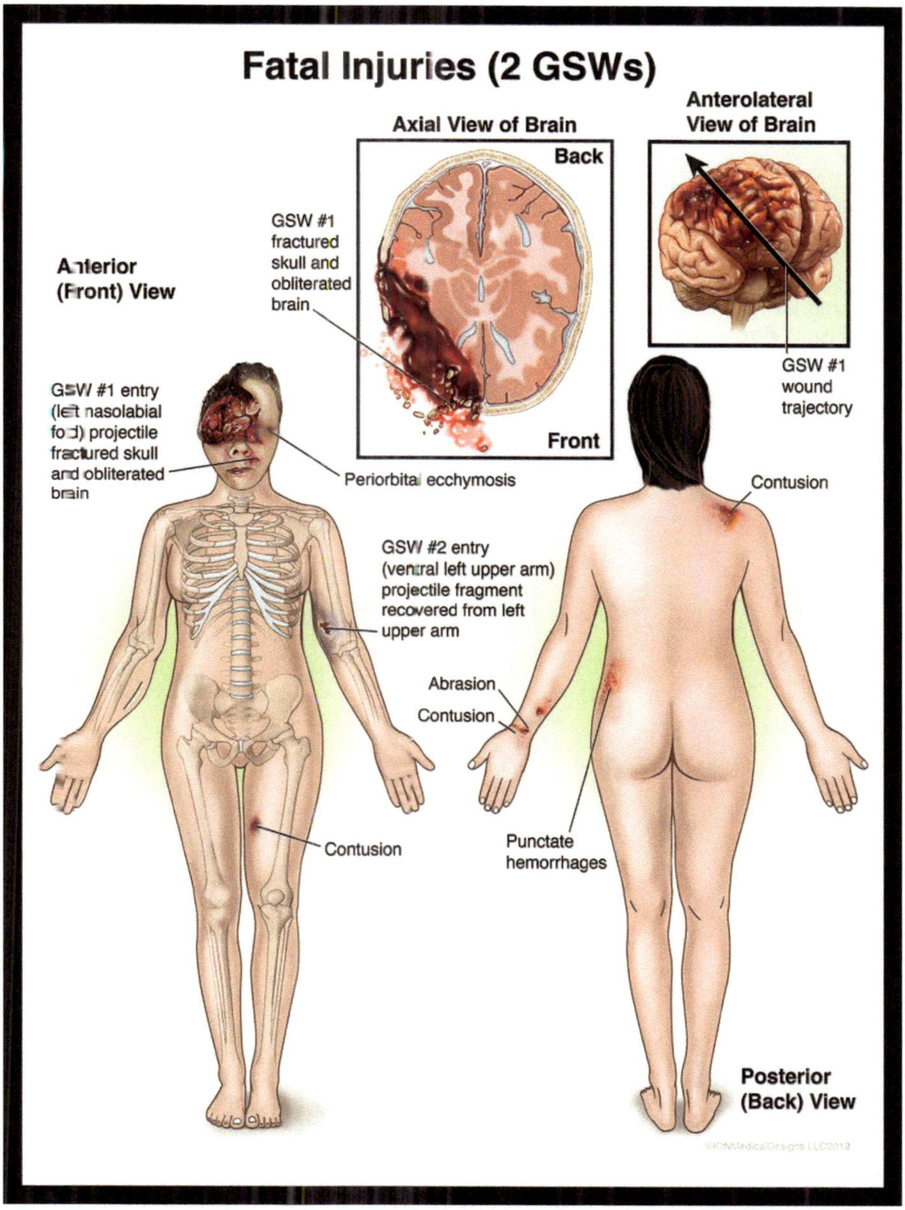

FIGURE 6.14 This is an illustration board depicting all the bullet wounds and trajectories of the bullets sustained by the plaintiff. The large inset illustrations are of the plaintiff's brain injuries and bullet trajectories through the head. She passed away due to multiple gunshot wounds.

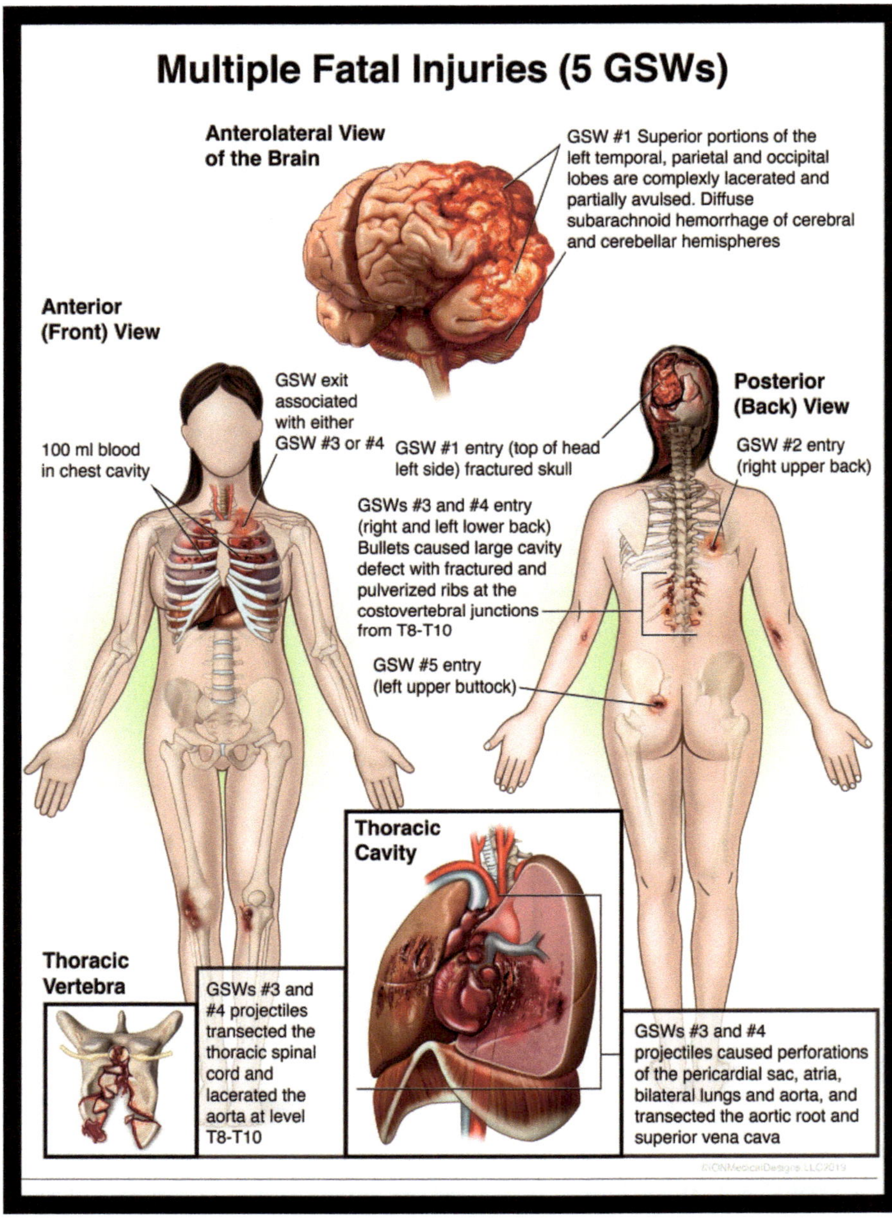

FIGURE 6.15 This is an illustration board depicting all the bullet wounds and trajectories of the bullets sustained by the victim. The large inset illustrations are of the brain injuries, axial view of the thoracic spine vertebra fracture, spinal cord laceration, heart, and lung injuries. Tragically, she passed away due to her gunshot wounds.

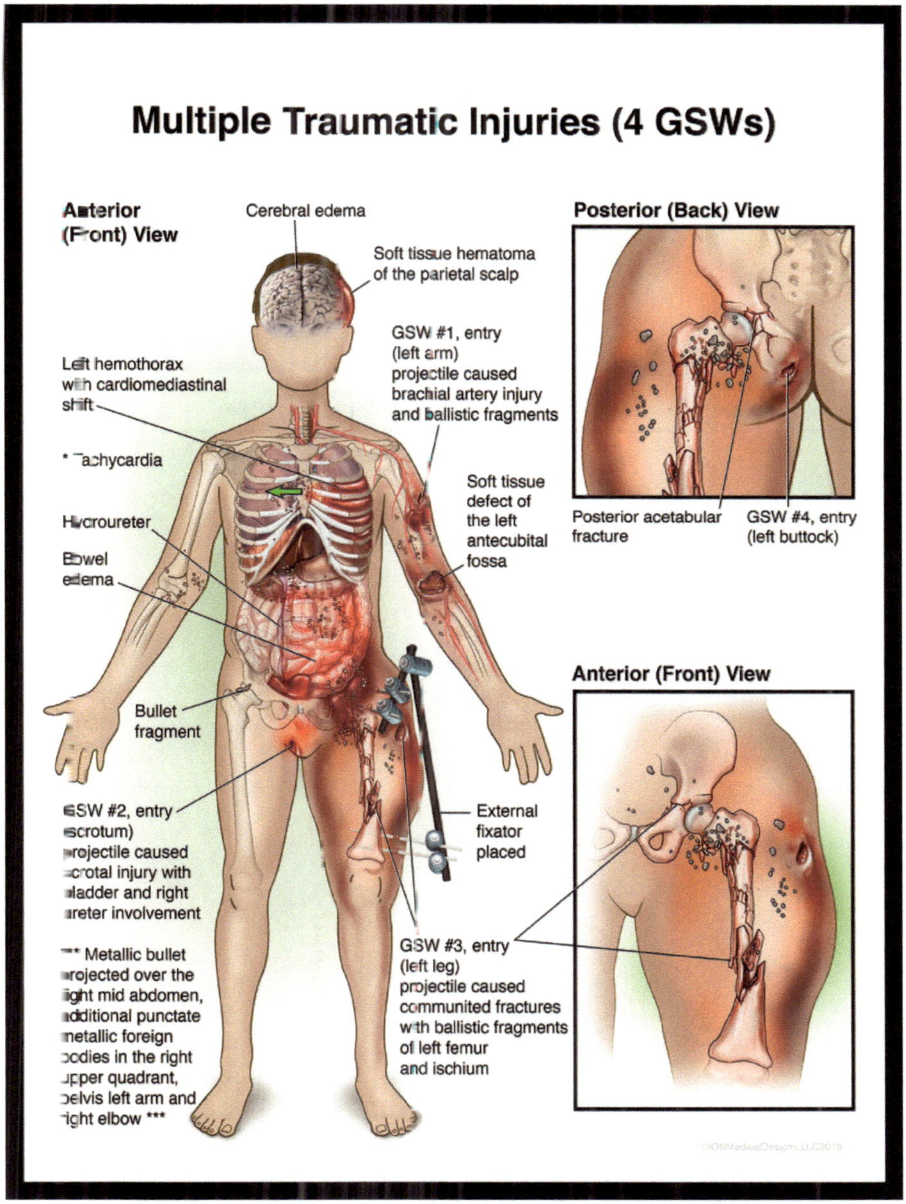

FIGURE 6.16 This is an illustration board depicting all the bullet wounds and trajectories of the bullets sustained by the surviving plaintiff. The large inset illustrations are of the plaintiff's femur fractures, bullet wounds, and location and nature of the shrapnel within the body.

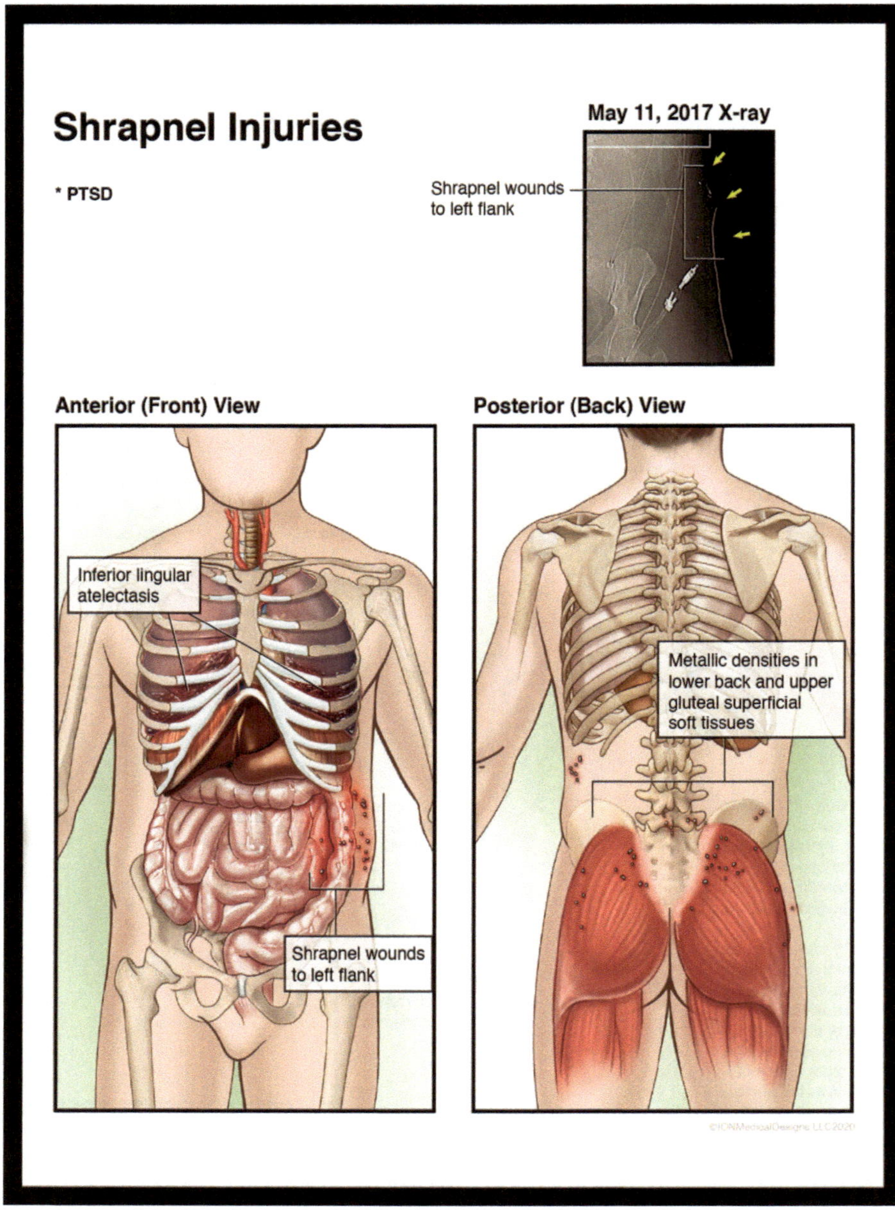

FIGURE 6.17 This is an illustration board depicting the shrapnel wounds sustained by the surviving plaintiff. Anterior and posterior views of his body are shown due to the extent of shrapnel injuries to his abdomen and buttocks, as well as the various organs and tissues affected.

6.9 $230,000.000.00 VERDICT!

Judge Xavier Rodriguez found that the Air Force was 60% liable for the mass shooting because they did not report the gunman's prior assault conviction to the FBI. If they had reported the assault, it was argued that may have prevented Devin Kelley from purchasing the semi-automatic rifle that he used to kill 26 people and injure 20 additional.

6.10 IN NEWS TODAY—DEPARTMENT OF JUSTICE SET TO APPEAL—VICTIMS WILL RECEIVE 144.5 MILLION DOLLAR SETTLEMENT

THE UNITED STATES
DEPARTMENT of JUSTICE

ABOUT | OUR AGENCY | OUR WORK | NEWS | RESOURCES | CAREERS

Home » Office of Public Affairs » News

JUSTICE NEWS

Department of Justice

Office of Public Affairs

FOR IMMEDIATE RELEASE — Wednesday, April 5, 2023

Justice Department Reaches Multimillion Dollar Civil Settlement in Principle in Sutherland Springs Mass Shooting

The Justice Department announced today an agreement in principle to settle the civil cases arising out of the tragic November 2017 mass shooting at the First Baptist Church of Sutherland Springs, Texas, that killed 26 worshippers and injured 22 others.

These tentative settlements will resolve claims by more than 75 plaintiffs arising out of the shooting. Plaintiffs' claims alleged that the Air Force was negligent when it failed to transmit to the National Instant Criminal Background Check System (NICS) information about the shooter that would have prevented him from purchasing guns from a federally licensed firearms dealer. A federal district court in Texas concluded that the United States was liable for damages caused by the shooting. This tentative settlement would resolve the pending appeals.

The agreement in principle would settle all claims for a total of $144.5 million. The settlement agreement has been approved, subject to the plaintiffs' securing the required court approvals. Under applicable law, a court must approve some aspects of the settlements.

"No words or amount of money can diminish the immense tragedy of the mass shooting in Sutherland Springs," said Associate Attorney General Vanita Gupta. "Today's announcement brings the litigation to a close, ending a painful chapter for the victims of this unthinkable crime."

The NICS plays a critical role in combatting gun violence, and the federal government is always striving to improve the functioning of that system. The department continues to work actively to combat gun violence as part of its comprehensive violent crime reduction strategy.

Component(s):
Civil Division
Office of the Associate Attorney General

Press Release Number:
23-371

Updated April 5, 2023

FIGURE 6.18 This is a screen capture of the Department of Justice's press release for the civil settlement in principle in Sutherland Springs mass shooting.

6.11 CASE TWO—APARTMENT SHOOTING—CIVIL SUIT

Greg Bevel and Wesley Gould, Rochelle McCullough, L.L.P.

An apartment shooting that occurred with no criminal charges. Attorney Wesley Gould and Attorney Greg Bevel represented a woman who was shot through the front door of her apartment by individuals who thought her apartment was of the individuals they wanted to shoot.

Since the apartment the woman lived in didn't have adequate security, meaning that there were no security cameras or doormen, there was no way to identify and locate the criminals. Therefore, no criminal trial was held due to the negligence of the apartment owners.

The attorneys chose to use illustration boards as their modality to depict the plaintiff's gunshot wound trajectory (Figure 6.20), femur fracture, and residual shrapnel (Figure 6.19). They also wanted to illustrate the cephalomedullary femoral nail surgery. The cephalomedullary nailing is a procedure to fix the femoral shaft fracture (Figure 6.21). It helps to realign the bone, and the rod and screws help the bone stay in place and strong. Attorneys use the surgery to show pain and suffering or, if you're defense, to show the surgeon fixed the injury.

The illustrations were utilized to help the jury understand the plaintiff's pain and suffering. They were presented along with photographs for understanding of the medical terminology, helping to paint a picture of the plaintiff's experience before, during, and after the injury and treatment.

Please see the following illustration boards for the case.

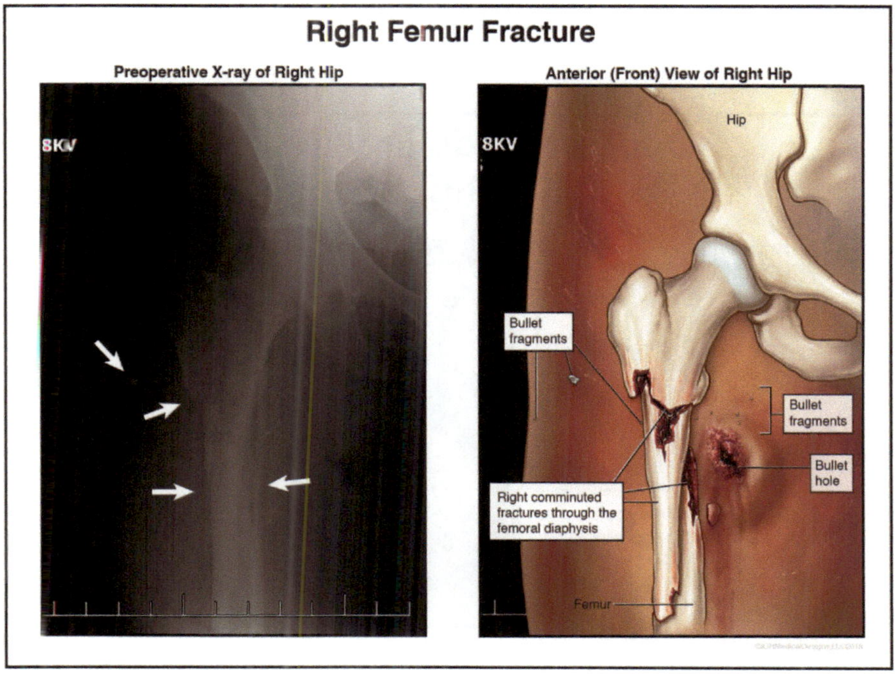

FIGURE 6.19 This is an illustration board depicting the gunshot wound to the right thigh and the associated femur fracture and soft tissue edema. It is a good example of a colorized x-ray.

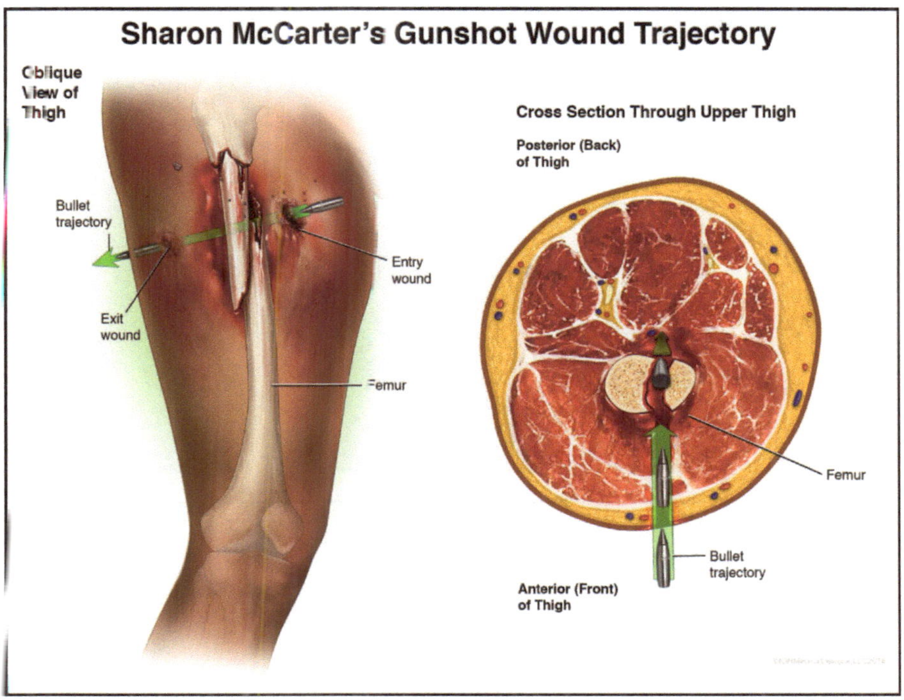

FIGURE 6.20 This is an illustration board depicting the gunshot wound to the right thigh, the associated femur fracture, soft tissue edema, and bullet trajectory.

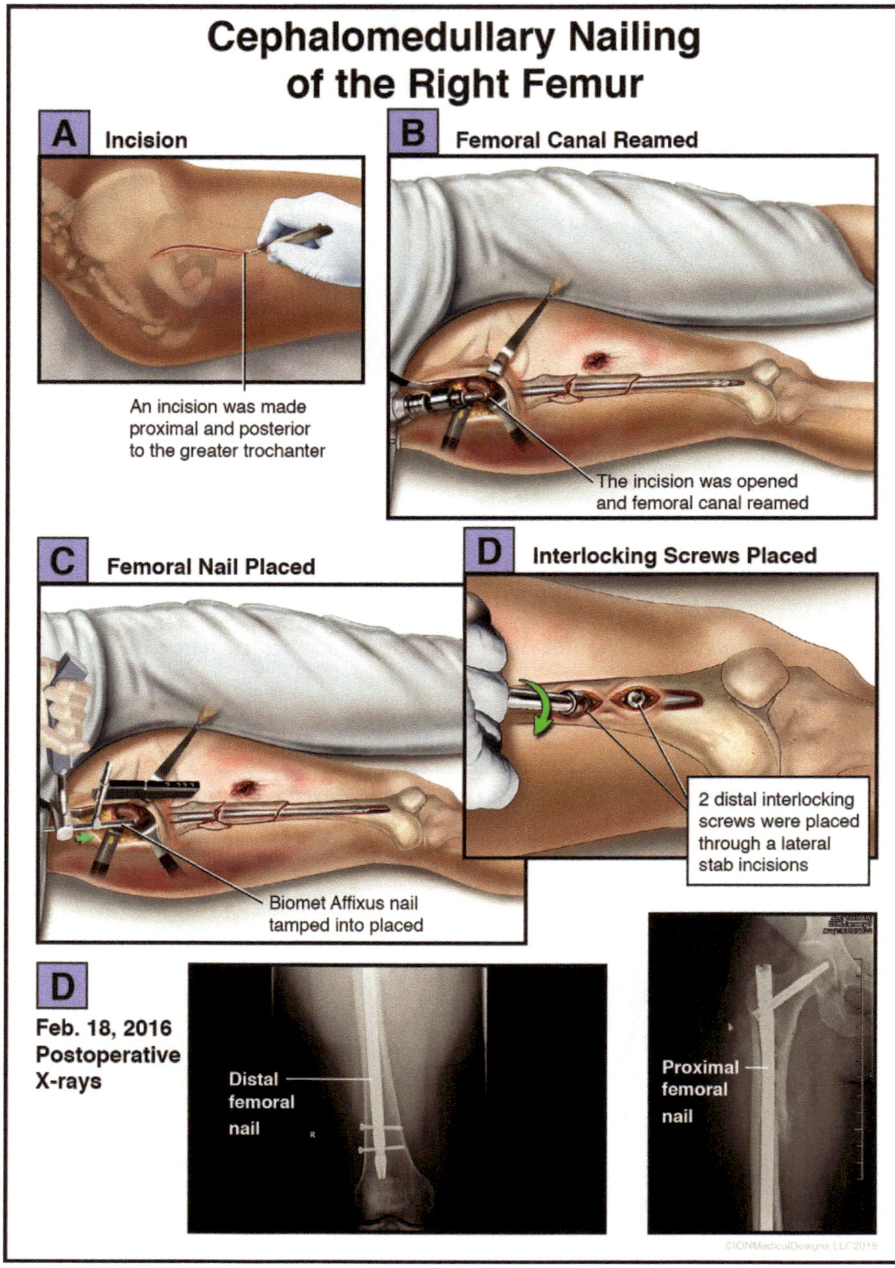

FIGURE 6.21 This is an illustration board depicting the femoral nail surgery to repair the femur fracture she sustained. In this surgery the femoral canal is reamed, and a nail is tamped into place across the fracture site and then is secured by screws. The nail helps to support the bone to keep it in place and for strength.

CHAPTER 7

Forensic Facial Reconstruction

> Forensic art is any art that is forensic in nature that would be valuable in legal proceedings.
>
> (*Forensic Art and Illustration*, 2014)

Art that aids in identification of a deceased person or suspect and/or age progression of a missing child and/or person. It can include digital or hand-drawn age progressions for cold or missing persons cases, sketches of potential suspects through witness interviews, injury and surgical procedures illustrated for court, cranio-facial reconstruction—either digitally or by hand using clay—and more. Forensic applies to how the art can help with investigations, as well as aid, in conjunction with court presentations, to provide justice for the victim (*Forensic Art and Illustration*, 2014).

7.1 FOUR CATEGORIES OF FORENSIC ART

Forensic art can be divided into four general categories with several subcategories which are the following (*Forensic Art and Illustration*, 2014):

- **Composite Imagery**—Graphics composed of individually described parts, they can be full body drawings or individually described object or evidence drawings.
- **Image Modification and Image Identification**—Methods of manipulating, comparing enhancing and categorizing photographic images.

DOI: 10.4324/9781003336310-7

- **Demonstrative Evidence**—Visual information used for trial display.
- **Reconstruction and Postmortem Identification Aids**—Methods to help identify human remains in a variety of conditions (*Forensic Art and Illustration*, 2014).

Forensic art is a blend of art and science, scientific principles depicted and presented in a visual format. Anatomy of the facial structure, craniofacial growth (age progression), pathology, anthropological, and odontological data are useful for the artist while creating postmortem drawings based on intact or relatively intact bodies.

Forensic artists use their artistic skill to aid in criminal investigation in many ways. Depending on the case, they may collaborate with other specialists such as forensic pathologists, who may advise and guide artists to create the drawings based on the condition of the body. They may also consult with odontologists, radiologists, craniofacial or maxillofacial surgeons, ophthalmologists, and even cosmetologists.

Taphonomy, anthropology, and odontological data are used in postmortem drawings or 2D and 3D facial reconstructions of the skull. While taphonomy is a paleontological term looking at the dispersal, fossilization, and burial of bones, for forensic anthropological purposes, forensic taphonomy factors in changes that have happened to a body postmortem. That can include disarticulation, decomposition, and disarticulation (separation of the bones from the deterioration of tendons and ligaments), movement through water sources, erosion, or scavenging, as well as other local environmental factors and impact on the remains.

7.2 THREE-DIMENSIONAL FACIAL RECONSTRUCTION OF THE SKULL

While studying for my bachelor's degree at the Cleveland Institute of Art, I had the pleasure of meeting and learning from a very well-known and prevalent artist who specialized in 3D facial reconstruction: Betty Pat Gatliff.

Betty worked with physical anthropologist Dr. Clyde Snow in 1967 at the Civil Aeromedical Research Institute at the Federal Aviation Administration in Oklahoma City. Her first case came from the Oklahoma Medical Examiner's office. Dr. Snow asked her to assist in sculpting a face for the skull.

Dr. Snow recommended that Betty read a book titled *The Human Skeleton in Forensic Medicine* by Dr. Krogman. There are many characteristics of the human skull in the book that help to identify and provide a person's individualization such as age, sex, and race that can contribute to cranial identification. The dead skull is a matrix of the living head with a bony core that brings the human face to life. After the cranial framework is prepared, the clay flesh is built bit by bit. When the clay shape is completed, a living head emerges that will help with identification of the dead.

Building a fleshy face from a skull is difficult because a skull doesn't give all the clues that it should. A person is recognized by so many little details, many subtle nuances, that are very hard to capture with just a skull to reveal someone's precise individuality. So only a gross likeness can be achieved. The average identification specialist is not necessarily gifted enough to sculpt a likeness from a skull. A competent sculptor directed by a medical forensic artist and/or anthropologist using a nuclear skull and data can achieve an accurate representation of a human likeness.

Betty's first attempt at a 3D reconstruction was to sculpt a face of a Native American Indian male. She was tasked to find a name to identify the remains so authorities could work towards a positive identification. She studied the text, sculpted, placed her sculpture tools down, and re-referenced the text until she completed her sculpted bust. She was able to complete the bust, and the authorities were able to make a positive identification.

In her career she has worked on over 200 cases and has successfully developed and taught a week's course on how do 3D facial reconstruction. She stated that in the one weeklong course you cannot expect to become an expert in the field. With discipline, practice, attending workshops, reading books, and purchasing the correct tools, you can become a competent forensic artist.

In addition to a lot of practice, Betty taught. Through teaching she was able to develop a process and/or method. Her method helped her to outline her process into steps to create a better workflow.

In 1987, her apprentice Karen Taylor and herself attended a workshop in Scottsdale, Arizona, taught by Jon Zahourek. The class taught craniofacial anatomy. Zahourek taught a hands-on approach to learning anatomy that involved building the muscles with clay over the skeletal framework. The mind eventually takes over, with muscle memory and practice.

They also studied anatomy with Dr. Wilfred Stedman, who taught anatomy with a hands-on approach. He was a retired orthopedic surgeon and sculptor. He encouraged them to use anatomy in their facial reconstruction techniques.

7.3 CIRCUMSTANCES FOR CREATING 3D FACIAL RECONSTRUCTION—METHOD

3D facial reconstruction is a process of taking human remains, typically a skull, and then working with a physical anthropologist to create a likeness for identification purposes.

Law enforcement, along with medical examiners, are often presented with cases of unidentified homicide or sudden death cases. There are many reasons to want to identify a missing or unknown person. In a homicide case it will hopefully bring closure and justice to the family. There also may be lingering estate and business matters to attend to.

Climate can have an effect on the condition of the body and body's position. If a body is intact, it can be photographed postmortem.

Skeletal remains require a facial reconstruction method. Constructing a 3D face from a skull allows the audience to see a person in 3D, which gives them a full perspective of how the person once looked (*Forensic Art and Illustration*, 2014).

Facial reconstruction is a two-phase process. The steps of the phases for 3D reconstruction are listed subsequently:

7.4 TECHNICAL PHASE

In the technical phase case, information is gathered and applied to the known data. All the pertinent material should be gathered, and the skull should be prepared and protected with the mandible securely glued to the skull.

After the skull is prepared, it is mounted on an adjustable skull stand in the Frankfort Horizontal plane. The Frankfort Horizontal plane is an anthropological standard that closely replicates the natural position of the head in life. This position can be achieved using a triangle and a straight-edge ruler. Always keep the head in this position for the best results and to avoid distortion.

The following is a list of the step-by-step process to create the best facial reconstruction possible.

- Receipt of skull, transfer of evidence and record keeping
- Scientific input and case material gathered
- Preparation and protection of the skull
- Gluing the cranium to the mandible
- Placing the skull into the adjustable stand
- Orientation into the Frankfort Horizontal
- Cutting and application of the tissue markers
- Prosthetic eye setting
- Establishing facial contours by connecting tissue depth markers

List from Karen T. Taylor's book *Forensic Art and Illustration* (2014, page 422).

7.5 TISSUE DEPTH MARKERS

There are different techniques of facial reconstruction. The tissue depth method, or American 3D facial reconstruction method, uses average skin-thickness measurements at specific points on the skull to guide soft-tissue reconstruction. The American (modern) way of tissue depth measurement is used mostly in law enforcement. Average skin-depth measurements are collected on the human skull at 21 different points for males and females from three different races. The data is then collected using needles, x-ray, and ultrasound techniques. Before the reconstruction begins, an attempt is made to guess the individual's sex and race.

Once the appropriate tissue depth data is collected, the tissue markers are cut from eraser tips. The tissue markers are then adhered to the skull with cement. The face is constructed by rebuilding the face from the skull by placing uniform clay strips to accomplish a general face shape. After the general face shape is achieved, you would apply the features and transitions.

A secondary method of facial reconstruction is the Russian method. In this method the face would be rebuilt by the skull by sculpting the muscle at the origin and insertion points. This method is attributed to Mikhail M. Gerasimov, a world-renowned anthropologist. With this method, a considerable understanding of anatomy would be required. This method is predominately used on fossil skulls where the reconstructionist has limited resources for tissue depth measurements. Depending on your work situation, this may be your best option; however, this type of reconstruction takes many hundreds of hours and can be expensive. This method offers no testing or comparison likeness; however, Richard Helmer of Bonn, Germany, says Gerasimov reported almost all the 140 court-ordered carried out in the laboratory could be identified.

Many forensic reconstruction artists use a combination of the two methods. A wise reconstructionist uses the best aspects of each method. Richard Neave, an English medical reconstruction artist, uses the combination method by applying his knowledge of facial anatomy as well as the available tissue marker measurements. His reconstructions are done with plaster castings of human skulls. He then covers the skull with facial musculature at the origin and insertion points with a layer of clay.

Your methodology should be determined by your work situation. If you work in law enforcement, the tissue depth technique is the practical choice given the time constraints. If you work in a research facility and have the time for skull casting, muscle building, and adding detail, the anatomical modeling method would work. Or the popular choice—a combination of the two! The following is a list of the phases as well as tools and materials derived from Karen T. Taylor's book *Forensic Art and Illustration* (2014).

ARTISTIC PHASE

- Mouth development
- Eye development
- Nose development
- Cheek development
- Ear development

- Surface texturing and detail
- Hair and/or wig
- Photography

7.6 TOOLS AND MATERIALS

The following tips and materials are from Karen T. Taylor's book *Forensic Art and Illustration* (2014). There are various tools and materials that are required for the sculpture busts. Specific sculpture tools such as a flat wooden spatula, wire tool, and pointed wooden stick are helpful. A boley-style gauge, metal scale, plastic brayer, or ruler, and an X-Acto knife and blades are also helpful.

The following materials are also helpful in the modeling process: clay such as oil-based modeling clay, Duco cement or other adhesive, cotton balls and swabs, vinyl machine erasers, #40 grade sandpaper, aluminum "gutter guard," or flexible mesh.

These are the minimal tools you would need, and over time you may find others that suit you well for modeling, and fingertips will work as well! (*Forensic Art and Illustration*, 2014, page 422).

A few pictures of 3D reconstructions:

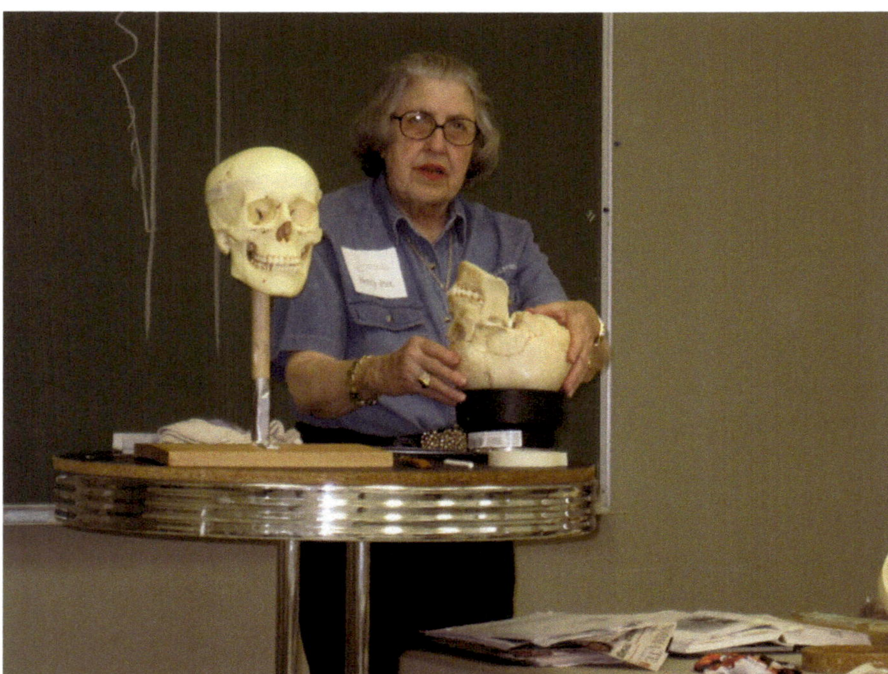

FIGURE 7.1 This is a photograph of Betty Pat Gatliff teaching her method of facial reconstruction. Photo credit: Chris Saper (*Chris Saper (Chrissaper)—Profile | Pinterest*, n.d.)

Identified...Identified...Identified

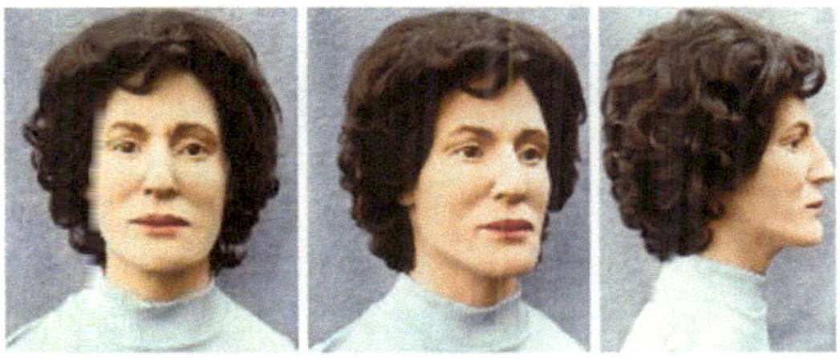

Reconstruction by Betty Pat Gatliff.

Date of Discovery: April 24, 1995
Location of Discovery: Caddo County, Oklahoma
Estimated Date of Death: Months prior
State of Remains: Decomposed
Cause of Death: Unknown

Physical Description

Estimated Age: 16-25 years old
Race: White
Sex: Female
Height: 5'7"
Weight: Unknown
Hair Color: Light brown
Eye Color: Unknown
Distinguishing Marks/Features: Possible one term or near-term pregnancy. Right handed.

FIGURE 7.2 This is a photograph of a facial reconstruction created by Betty Pat Gatliff. The person was identified because of her excellent reconstruction work! (*1386UFOK*, n.d.)

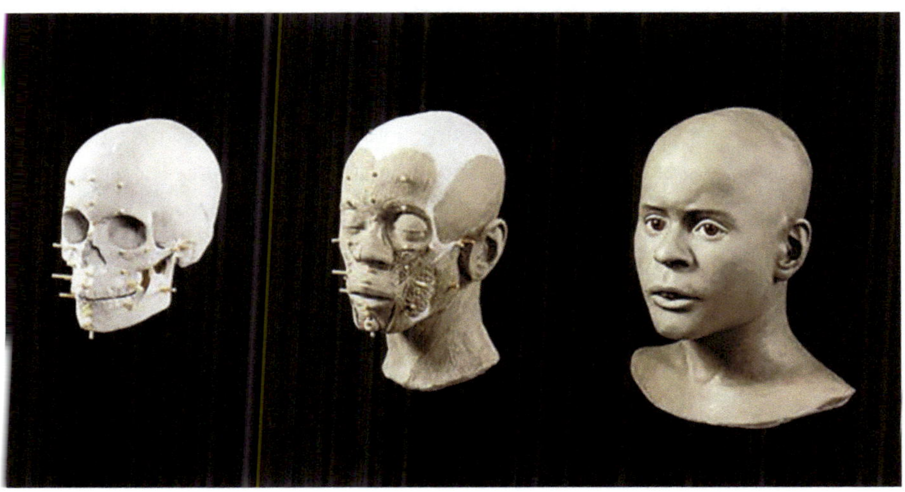

FIGURE 7.3 This is a photograph of the Russian process of 3D facial reconstruction, which includes tissue markers with anatomy sculpted with clay and then a face built. This is a photograph of the digital facial reconstruction created by Oscar Nilsson of the Paleolithic teenager (*Facebook*, n d.).

7.7 MODERN 3D FACIAL RECONSTRUCTION WITH ARTIFICIAL INTELLIGENCE (AI)

Meet Vistegutten: The Lonely Boy in the Cave (Norway)

The case that intrigued me most to profile here is the 3D facial reconstruction done by Oscar Nilsson of a Paleolithic teenage boy from more than 30,000 years ago. In the late nineteenth century, archeologists found an ancient human skull deep inside the cave of Mladeč, in the Czech Republic. The sex of the skull was thought to be male due to the male characteristics it had. Then female, and then proven male by DNA testing of the bones according to the facial reconstructionist Oscar Nilsson.

The boy was very short for his age, standing just 4 feet and 1 inch. He also had a skull pathology called scaphocephaly, meaning your skull grows backward instead of sideways, giving him an unusual appearance.

Over the course of the archeologist's modern investigation, they found that the skull belonged to a 15-year-old male who lived between 26,000 to 43,000 years ago. Using 3D graphic tools and modern forensic techniques, they were able to construct his face.

Several researchers including a Brazilian graphics expert Cicero Moraes, a surveyor with GEO-CZ Jiri Sindelar, and the Czech Republic deputy director of the Cave Administration, Karel Drbal, gathered and studied the ancient remains. The measurements of the skull and dig descriptions were included with the research materials.

To digitize the skull, they performed CT (computed tomography) scans of the skull. However, the skull was missing the lower jaw. Then 200 CT scans from modern humans as well as archeological excavations were collected by the researchers. Statistical methods were used to find an estimated jaw shape to best fit the Mladeč skull for the full reconstruction.

The next step in the process of reconstruction of the skull was the soft tissue marker application across a 3D digital reconstruction of the skull. The application of skin, fat, tendons, and muscles to construct his face was done. There was only so much data to construct the face, so the shape and size of the mouth, eye color, and shape and size of the nose couldn't be determined this way. They were done neutrally to best represent the time era. They chose brown skin and brown eyes, estimating the indigenous people of that time which was of Mediterranean descent.

To complete the data set for the reconstruction of the teenage boy's face, the researchers imported the live subjects CT scans. The anatomy of each CT scan was then deformed using the computer, and the soft tissues and bones from the CT scans were used to approximate his face and then manipulated to fit his skull. With the Mladeč fossil, a CT scan of a man and woman were converged to a similar result.

On the digs, archeologists did discover a few stone artifacts, fishing hooks, food remnants, bone tips, and teeth, leading us to believe this was a cave for living and working for the ancient people. There is little known about this young man. He lived more than 20,000 years ago, before our modern conveniences of medicine, agriculture, and writing (Puiu, 2022).

Please see the following computer graphics made of his 3D reconstruction.

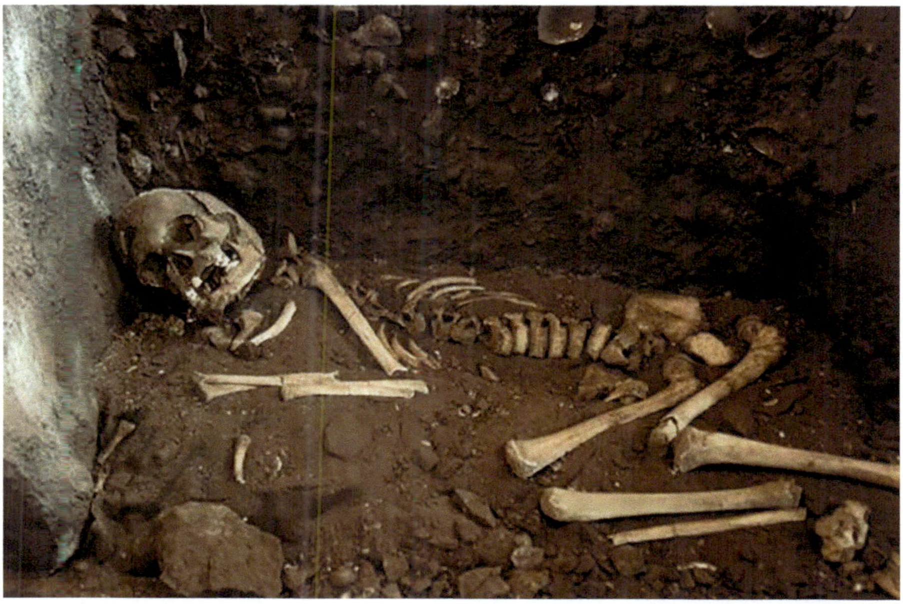

FIGURE 7.4 This photograph is of the skeletal remains of the ancient Paleolithic teenage boy. Vistegutten's skeletal remains were found in a cave once used by Mesolithic hunter-gatherers. The teenager's skeleton is on display at the Archaeological Museum in Stavanger (Terje Tveit/The Museum of Archaeology/University of Stavanger/CC BY-SA 3.0).

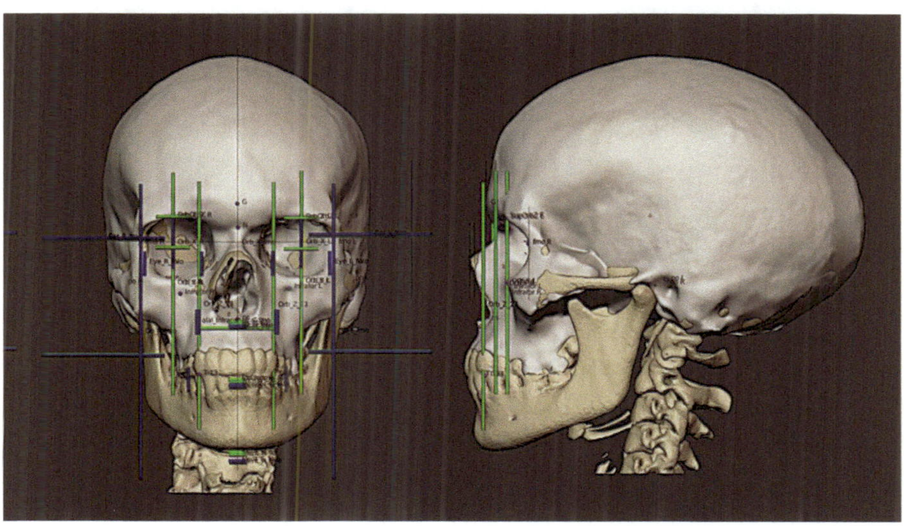

FIGURE 7.5 This is a photograph of the skull with the digital facial markers. The CT scan of the ancient boy's skull combined with CT scans of other human beings. Credit: Cicero Moraes/Jiri Sindelar/Karel Drbal (Puiu, 2022).

The forensic artist Oscar Nilsson invested many months in creating the reconstruction of Vistegutten based on the boy's skull (Oscar Nilsson).

(*Art & Science by O D Nilsson—the Sculptor's Studio*, n.d.)

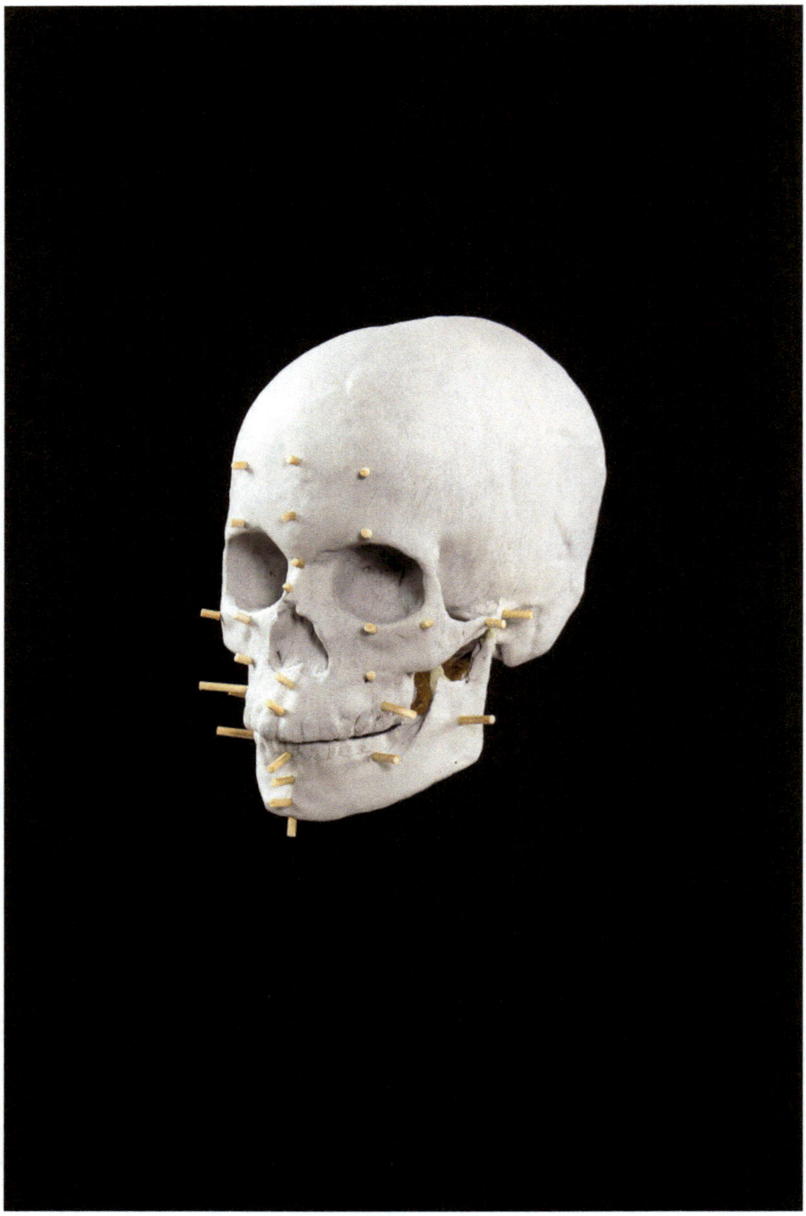

FIGURE 7.6 Photograph and reconstruction work created by Oscar Nilsson. The skull here has the measured soft tissue depth markers.

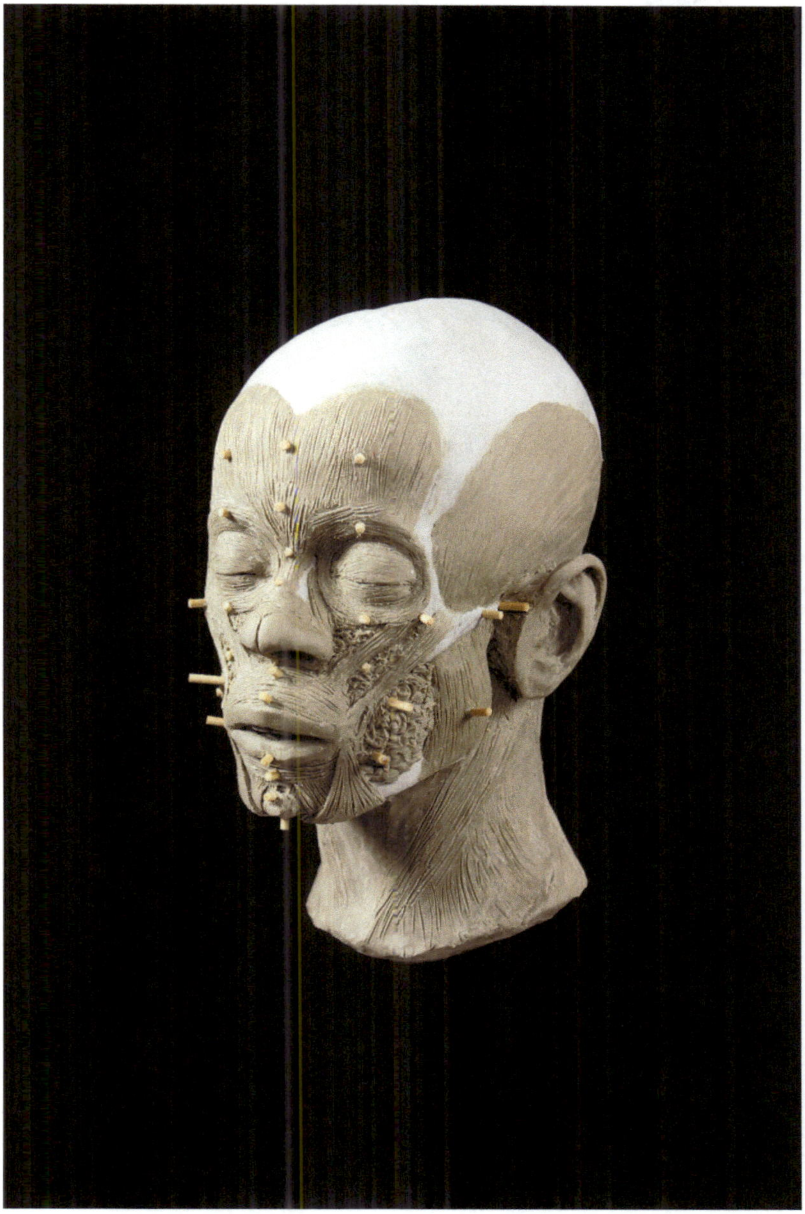

FIGURE 7.7 Photograph and reconstruction work created by Oscar Nilsson, where he has started to sculpt the muscles onto the skull.

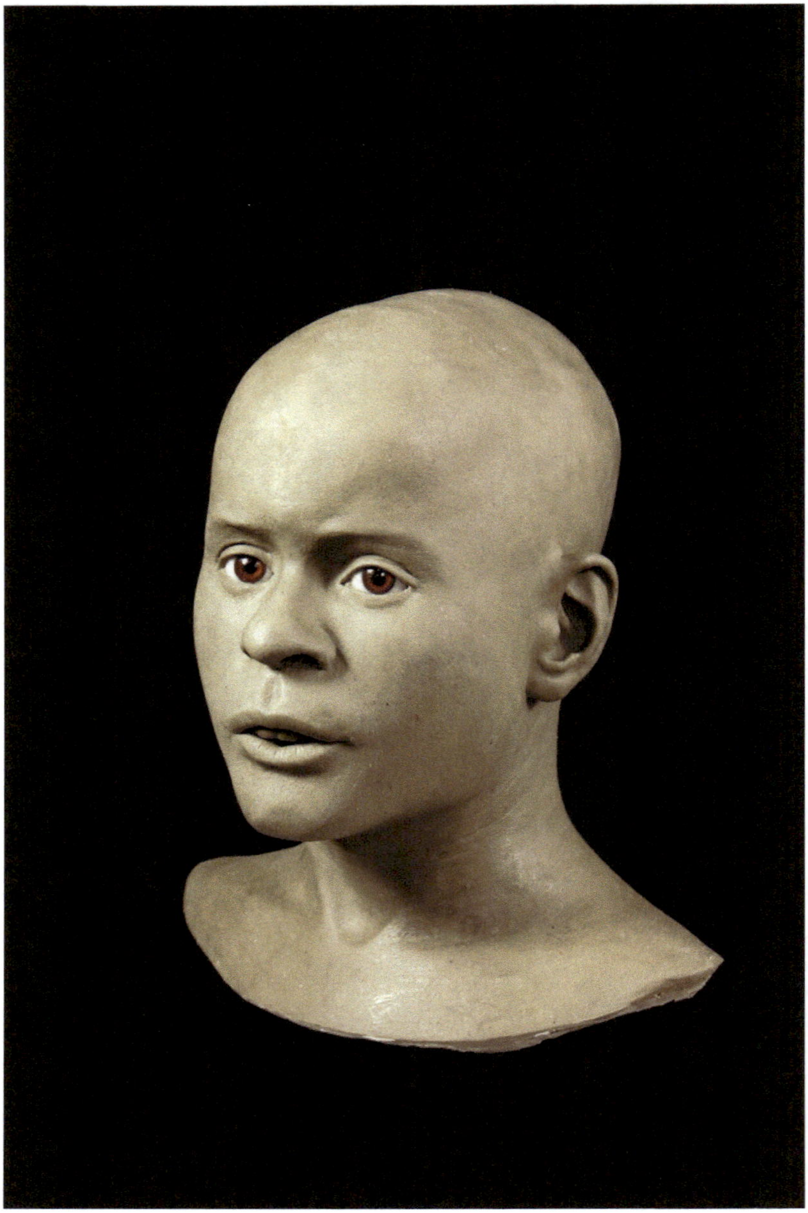

FIGURE 7.8 Photograph and reconstruction work created by Oscar Nilsson, where the skin and eyes have been modeled.

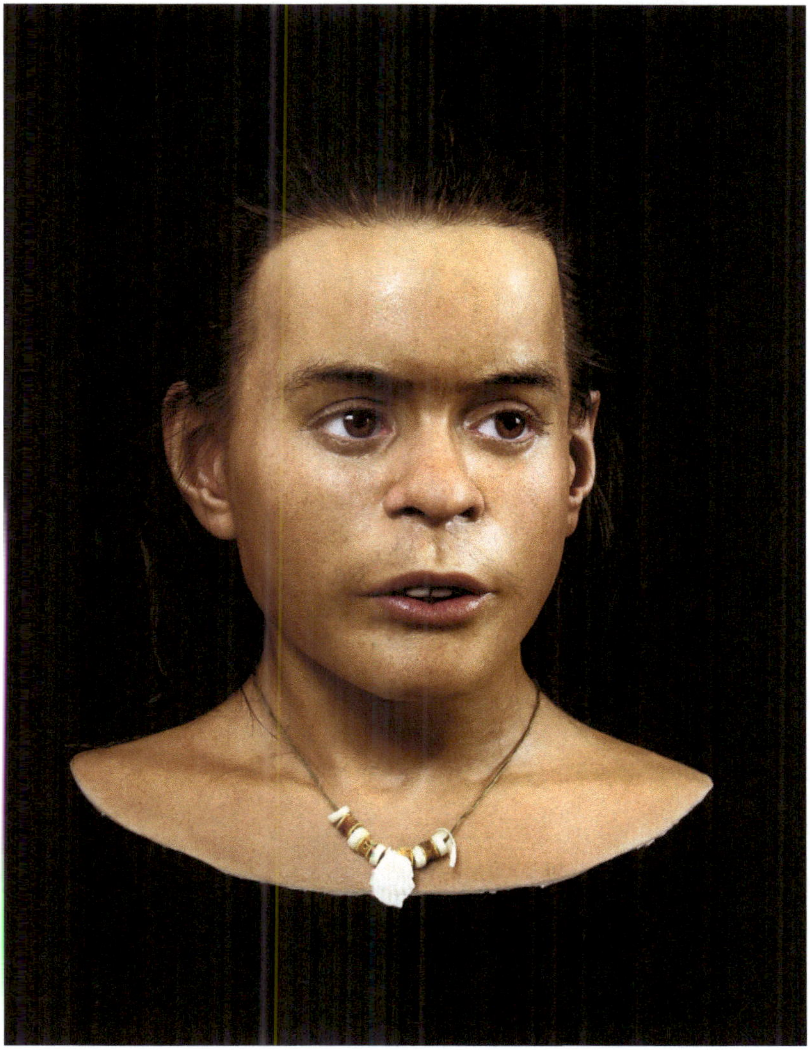

FIGURE 7.9 This is a photograph of the digital facial reconstruction created by Oscar Nilsson of the Paleolithic teenager.

The forensic artist Oscar Nilsson invested many months in creating the reconstruction of Vistegutten based on the boy's skull (Oscar Nilsson) (*Facebook*, n.d.).

CHAPTER 8

Medical Legal Illustrations Are Useful in Every Stage of Litigation—Not Just Trial!

The common assumption is that medical demonstrative aids are only utilized or helpful within the courtroom, only for cases that proceed to trial. However, medical graphics can be utilized at all stages of litigation. The following list outlines the various trial stages where they can be most helpful:

- Prelitigation—Attorneys can utilize medical demonstrative aids to educate themselves about their case before filing a claim. They may also reveal, and allow time, to resolve any potential ambiguities in the case ahead of time, before the issue arises in the courtroom and prior to settlement discussions.
- Demand packages—Sending medical illustrations along with the demand letter is a powerful way to ensure that the opposing counsel understands that you are serious and prepared for litigation.
- Depositions—Utilizing client-specific medical demonstrative aids, for when your medical expert is deposed, allows them to approve the accuracy of the exhibits on the record.
- Mediation—Presenting medical illustrations will indicate readiness for trial to opposing counsel.
- Trial—Using the demonstrative aids to help narrate the case to the jury and make a visually dramatic, illustrative, and/or memorable impact.

DOI: 10.4324/9781003336310-8

8.1 SUBMITTING MEDICAL DEMONSTRATIVE AIDS TO TRIAL

How do I get medical demonstrative aids into trial? The following list is a recommended course of action:

1. Find a qualified medical artist.
2. Find a qualified medical doctor expert.
3. Utilize client medical records and medical imaging for accuracy in depicting the injury(ies) and/or medical procedures.
4. Utilize such demonstrative aids in depositions, mediations, and trial.
5. Exchange/submit the medical demonstrative aids.
6. Know the courtroom. If the judge is more conservative, too much blood may be inappropriate. Or maybe the courtroom isn't high tech, so you may need to print your illustrations for the jury to review.

8.2 FIND A QUALIFIED MEDICAL/FORENSIC ILLUSTRATOR

You have something important to communicate and need a unique image that will educate, as well as clarify, a specific injury or surgery. Medical illustrators are in the business of visualizing science and medicine for the lay person, and they are (or at least should be!) trained in art and science. As such, they are able to communicate the complex information in an accurate, educational, and visually captivating way.

Working with a medical illustrator—and purchasing illustrations, animations, and interactive applications—may be new to you. Take your time and do your due diligence before hiring an artist.

Ideally, the artist would have a bachelor's and/or master's degree in medical illustration, or relevant experience in the field, and hold a board certification from the Association of Medical Illustrators.

The artist needs to be trained artistically and medically to be able to appropriately work on medical legal cases. They preferably would have experience working with a medical legal firm and working independently with personal injury and medical malpractice attorneys in the medical legal or forensic fields.

Having direct experience is important. The artist should be able to interpret radiologic images and decipher the medical reports. They should be confident conversing with the medical experts to be able to convert the complex information into effective visual aids. The artwork should reflect the medical records and be simple enough for a juror to understand.

The medical doctor expert will then utilize the illustrations throughout the case to educate individuals in depositions, mediations, and trial.

Most artists have websites with their online portfolios showcasing their artwork. Asking for samples or looking through their portfolios to see their style of art before hiring them is important. Look at Google reviews, or, even better, ask your colleagues for referrals.

Make sure you address the usage rights. Medical illustration is a service. There are typically digital files, and sometimes prints are provided. For legal purposes, an unlimited, nonexclusive copyright is typically provided. Meaning the copyright permits the buyer use of the image across all media platforms. However, the content creator may grant the exact same rights to other buyers.

8.3 FIND A QUALIFIED MEDICAL EXPERT

An expert witness is someone who possesses key knowledge in a particular field and is qualified to give testimony in court. The testimony can be based—collectively and individually—on their experience, education, research, and medical training. The expert witness must provide an educated, researched, unbiased opinion. For the purposes of personal injury and medical malpractice on behalf of attorneys, specifically the testimony would be related to the client's current condition, injuries, and surgery(ies). The client analysis would be presented to the jury so that they can comprehend the information presented to them.

The expert witness can be called by the prosecution or the defense on a given case. The expert will typically provide reports, opinions, case analyses, life care plans, and their expert opinions. They often must testify in court, explaining their opinions to the jurors.

Expert witnesses are very helpful in personal injury and medical malpractice cases. They can utilize their knowledge and expertise to provide insights and opinions on client specific injuries, standard of care procedures, and future medical care required for the client.

8.4 EXPERT WITNESS DIRECTORIES

- Expert Institute—Services include expert witness candidates, assistance in case validation, deposition preparation, expert testimony, and affidavit of merit.

- Round Table Group—Services include expert witness candidates, expert CVs provided, no fee until retained policy, experts who work solely for one side and provide free consultations.
- IMS Consulting & Expert Services—Services include an expert witness candidate search globally, handling the administrative demands of your case, consider various attributes such as depositions, litigation history, academic and industrial experience, jury consulting, graphic design services, and helping experts prepare for testimony and communicating their opinions effectively and persuasively.
- Prime Experts Group—Services include: No fee for locating an expert, strategic approach to cases to review experts thoroughly before recommending them, fees cover case reviews and obtaining an opinion, no hourly rate or large upfront retainer, case review and submission to experts to receive feedback before formal opinion, experts will not submit a formal opinion and will not review records without retention.

Be sure to use the demonstrative aids as tools to help the expert in explaining or illustrating their testimony for the jury as the court will allow it (Barreto, 2022).

8.5 UTILIZE YOUR MEDICAL IMAGING/REPORTS

Make sure to gather and organize the client's case materials including medical imaging, radiology and surgical reports, autopsy reports, autopsy photographs, police reports, and medical record summaries. Then send these to the medical artist to review before creating the demonstrative aids. It is important that they have as much information possible to create accurate demonstrative aids for a client-specific case.

8.6 EXCHANGE/SUBMIT THE DEMONSTRATIVE AIDS

When your artwork is completed by the artist, and reviewed for medical accuracy by the medical expert, exchange it to opposing counsel for their review. Submitting your demonstrative aids early, before mediation discussions and trial date, will help to ensure admissibility.

Many trial courts set deadlines to exchange exhibits within the court's pre-trial order. Attorneys for both parties (prosecution and defense) may be ordered to produce their trial exhibits within 60 days or else lose the chance of submitting them at all. If the court is unclear, clarifying with opposing counsel and the court is imperative.

Effective demonstrative aids are a powerful weapon at trial. Images are compelling and will hold attention, along with a good presentation and education on what the case focuses on. Medical demonstrative aids, along with a strong medical expert testimony, will greatly increase your chances of a successful outcome at trial.

8.7 KNOW THE COURTROOM

You may want to also consider the courtroom before deciding what type of demonstrative aid to have created. Is it low-tech? If so, you may not want to order an animation or interactive project. If you still want to, you may have to make sure you provide the technology and capability to present it yourself, or to hire a presentation tech to do that for you. Is the judge conservative? Then you may go easy on how much blood is portrayed in the artwork.

To maximize the chances of a successful settlement or verdict, confirm that the judge can clearly see the demonstrative aids from where they are presented. Create a narrative around the medical graphic before it's revealed; the best presentation wins! Again, be sure to present your demonstratives to opposing counsel before mediation and trial date discussions begin.

CHAPTER 9

Utilizing Focus Groups for Review of Demonstrative Aids

Given the unpredictability of juries, resources such as focus groups provide great insight for attorneys when preparing for trial. They are very similar to a brainstorming session, only the advantage is that you can assemble a group from a variety of different backgrounds, including gender, racial, cultural, and socioeconomic, much the way a jury is assembled to hear case summaries. They can review key pieces of evidence, demonstrative aids, and answer questions—as well as provide feedback on the case materials—all prior to court proceedings.

9.1 ADVANTAGES OF FOCUS GROUPS DURING TRIAL PREP

A focus group can be organized at any stage of the litigation process, although it is usually more beneficial if held early in the process, generally before the depositions are taken is ideal. A few of the many advantages of focus groups are the following:

- Discovering problems in the case, so there is time for correction
- Maintaining objectivity
- Gauging the effectiveness of demonstrative aids
- Helpful in jury selection
- Understanding the significance of the jurors' answers
- Showing what strategies/arguments are the most, and least, effective

DOI: 10.4324/9781003336310-9

- Helping the attorney(s) with realistic goal setting
- Helping to maximize objectives during the discovery process
- Helping to see if it's just a bad case that may be difficult to win—and thus needs to be settled before investing a lot of time and resources

Focus groups are an economical and quick way for an attorney to garner feedback and collect critical knowledge on their case before jury selection and trial begins. Having a recording of the focus group data, to reference later, also helps with trial preparations (*Demas Law Group*, 2024).

9.2 HOW TO HIRE A FOCUS GROUP

Focus groups meetings can be convened in person and virtually. Hiring can be done from social media, Craigslist, legal focus group platforms, and even staffing agencies. Small to large groups can be used, and questionnaires can be given, to better find out who the individuals are as people.

The following is a sample questionnaire to provide potential focus group candidates.

Following is the questionnaire that you should have members filled out in its entirety:

Full name:

Cell phone:

Home phone:

*Number you can be reached at between 9am and 5pm:

*Gender:

*Age:

*Race:

*Political affiliation (Democrat, Republican, or other):

*E-mail address:

PayPal address:

City you live in:

Marital status:

Children?

Highest grade in school:

Place of birth (city/state):

U.S. citizen?

Ever served in the armed forces of the U.S?

Current employer and how long employed?

Position or title:

Self-employed (Y/N):

If yes, name of company and type of business:

Location of employer (city/state):

Total family income? $0-$40K, $41K-$75K, $75K-$100K, $100K+:

Do you own your own vehicle?

Make/model/year:

Do you rent/own home?

*Ever been a party to a lawsuit, other than divorce?

*If, yes then what kind of lawsuit?

*Ever served on a jury?

*Have you ever participated in a focus group? If so, what kind?

Name of last book you read:

What magazines do you like to read?

How many times a week do you watch the news?

From where do you obtain news? (Check one or more):

Social media (Facebook, Twitter, et.) Television, YouTube, online news outlets, newspaper(s) (Please list): ____________________

Favorite movie genre?

Hobbies?

If you or a family member have ever had a serious injury or have a disability, please describe:

If you or a family member have any relationships to the medical or legal field, please describe:

(*Omaha Personal Injury & Wrongful Death Trial Attorneys*, n.d.)

9.3 DO FOCUS GROUPS ENHANCE SETTLEMENT NEGOTIATIONS?

After reviewing your case in its entirety, you may want to test how strong it is to a diverse group of individuals reflecting a realistic, or otherwise anticipated, jury pool.

In some cases, both parties will hold a joint focus group as a mock trial. Since focus groups can reasonably predict the outcome of the trial, each party would more clearly see the holes and issues of their case. They are even more cost-effective if such expenses are split between multiple parties; in addition, all parties can potentially save time—and the expense of a pricey trial—as well as give insight on whose favor the verdict may be decided (*Demas Law Group*, 2024).

9.4 HAVING YOUR MEDICAL ARTIST LISTEN IN ON THE FOCUS GROUP

After hiring your focus group, you may want to invite your medical artist to listen in. I have had the pleasure of listening in on the focus group while the demonstrative aids were being presented, and that process vastly improved how my artwork is presented. Meaning how some of the art is positioned on the illustration board and not having too many surgical steps on one illustration board, adding a normal/healthy illustration for their reference to compare to the injured anatomy. Most people in the focus groups have trouble understanding the medical terminology. There is a balance between reflecting the medical records for accuracy and simplifying the terminology for the jury. That's where your medical expert comes into play to help the jury understand some of the terminology. Some of the key factors I took away from the focus groups reviews were the following:

- Having a normal (healthy) anatomy reference—Most people don't know what healthy tissue looks like or where in the body the injury is located, so it is helpful to include that in your presentation (Figure 9.1).
- Language—People who are not trained in the medical field do not know medical terminology. It requires a thought-out balance of working from the reports and labeling correctly and labeling anatomy so that people will understand what is. This is why it is very important to have the medical experts working with the artists and to have a medical expert testify on your client's behalf (Figures 9.2, 9.3,9.4,9.5).
- Too many illustrations on one page—If you have a surgery with several steps, or a client with a lot of injuries, don't present such on a single illustration board. It is helpful to split it up. I have generally been limiting surgery boards to four steps on a page, maximum. If you wanted an injury summary board created, you may also split the illustrations into categories, for example, brain injuries (Figure 9.4).
- Number or letter the steps—Number each step so that people can follow the order, especially if it is a surgical illustration board; that way, people can follow along easily (Figures 9.3, 9.4).

- Conventional reading format—Keep the conventional reading format, top to bottom, left to right. It's a convention for a reason! (Figures 9.1, 9.2, 9.3, 9.4,9.5).
- Reproduce colorized x-rays adjacent to the illustrations—People can be easily confused. Make sure that your x-ray and/or medical imaging is reproduced adjacent to the illustration. In some cases, include the number and film series so that it can be easily referenced by the attorney or the medical expert testifying on the client's behalf (Figures 9.1, 9.2, 9.4).
- Client likeness evokes emotional response—A more realistic likeness of a suffering or deceased human being will create an emotional response. Make sure that is what you want to portray to the jurors (Figures 9.3, 9.4, 9.5).

The following illustrations are examples of the key points learned from attending focus groups.

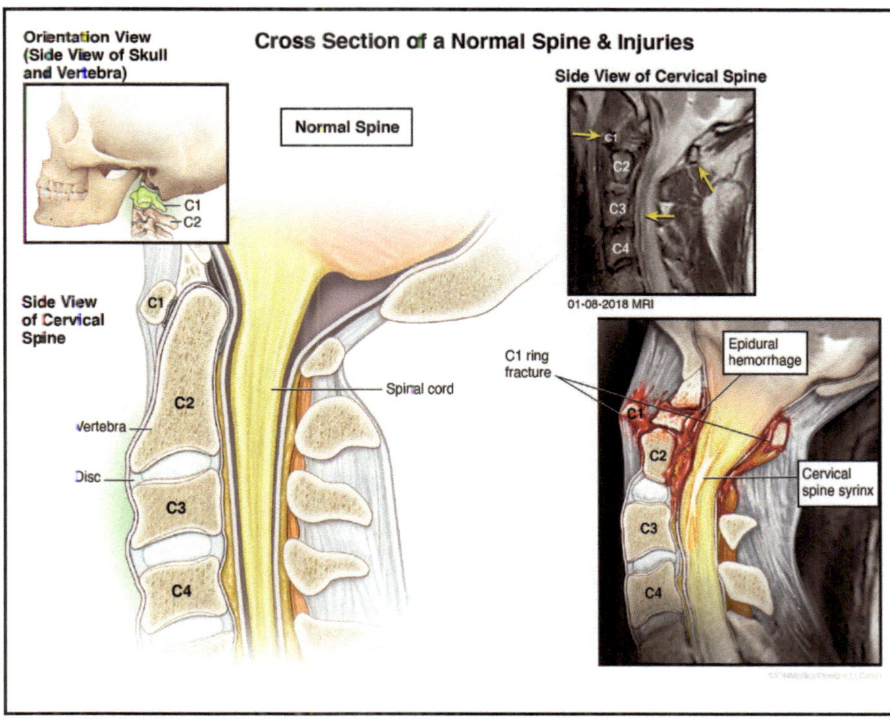

FIGURE 9.1 This illustration board presents a normal (healthy) cervical spine, skull, and relative anatomy next to a fractured C1 and C2 vertebra. It is also an example of the medical imaging reproduced next to the illustrated MRI. It is important to show the jury that these injuries are based on, and derived from, medical imaging. This illustration was a part of a series of illustrations. At first the normal/healthy anatomy illustration was a separate exhibit. I then placed the normal/healthy anatomy of the cervical spine next to the injured spine so the focus group and jurors could see how the cervical spine was injured.

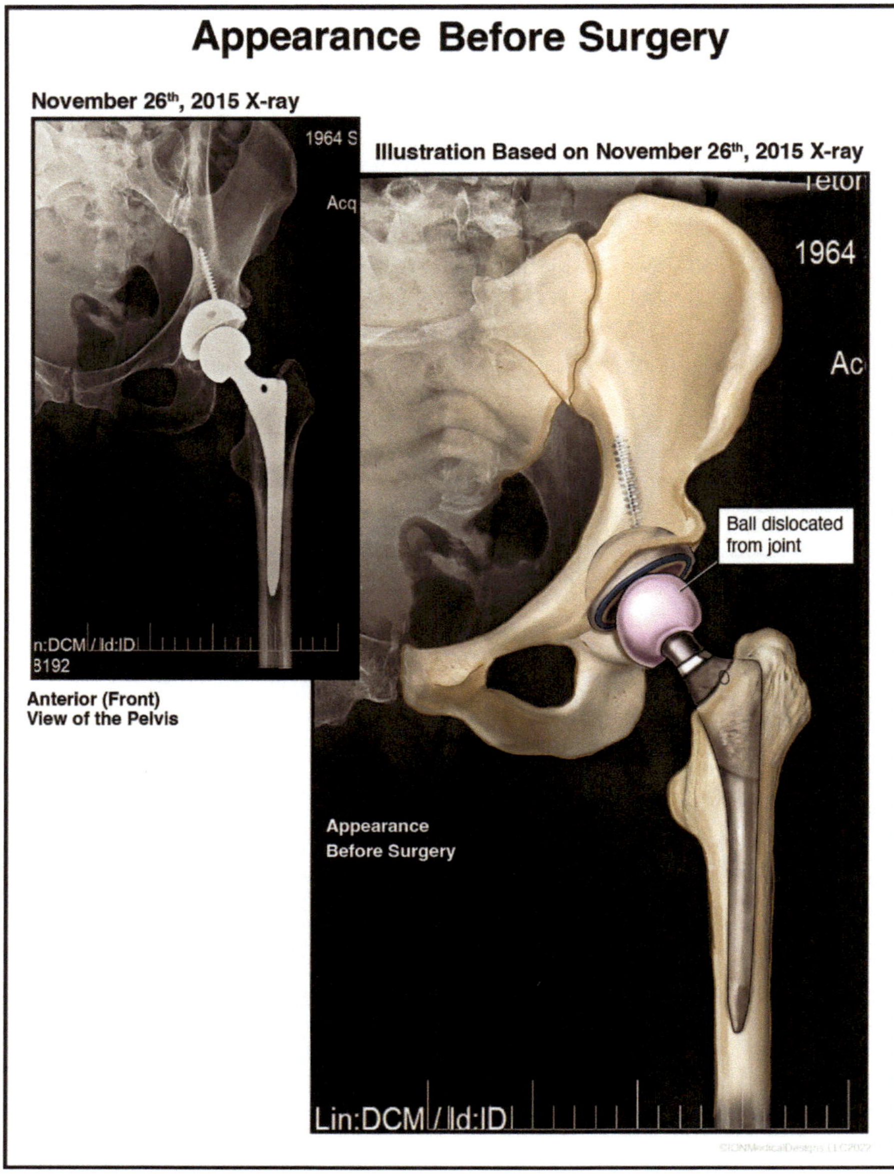

FIGURE 9.2 This illustration board is an example of an x-ray reproduced with an illustrated/colorized x-ray, simplified text, and not too many images on one page. This illustration was changed/improved by simplifying the language. For example, instead of "pre-operative appearance," we changed it to "appearance before surgery."

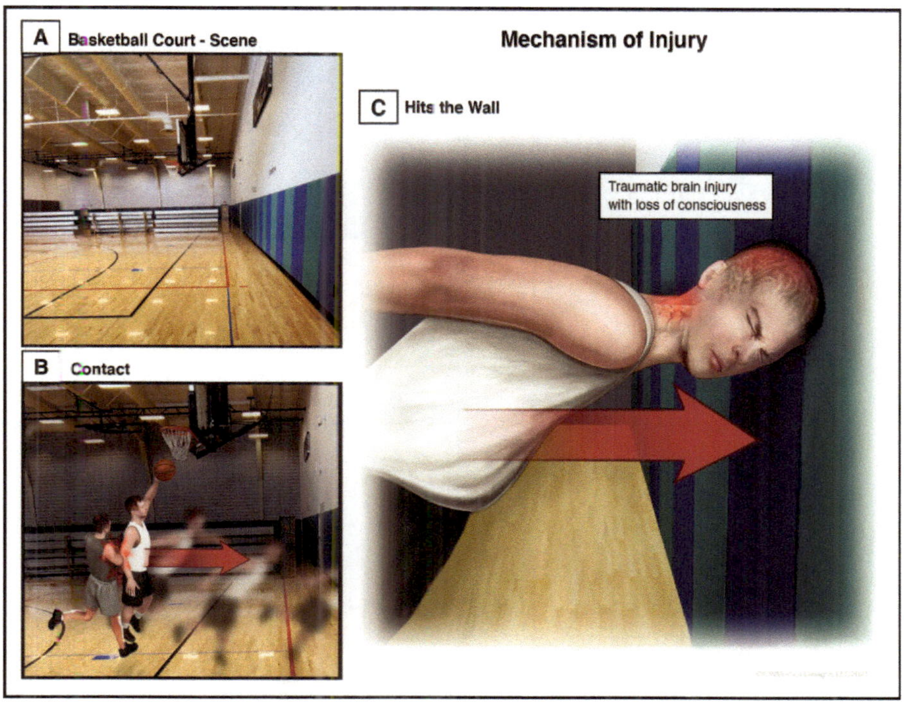

FIGURE 9.3 This illustration board is an example of client likeness, conventional left-to-right format, lettering steps, and simple text. This illustration was improved with a simple layout that was lettered in a left-to-right pattern. Also, to show the force of his head hitting the wall, a few bright red arrows were added to show the motion as well.

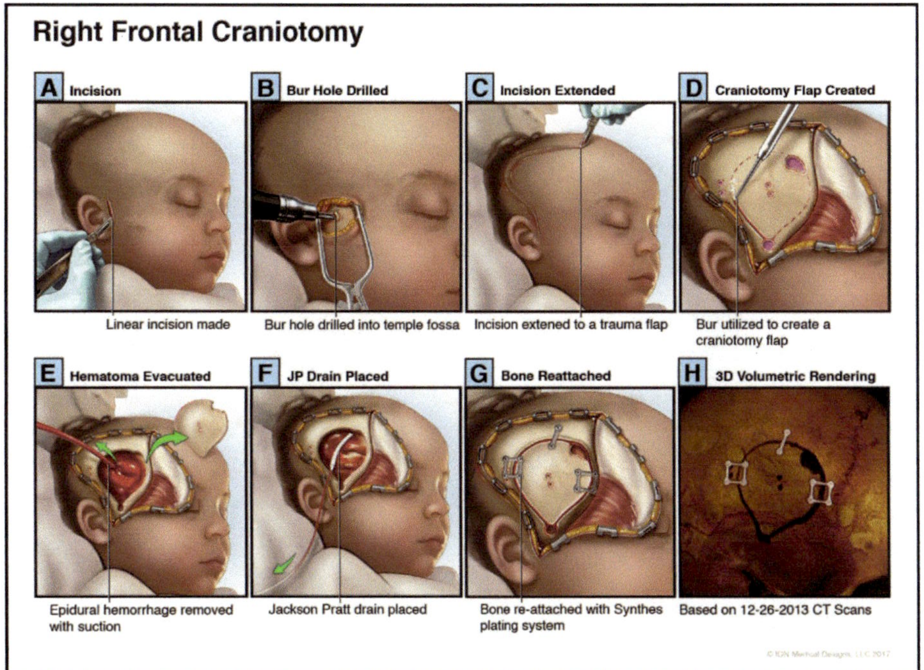

FIGURE 9.4 This illustration board is an example of conventional left-to-right format, lettering steps, simple text, and client likeness. To improve this illustration board, I would split it into two illustration boards of four illustrations each.

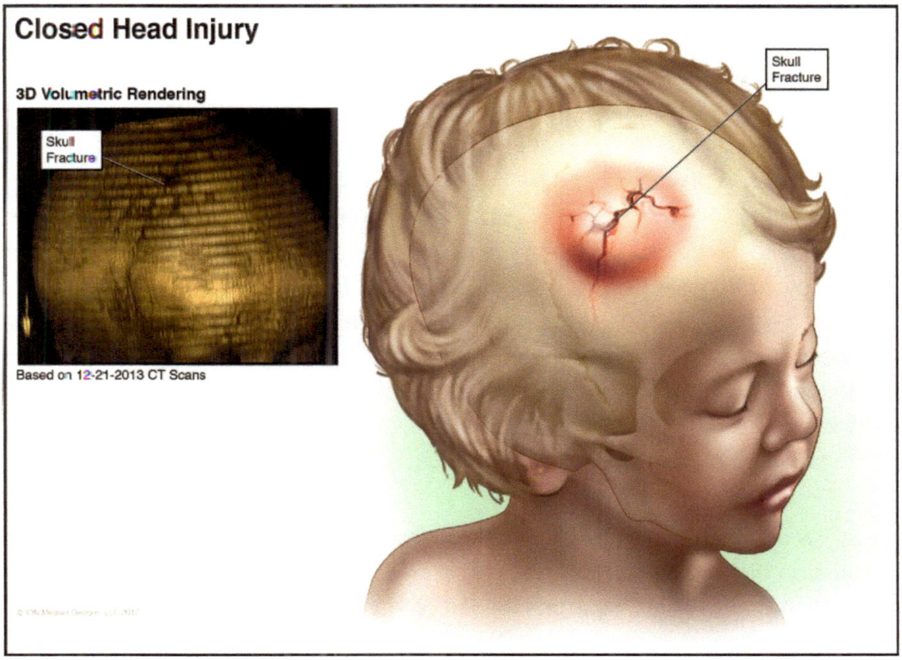

FIGURE 9.5 This illustration board is an example of a client likeness and medical imaging reproduction. I distinctly remember this likeness provoking an emotional response from the focus group. We had a comment from a member in the focus group that the client likeness of the child was too sad and evoked an emotional response. Using a likeness for an emotional reaction is a strategy and is the goal of some of the art. We didn't change this illustration.

A few questions about focus groups are featured here and answered by Howard Thigpen, Bachus and Shanker (Akter, 2024):

Do you have any feedback that would be helpful for other professionals on how insightful focus groups are?

Answer: Focus groups can be used for a variety of reasons to help attorneys better understand how a wide cross-section of people in the community—where the trial will be held—think about issues in their case. Most of the time the focus group will identify issues that, in my case, I had not even considered. Being able to identify these issues prior to trial will allow you to take control of the issue and address it on your terms, instead of leaving it either to opposing counsel or jurors themselves to resolve without your input. The focus group can be held before a lawsuit is filed, shortly after a lawsuit is filed or even shortly before the trial. They can be used to see how the community:

- Values the particular damages in your case
- The community's beliefs on key issues

- The community's position on contentious issues
- How the community views each party and their witnesses, as well as identify strengths and weaknesses for both sides

The focus group can last just a couple of hours or take all day, depending on the breadth of the issues you want covered. I have used pre-suit focus groups to identify issues that a jury might address, which can shape my written discovery and depositions. Also, I have used focus groups to address which issues might sidetrack jurors from the ultimate issue(s), so that I can address these during *voir dire* and opening statement. Lastly, I have used focus groups to identify whether my presentation of the case can be more simplified so that the jurors fully understand what happened and what should have happened regarding the applicable standard of care.

I highly recommend the use of focus groups throughout your investigation and preparation of the case for trial. Many attorneys avoid using them due to the misconception that they are cost prohibitive. With the emergence of Zoom, you can run a short focus group online cheaply with the potential benefits far exceeding any cost. It is important to ensure that, whoever oversees gathering the focus group together, that they get a variety of backgrounds from the county where the trial will occur. You don't want to have all of one demographic participate. The more diverse your focus group participants are, the more information you will gather to help you prepare for settlement or trial. Diversity in the focus group will also help you determine what type of juror you will fight to keep on the jury at trial. What are the statistics of helpful feedback vs not helpful?

Answer: 100% of the focus groups that I have ever run have provided me with helpful insight into my case. It is important to approach focus groups with the mindset that you are working to win the trial and not the focus group. Make sure that you present all the bad facts for your case so that you can get participants' thoughts and reactions to those bad facts. This will help you to shape your presentation of the case for trial and get out in front of issues that may damage your ability to obtain a favorable verdict.

Did hosting a focus group ever persuade you to settle a case?

Answer: Responses or reactions within a focus group have persuaded my client to settle a case. Make sure that your client attends the focus group. You don't want your client to be seen by the focus group participants, but you do want your client to see how actual members from the county, where the trial will take place, are responding to them as a witness, the case in general, the value of the case, as well as the key issues. This is one of the most effective tools that I use to help my clients grasp a very real, unbiased picture of their case and the value of their case.

Have you ever hosted a focus group with defense counsel as a mock trial?

Answer: I have hosted a focus group with defense counsel. It is a great tool for making sure that those participants from the county where the trial will be held are receiving a strong presentation of the case from both sides. It is hard for some attorneys to present the case equally as strong from both the Plaintiff and Defendant's perspective. Doing a focus group with defense counsel will ensure that you aren't just making your client's case the strongest and that the participants are hearing the good and the bad facts on both sides. Your feedback from the participants will be truer to that of a real jury, since they are getting a more robust presentation of the facts.

Have you noticed a difference in feedback if you use a different artist? Or does a particular artist provoke similar feedback?

Answer: Yes, I have noticed a difference in feedback. The artist that you use for your demonstratives or aiding in the presentation of the case matters. I have worked with a handful of different artists. The work product that I get from Lindsay Coulter and ION Medical Design has been much more accurate, detailed, and effective, whether it has been used with mediators in settlement conferences or jurors during trial. From my perspective, utilizing the talents of Mrs. Coulter and ION Medical Design has been amazing. Most artists don't have the medical background and expertise that she brings to the work. With Mrs. Coulter it's more of a collaborative process with my experts. The experts are constantly impressed with the accuracy and detail that Mrs. Coulter brings to each project, which allows them to be more persuasive with the jury when utilizing the artwork during their testimony. I highly recommend using Mrs. Coulter and ION Medical Design for all your trial artwork presentation needs.

9.5 IN CLOSING—UTILIZE FOCUS GROUPS!

I would highly recommend having a focus group for your cases. They provide valuable insight that would not have been realized and acquired without hosting one. If you hire a focus group in enough time that you can change your presentation positively, it is worth the effort.

I have listened in on a few focus groups. I personally do this free of charge. It helps me to learn how to better serve my clients, as well as the people suffering from these injuries, to create more effective illustration boards in future cases.

CHAPTER 10

How Media Has Affected Learning

There are so many types of media such as books, magazines, newspapers, the internet, tv, radio, podcasts, and social media giving us modalities for learning and for information to be broadcast worldwide. When I was in grade school, we had to go to the library to research a project, and AOL chat was all the rage. With all these resources at our fingertips, we have an amazing and historically unprecedented way to access information worldwide. Now with smartphones, we have minicomputers in our pockets and purses. There are also all types of online learning possibilities such as online universities and continuing education credits to allow us to educate ourselves on our own timelines and when convenient for our busy schedules.

10.1 THE TECH GENERATION—IMMEDIATE ACCESS

We live in a digital ecosystem, and it's time for our society to adapt. No matter how strong the resistance, technology progresses, and new trends will eventually become standard practice. This, of course, applies largely to developed countries with a standard well-structured economy and educational system.

Thus, creating a society with little to no attention spans makes it even harder for teachers to educate at present, and will even effect jury trials. This new generation is going to require unique and captivating trial presentations to focus their attention.

DOI: 10.4324/9781003336310-10

10.2 COMMUNITY STRENGTH THROUGH SOCIAL MEDIA

There are many benefits of social media within communities such as newsletters, social networking, company updates, case updates and/verdict information, tips and tricks for your business, and events. This list can go on and on! It is easy to build a network and broadcast this news to everyone in their network who can share with their network, etc.

Social media is a good way to hire focus groups. You could post the job description over multiple platforms such as Facebook, LinkedIn, Indeed, Nextdoor, etc.

When I started moonlighting doing my current work, before forging out on my own and starting my business, I used social media platforms to build my business. One of the best professional social media platforms is LinkedIn, which was founded in 2002 and purchased by Microsoft in 2016. I was personally able to connect to my target audience by searching for the professions relating to my business, such as lawyers and surgeons, and inviting them to connect. LinkedIn is especially helpful because you can see the individual's credentials before deciding to connect with them. After building my contacts, I then posted relevant content to engage my target audience. There is continuing education available to keep your skill sets fresh. Follow companies with content that interests you.

LinkedIn Autopilot allows a computer-generated connection through an automated system. Open the autopilot account, and within minutes it will start generating sales leads and opportunities.

LinkedIn will also filter your sales leads with their program called Sales Navigator or Recruiter. You select the level of engagement you'd like to initiate.

After setting up your account, you can expect dozens of leads. LinkedIn is the social media platform that I have had the best luck with.

While I have also tried Facebook, I haven't done much with it for my business; I have found it to be more of a social platform than a business tool.

I use Mailchimp for my automated email platform. It is nice because it allows for the creation of campaigns, email mailers, and ads—among other things. You can track your marketing campaigns by geographical area and even see who has read your campaign and how many clicks your campaigns get. It shows how you rank in comparison to others and even allows for product sales. One other nice feature is that it allows you to generate your mass emails by info@. You can put each client's first and last name in, and the program will generate a personal email, though it does take a little time. You must create an account for each person, but it's worth it. People love a personal touch.

10.3 THE TECHNOLOGY "WOW" FACTOR

Our company provides clients a very wide range of services to choose from. We offer something as simple as black and-white line illustrations all the way up to augmented reality. I want to focus on the augmented reality portion here briefly.

Augmented reality is a 3D holographic image projected from a 2D picture plane. The 2D plane can be the floor, a T-shirt, business card, a QR code, or a tangible model.

We have created several interactive 3D holograms. I mostly use them for trade shows to bring people to my booth. People talk about them at the lunches and then there is a line at my table. They are special technology "wow" pieces. Most people are afraid to pick up the iPad at the booth or at a lunch and learn, like they will break it or something. I encourage them to pick it up, try it, and see how easy it is to use. It's something unique to potentially utilize that has a lasting impression (Figures 10.1, 10.2, 10.3, 10.4).

We have sold them to attorneys for trial. One that I can recall was of a posterior cervicothoracic spinal fusion. This piece didn't show skin; it was just skeleton and hardware, which can just as easily get the point across. The skeleton turned from front to back and then the hardware, rods, and screws came into the picture plane, into each spinal level. It was an interactive application, meaning the user interacts with the application and runs the presentation. Since the COVID-19 pandemic, we have sold quite a few stand-alone interactive applications, which is another tech "wow" application. They are self-sustaining applications with all the information included. For example, a catastrophic injury case would include all the injuries as well as all the surgeries in one application that can be downloaded to an iPad, laptop, or computer desktop. They are cross-platformed, meaning they can be built out for PC or Mac. (Figures 10.5, 10.6, 10.7, 10.8, 10.9, 10.10).

These interactive applications allow you to present material yourself. They are user-friendly and are certainly conversation starters. They can be easily run in the courtroom, and they leave a lasting impression on the viewer, making it easier for them to hold onto the information just presented to them. The artwork contained in the application can be individually printed and handed out to the jurors during trial. They can be printed large (36″ x 48″) and left out during the trial to refer to.

Please see the following screenshot examples of our technology pieces. I suggest you embrace these emerging technologies, as we have, and captivate your audience when the opportunity arises.

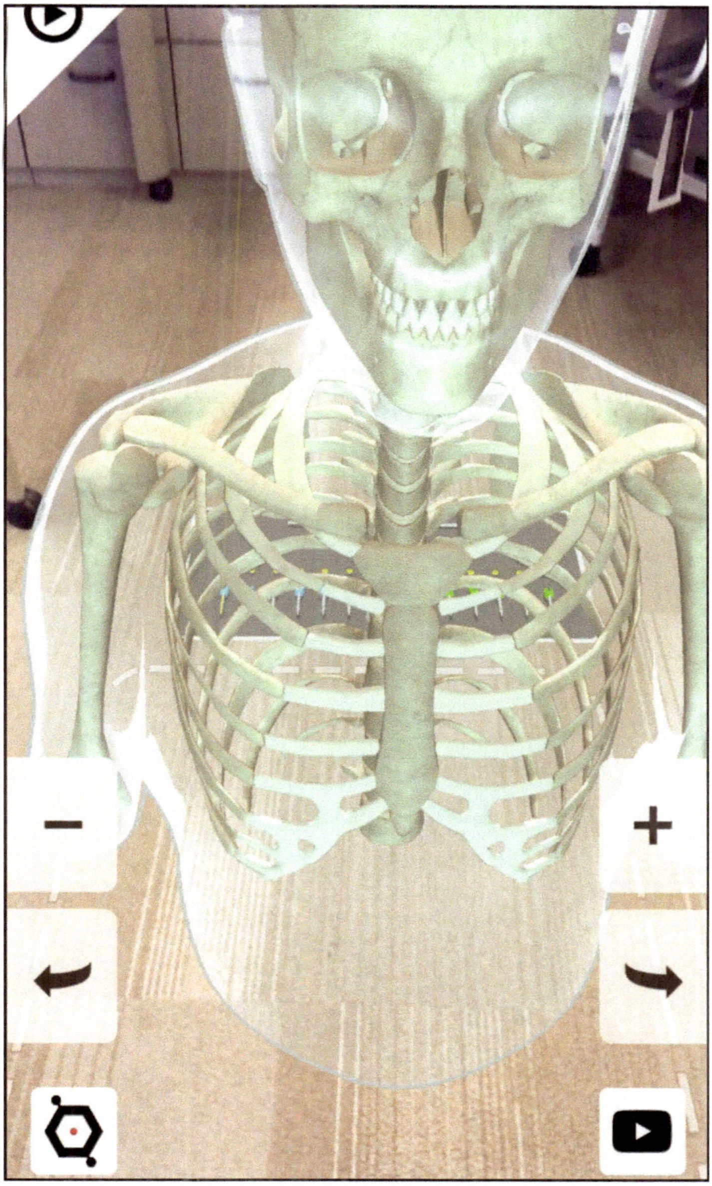

FIGURE 10.1 This is a sample of augmented reality (hologram). It was the posterior cervicothoracic case mentioned in this book that went to trial! This is a front view of the skull and rib cage.

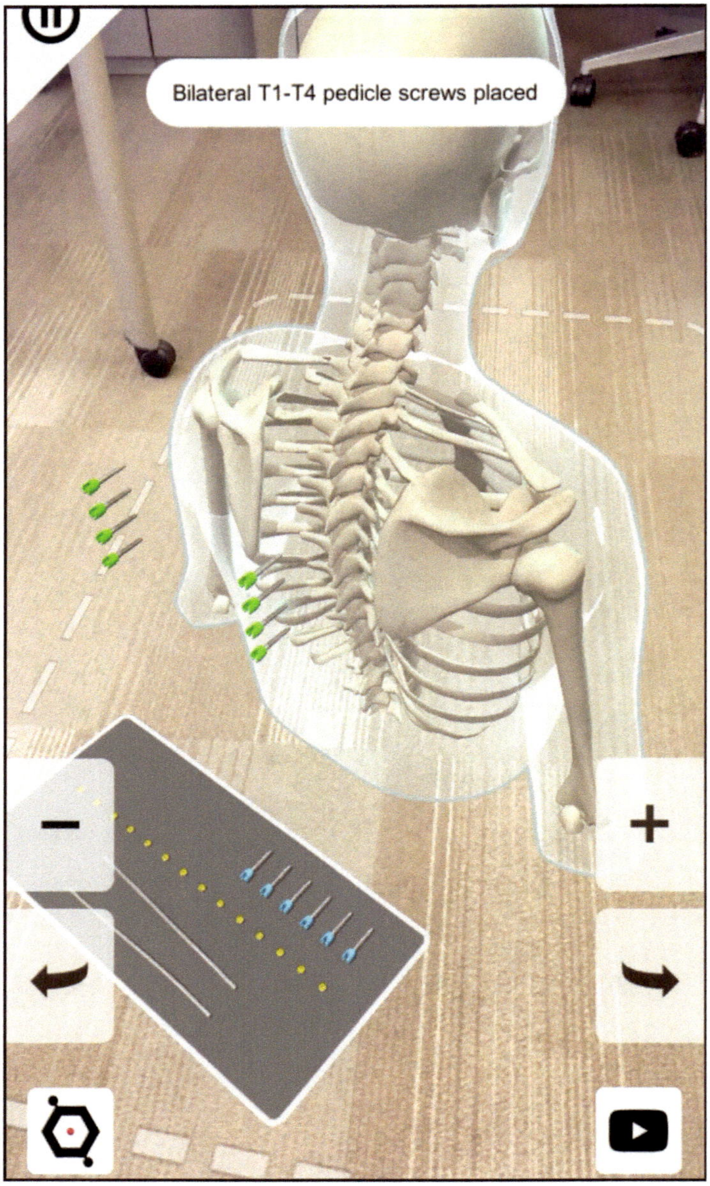

FIGURE 10.2 This is a sample of augmented reality (hologram). It was the posterior cervicothoracic case mentioned in the text earlier that went to trial! This is a back three-quarter view of the skull, rib cage, and spine with a tray of the pieces of the implant on the floor.

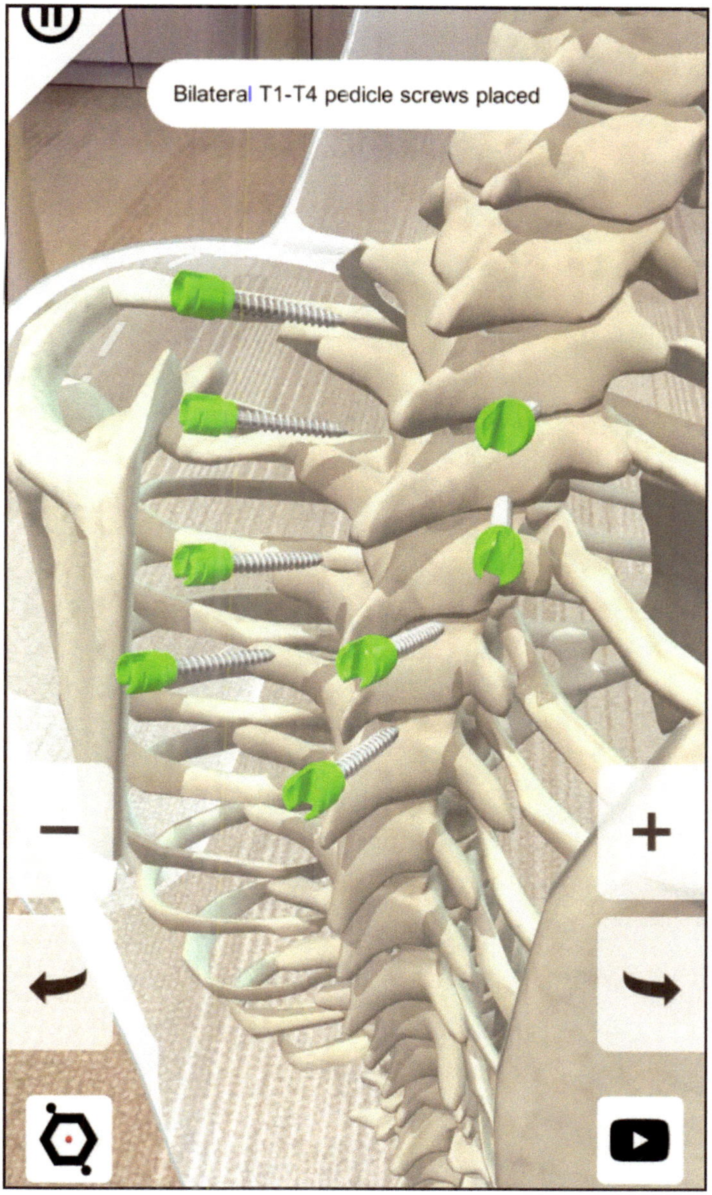

FIGURE 10.3 This is a sample of augmented reality (hologram). It was the posterior cervicothoracic case mentioned in the text earlier that went to trial! This is a back three-quarter view of the skull thoracic spine, showing the pedicle screws placed into the pedicles.

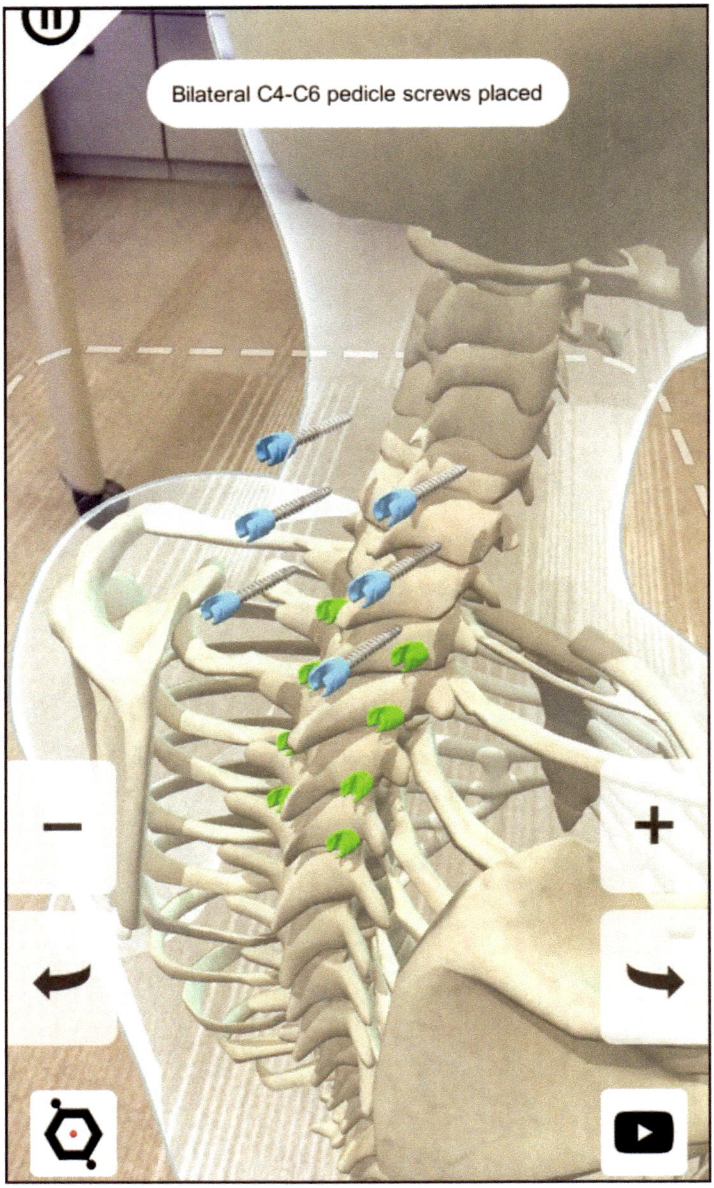

FIGURE 10.4 This is a sample of augmented reality (hologram). It was the posterior cervicothoracic case mentioned in the text earlier that went to trial! This is a back three-quarter view of the skull and thoracic spine, showing the pedicle screws placed into the pedicles.

For an interactive brain slice chooser, multiple levels of brain injuries need to be present to best utilize this application. Approximately five MRI scan slices that best represent the client's injuries would be chosen and illustrated over. Once the scans are illustrated over, the files can be placed into Unity. Unity is an interactive/gaming engine.

Please see the following screenshots of the application.

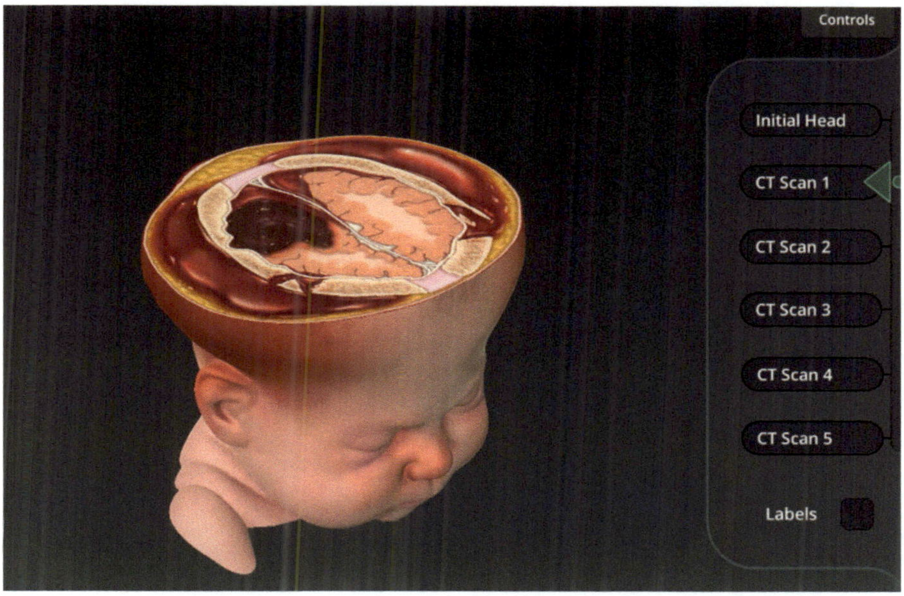

FIGURE 10.5 This is a sample of an interactive brain slice viewer. This baby head was created custom, meaning a client likeness created with a front view close-up view of the child's head. This application is great for multiple brain/skull injuries. You can click on the panel on the right to go to each slice and toggle the labels on and off. To create this type of application, you first need to illustrate over the MRI scans. After your illustrations are created, they are input into Unity (a computer software program). After the programming is complete, the application is built out for PC, Mac, iPad, or Android.

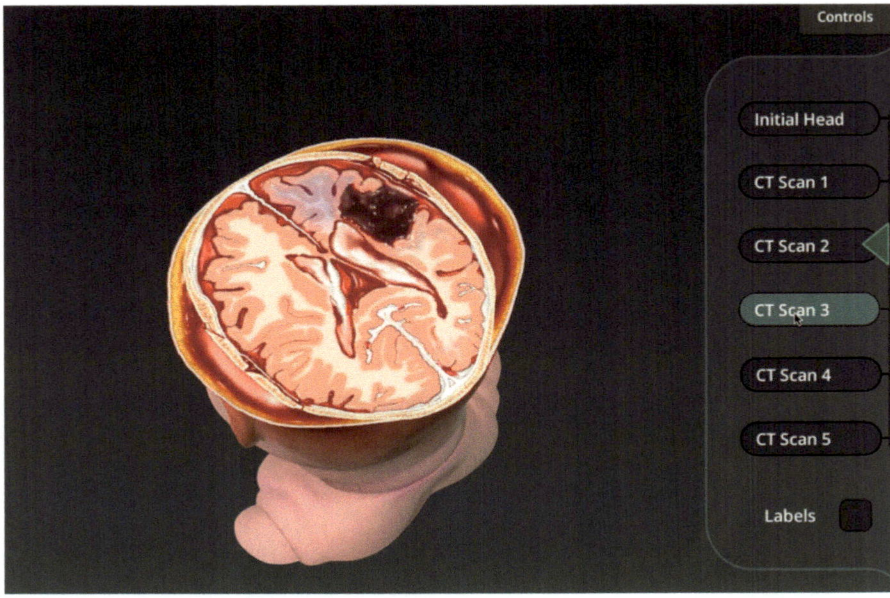

FIGURE 10.6 This is a sample of an interactive brain slice viewer. This baby head was created custom, meaning a client likeness created with a front view close-up view of the child's head. This application is great for multiple brain/skull injuries. You can click on the panel on the right to go to each slice and toggle the labels on and off. It is a depiction of the same application from another angle.

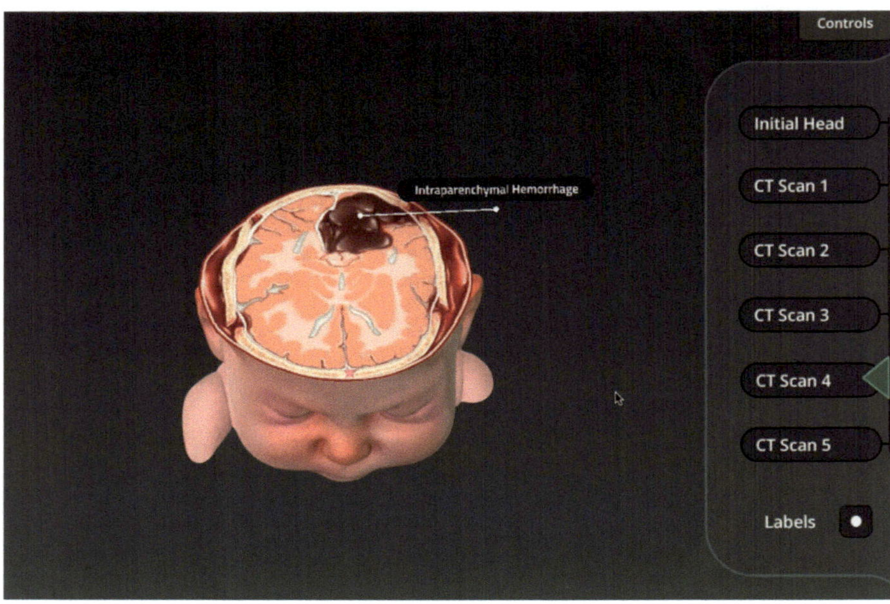

FIGURE 10.7 This is a sample of an interactive brain slice viewer. This baby head was created custom, meaning a client likeness created with a front view close-up view of the child's head. This application is great for multiple brain/skull injuries. You can click on the panel on the right to go to each slice and toggle the labels on and off. This is the same application from another angle.

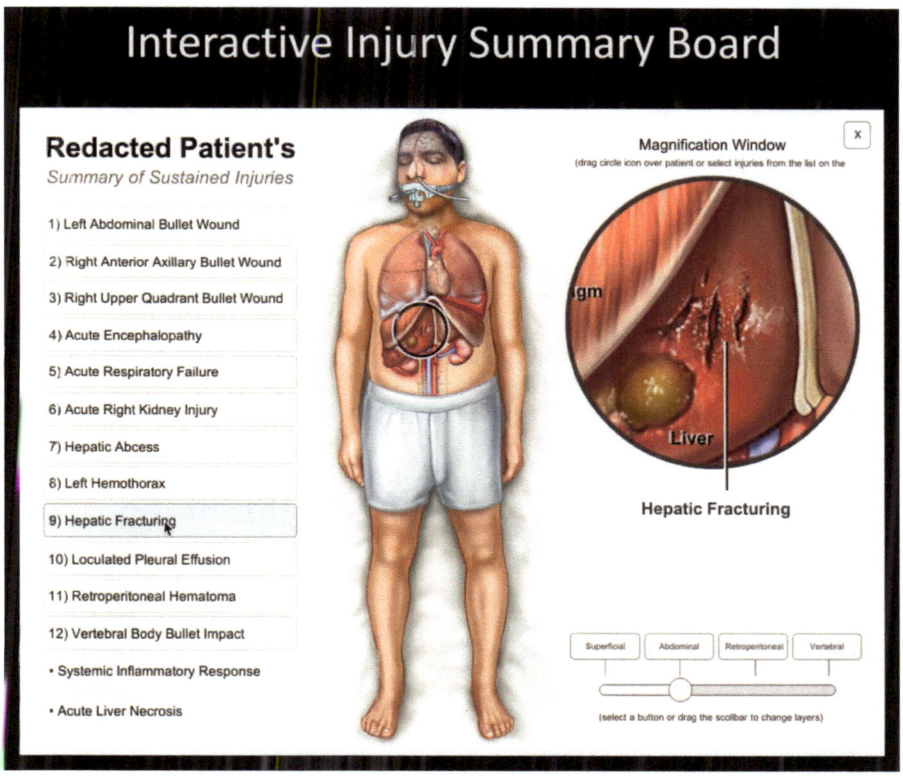

FIGURE 10.8 This is a sample of an interactive injury summary application. A likeness, all the injuries and surgeries are included if applicable. This application was created starting with illustrations that were then placed into Unity to program for an iPad application.

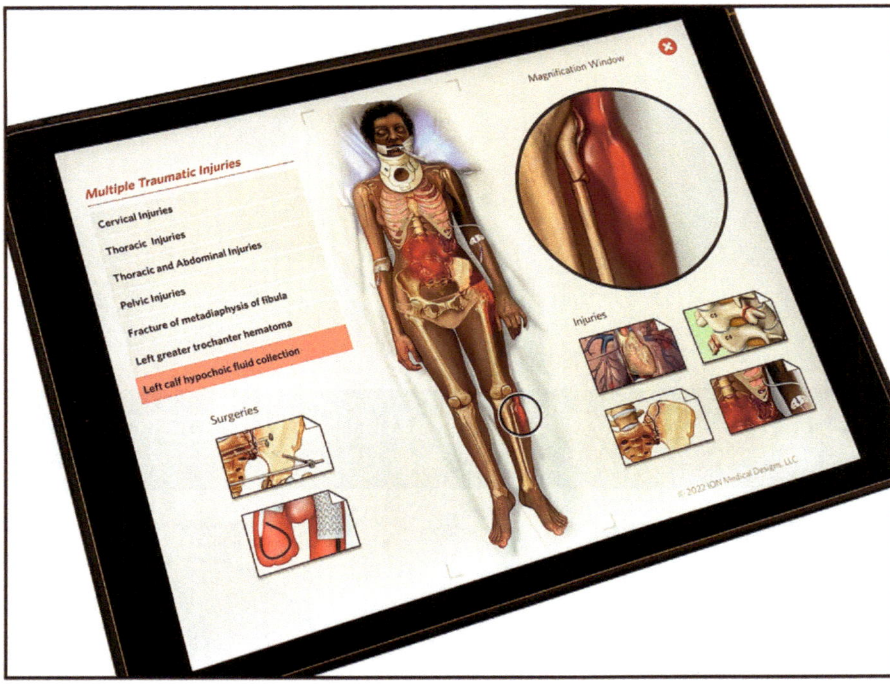

FIGURE 10.9 This is a sample of an interactive injury summary application. A likeness as well as all the injuries and surgeries were created and then placed into Unity to be programmed and built out for an iPad application.

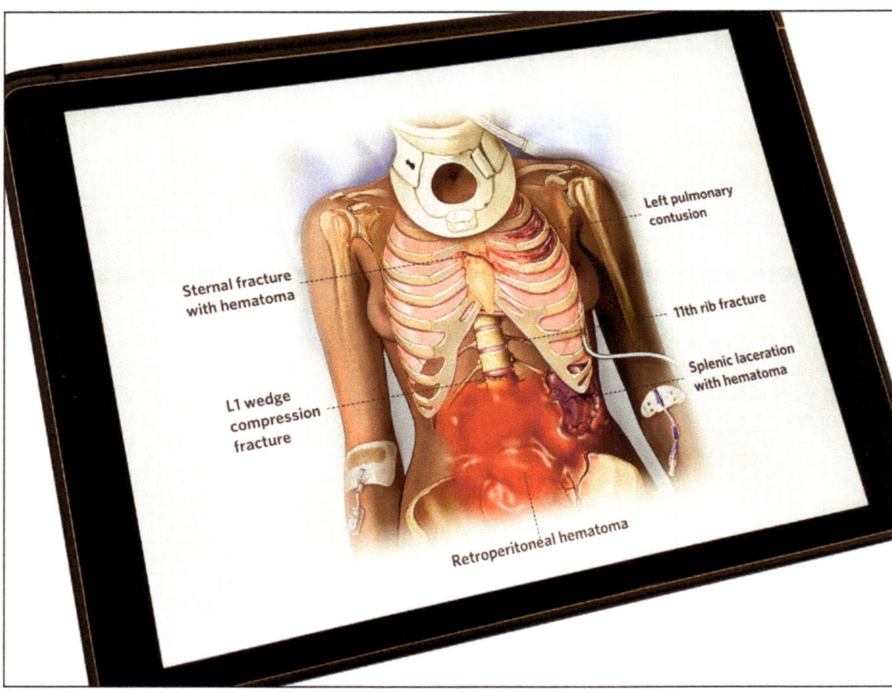

FIGURE 10.10 This is a sample of an interactive injury summary application. A likeness as well as all the injuries and surgeries were created and then placed into Unity to be programmed and built out for an iPad application.

CHAPTER 11

Conclusion

After reading this book, you will be competent—and have a full understanding—of what medical illustration is, its history, and how to hire a medical/forensic artist and utilize their skill sets in the courtroom or in all the various stages of litigation.

Visuals are powerful tools that—when used correctly, with the proper medical illustrator and an attorney passionate about their case—can evoke an educated and emotional response from the jury (aka our fellow human beings!).

We covered the myriad choices of services provided by medical/forensic artists, ranging from line drawings to videos and augmented reality. We also covered the subdiscipline of traditional and artificial intelligence forensic facial reconstruction.

We discussed how to hire medical experts and use them with your medical artwork to make sure the expert presents your client's injuries, surgeries, and future care correctly and in a way that captures the jury's attention.

We reviewed the media, how to use it, and even social networking possibilities for learning to promoting yourself and/or business.

Focus groups are an important process to educate yourself on the cases you take on and the tools that lead to success in the courtroom. Will they all be winners? Probably not. You can, however, test your presentation with a group of hand-selected people hired to review the logistics of your case. Then you do have choices about what to do with the case once it is properly reviewed.

As for the future of medical illustration, AI (artificial intelligence)-generated images are a hot topic in the world right now. AI is an intelligent agent able to achieve a

DOI: 10.4324/9781003336310-11

goal defined by humans. Meaning you teach the computer by repetition and explanation. For instance, with the new AI-powered stethoscope, the developers fed the AI machines thousands of heart sounds, distinguishing normal from those that may have a problem such as a murmur. With the repetition, the computer learns to distinguish the heart sounds on its own so the stethoscope can screen for heart disease in 15 seconds.

As AI relates to art and medical illustration, currently there are several AI platforms used, including Midjourney AI, Stable Diffusion AI, DALL-E AI, and Imagine Art AI. AI generators can produce beautifully rendered pieces of art within seconds. They have not yet mastered anatomy and medical/forensic art or surgical illustration. They are restricted in what they are permitted to learn, and an abundance of medical terminology has been banned from their learning capabilities. A few of the words/terms including blood, bloodshot, bruises, laceration, surgery, wound, pelvis, and many more anatomical and procedural terms AI is not permitted to search and create image derivatives. So it may be a while, if ever that the technology is perfected enough, for AI to create accurate anatomical illustrations or surgical procedures.

To create an image in AI, you can utilize ChatGPT to create prompts that are then input into Midjourney AI for the image generation. This helps generate prompts for you that can often result in more refined image results. You can upload an image as a prompt to give the computer an idea of what you are thinking and as a starting block. You can upload a sketch and have the computer render it for you! I learned that from a recent graduate student. Young professionals are flush with technology knowledge and ideas.

People may think our world will soon be crawling with robots; however, currently, AI is being used for fast production and efficient working. In the art world, AI can create concepts and ideas from your head to work from using text prompts from ChatGPT. A starting block, so to speak!

I recently learned from a talk at the Association of Medical Illustrator Conference on AI as it relates to copyright that the creator (author) of artwork, as the laws stand today, is a human being. There are not yet laws written for machine creation. Artists have already begun lawsuits against the copyright office declaring that they create AI from prompts using their thoughts, and it's not just generated from one prompt (keyword). Others are suing Google for generating work derivatives of written pieces of to 20 pages of text, hence the writers' strike in LA. Since the AI platform creators take all the images that that they use to teach the machines from the internet without permission, the rights and usage laws are blurred.

Just for fun, I rendered a few images using Imagine Art and Midjourney AI platforms. I left the prompts in the screenshots so you can see what the computer came up with from my thoughts.

Please see the following images.

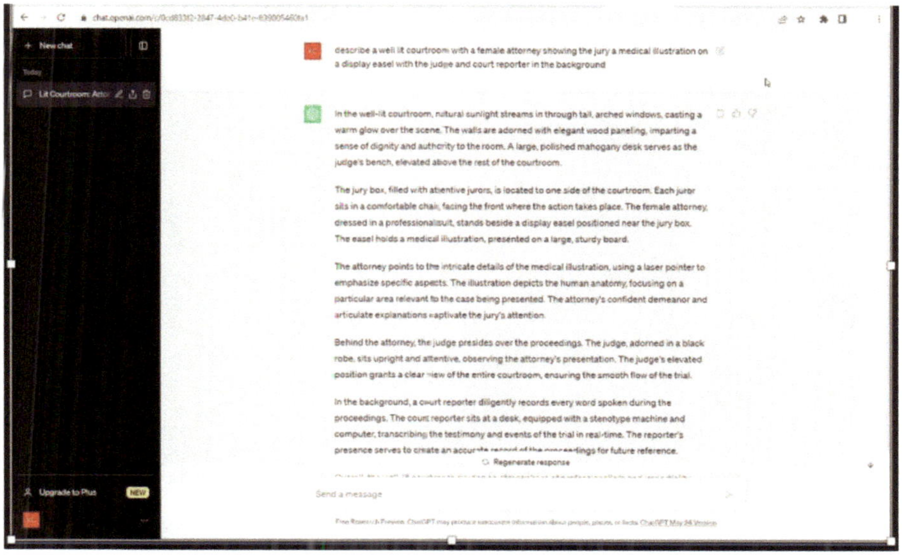

FIGURE 11.1 This screenshot is an example of text input from ChatGPT. You can copy and paste this text generated prompt into Midjourney AI and then an image will be generated for you based on the text input.

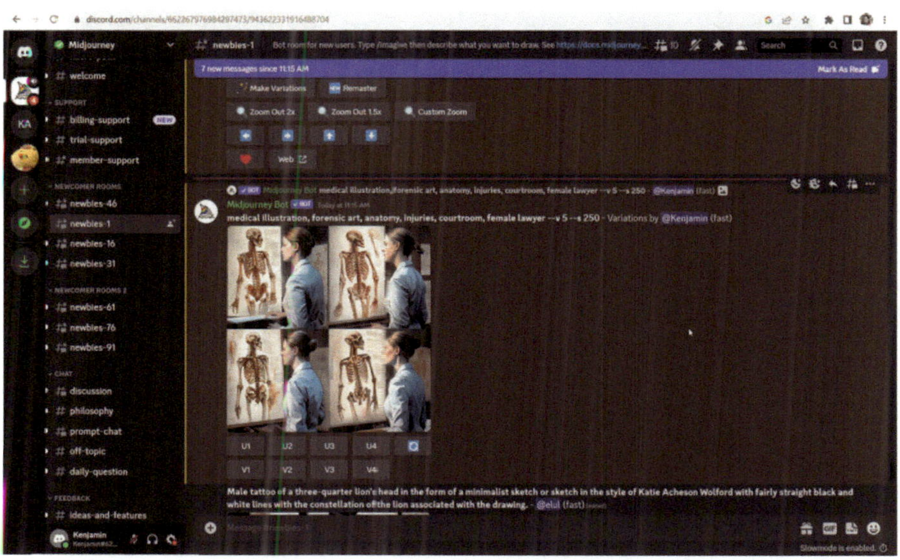

FIGURE 11.2 This screenshot is a series of computer-generated renders from Midjourney AI. After the text prompt is entered, a series of images is generated. You can select one of these images and continue to work from it by selecting the image you like. You can add more text prompts, refine your current prompts, or even start over.

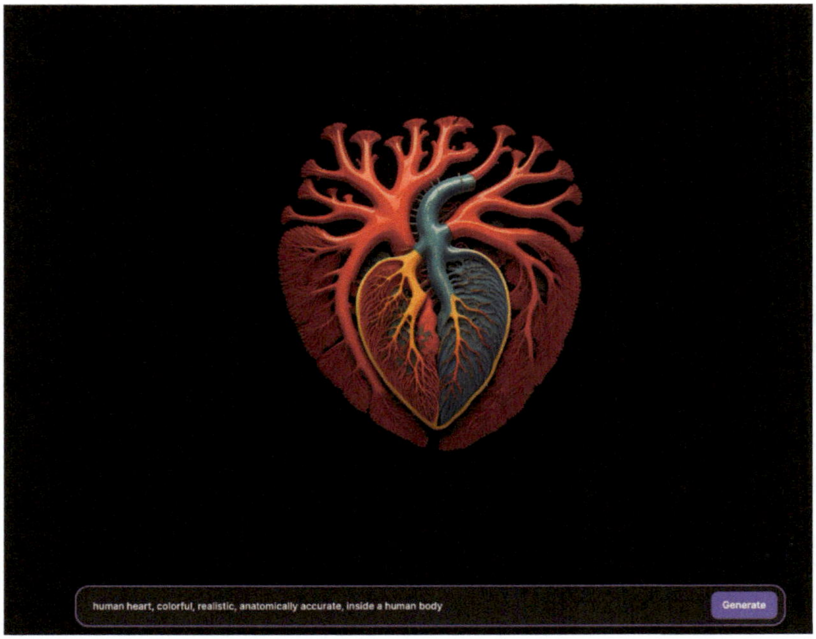

FIGURE 11.3 This screenshot is a computer-generated render from Imagine Art AI. The image was created from the following word prompts, human heart, colorful, realistic, anatomically accurate, inside a human body. As you can see, this is far from realistic, but very conceptual!

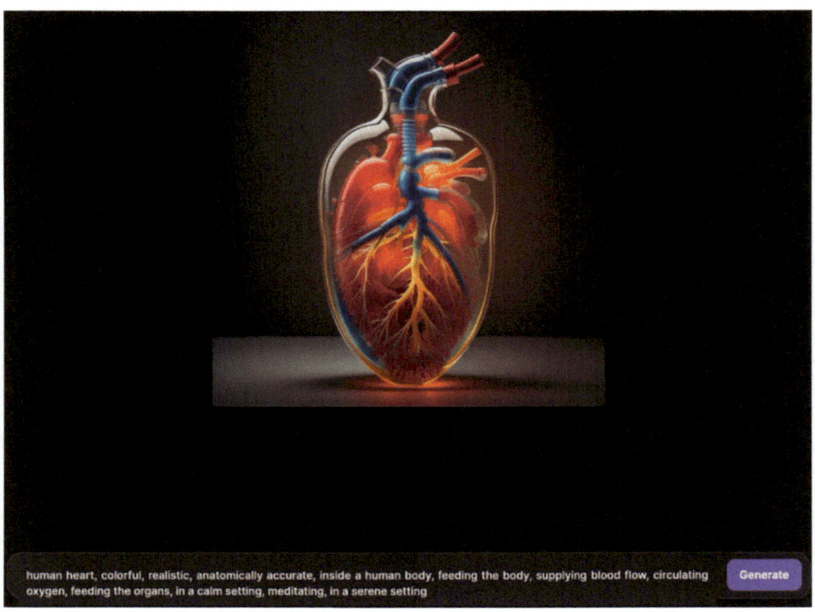

FIGURE 11.4 This screenshot is a computer-generated render from Imagine Art AI. The image was created from the following word prompts: human heart, colorful, realistic, anatomically accurate, inside a human body, feeding the body, supplying blood flow, circulating oxygen, feeding the organs, in a calm setting, meditating, in a serene setting. Since the first image generated was very artistic, I thought it would be fun to add feelings to the prompts. For example, how the heart functions and words associated with the word heart.

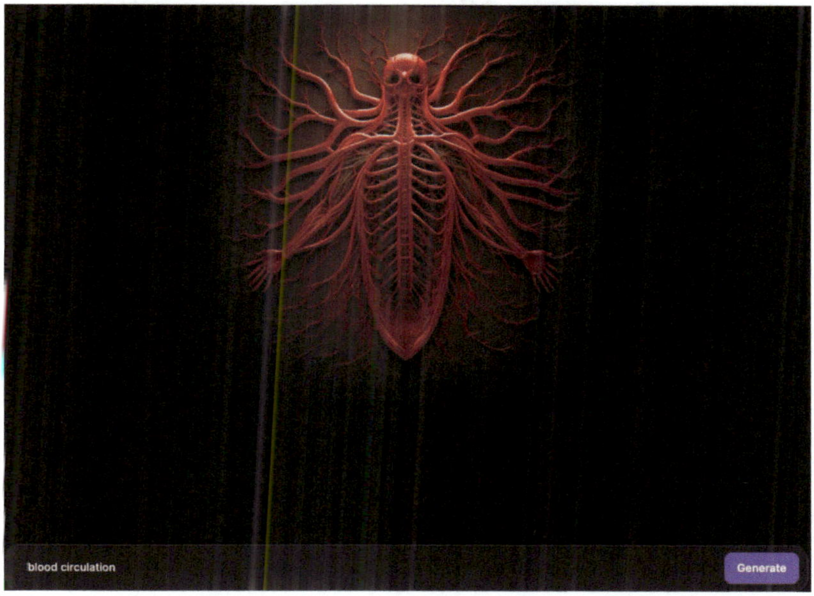

FIGURE 11.5 This screenshot is a computer-generated render from Imagine Art AI. The image was created from the word prompt blood circulation. I was interested to see what the computer came up with for the circulatory system. This is a very cool image, far from accurate. It is a great concept that could be expanded upon.

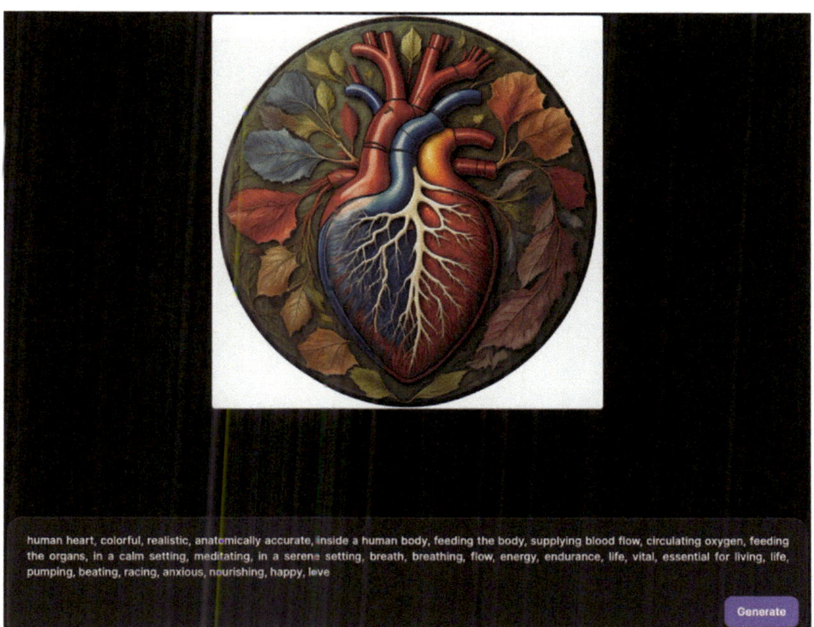

FIGURE 11.6 This screenshot is a computer-generated render from Imagine Art AI. The image was created from the same prompts as earlier, just expanded upon using prompts related to function and what the heart does for our bodies. I love this image, it's very conceptual.

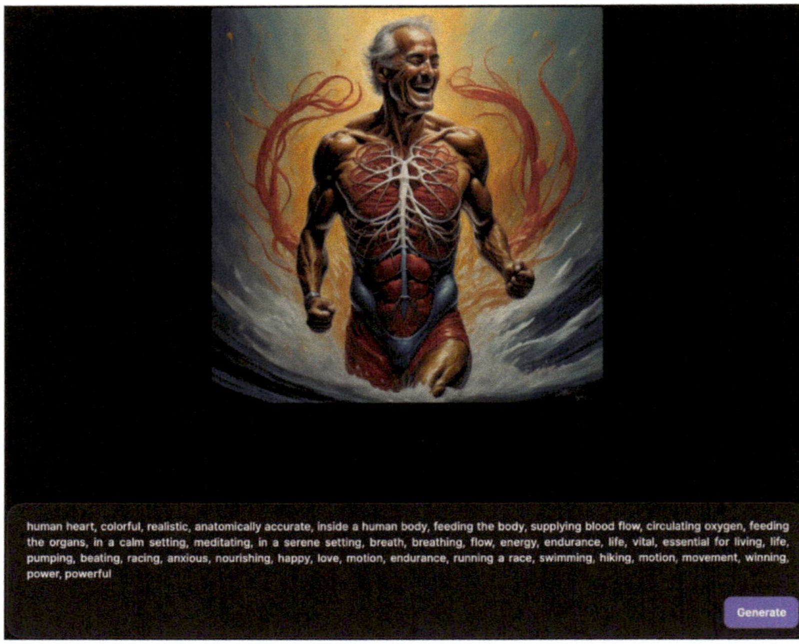

FIGURE 11.7 This screenshot is a computer-generated render from Imagine Art AI. The image was created from the same prompts as earlier, just expanded upon using prompts related to function and what the heart does for our bodies. Again, very conceptual.

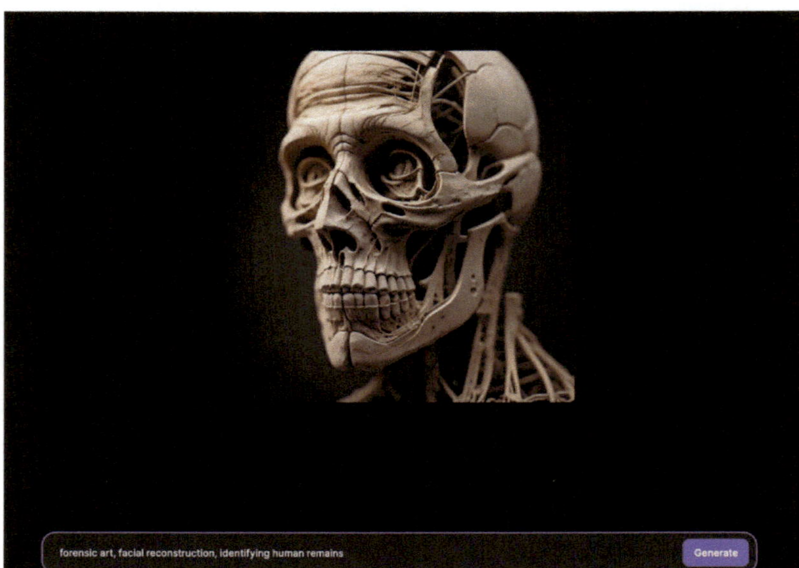

FIGURE 11.8 This screenshot is a computer-generated render from Imagine Art AI. The image was created from the following prompts: forensic art, facial reconstruction, and identifying human remains. As you can see, the anatomy isn't correct. Everything except the basic shape of the skull is inaccurate. It would be interesting to input an image of a volume rendering of the skull and see if the computer could be taught to build upon that.

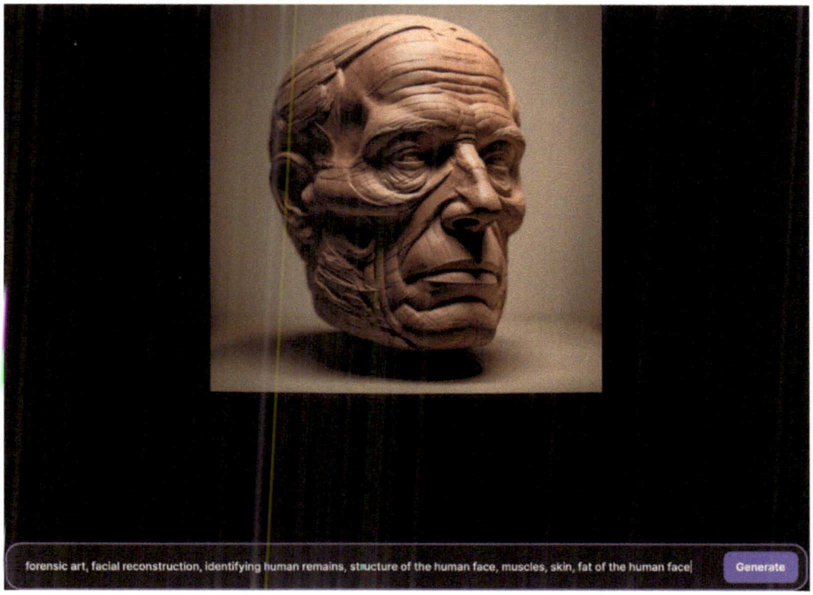

FIGURE 11.9 This screenshot is a computer-generated render from Imagine Art AI. The image was created from the following prompts: forensic art, facial reconstruction, and identifying human remains. This is the second version, expanded upon asking the computer to add fat and muscle. I love the clay look to it. It would be interesting to input images to AI of actual facial reconstructions to see what the computer generates thereafter.

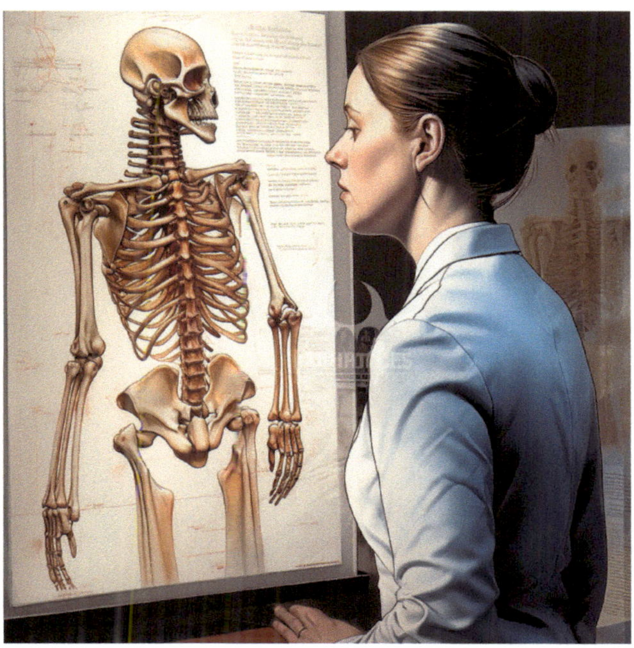

FIGURE 11.10 This screenshot is a computer-generated render from Midjourney AI. This image was created with the following prompts: female lawyer, anatomy, medical illustration, injury, courtroom, and presentation. The computer-generated image is a great place to start from. The concept can be refined and reworked. Notice how the skeleton is completely inaccurate. The cervical spine looks like a giraffe's cervical spine, and the femurs, pelvis, and skull stand out with inaccuracy. However, it could be reworked and expanded upon like an initial sketch.

It should be interesting to see how far this technology can be taken with how much it's taught by humans. Embracing technology with whatever field you are in will keep you in a good career.

11.1 THANK YOU!

I want to thank you all for reading this book! I hope you learned some things along the way and had fun reading it. This book is my life's work in a nutshell. Initially, I wanted to become a doctor but saw a flier in our mailbox advertising a school that offered medical illustration as a major and was immediately intrigued.

I think medical illustration is my life's calling, as it has been a perfect fit for me. I enjoy helping the attorneys to provide a voice to the dead and a brighter future to the living.

References

Akter, I. (2024, January 12). *Colorado injury lawyers*. Bachus & Schanker. https://lp.coloradolaw.net/bachus-and-schanker-v3/?gad_source=1&gclid=CjwKCAiAqY6tBhAtEiwAHeRopSZme57am_mALe4shrloECm6ltBJ34p1_W-Q5pTFXUZbXj7WUt2P9hoCowAQAvD_BwE

Barreto, Z. (2022, May 26). *How to find expert witnesses: The ultimate guide*. Expert Institute. https://www.expertinstitute.com/resources/insights/how-to-find-expert-witnesses-the-ultimate-guide/

Brödel, M. (n.d.). https://medicalarchives.jhmi.edu/portrait/brodel-max/

Demas Law Group. (2024, January 11). [Video]. Demas Law Group, P.C. https://www.injury-attorneys.com/

Facebook. (n.d.). https://www.facebook.com/profile.php?id=100063295443993

Forensic Art and Illustration. (2014, May 27). Karen T. Taylor, Facial Images. https://kttfacialimages.com/about/forensic-art-and-illustration/

Klatt, E. C. (n.d.). *Firearms tutorial*. https://webpath.med.utah.edu/TUTORIAL/GUNS/GUNBLST.html

Learn About Medical Illustration. (n.d.). AMI. https://www.ami.org/medical-illustration/learn-about-medical-illustration

Limited, A. (n.d.). *Entrance to first baptist church in Sutherland Springs, TX, 5 months after a gunman killed 26 worshipers during service. The simple sanctuary has been turned into a memorial for the victims*. Alamy Images. https://www.alamy.com/entrance-to-first-baptist-church-in-sutherland-springs-tx-5-months-after-a-gunman-killed-26-worshipers-during-service-the-simple-sanctuary-has-been-turned-into-a-memorial-for-the-victims-image178463281.html

The Metropolitan Museum of Art. (n.d). https://mymodernmet.com/wp/wp-content/uploads/2018/08/leonardo-da-vinci-vitruvian-man-1.jpg

Milesmartin. (2018, December 23). *Medical drawing and aims of drawing in general*. The Artful Scientist. https://artfulscientist.home.blog/2019/01/01/medical-drawing-and-aims-of-drawing-in-general/#jp-carousel-78

Omaha Personal Injury & Wrongful Death Trial Attorneys. (n.d.). Law Office of Matthew A. Lathrop, PC, LLO. https://www.lathroplawomaha.com/

Petoi. (n.d.). *Best robot kits for geeks, programmers, makers, engineers, developers*. https://www.petoi.com/pages/best-robot-kits-for-geeks-programmers-developers-vb?utm_source=google-ads&utm_campaign=&utm_agid=140300766205&utm_term=stem%20robotics%20kit&gad_source=1&gclid=CjwKCAiAqY6tBhAtEiwAHeRop-d71zx2spuThor51qLhVSav6NARzZDzXsV-pXNtNxCONWse8uuvBFhoCLp0QAvD_BwE

Puiu, T. (2022, October 1). *This facial reconstruction shows what a paleolithic teenage girl looked like more than 30,000 years ago*. ZME Science. https://www.zmescience.com/science/news-science/this-facial-reconstruction-shows-what-a-paleolithic-teenage-girl-looked-like-more-than-30000-years-ago/

Index

Note: Page numbers in *italics* indicate figures.

abdominal surgery, laparoscopic trocars placement for, *68*
accuracy of, 39, *39–41*
ACDF, *see* anterior cervical discectomy and fusion (ACDF)
AI, *see* artificial intelligence (AI)
angiography, 30
anterior cervical discectomy and fusion (ACDF), *75–89*
apartment shooting, 146–148, *147*, *148*
APGAR score, at birth, *98*
artificial intelligence (AI)
  3D forensic facial reconstruction using, 156–161, *157–161*
  platforms, 190
atypical entry wounds, 125
augmented reality, *181–184*
axonic brain injury, *5*

ballistics
  external, 124
  internal, 124
  terminal, 124
  see also apartment shooting; gunshot wounds; mass shooting
blood oxygen level measurement, *62*
body map, *13*, *120*
bony arthritis, *79*, *81*
bowel perforation, *69*
brain hemorrhage, *25*
breech position, 94, *95*, *97*
brief history of medical illustration, 15–20
bronchopneumonia, acute, *60*
buccal fat pad, repositioning of, *3*
bullet wounds, *132*, *133*, *138*, *140*, *143*
  see also apartment shooting; gunshot wounds; mass shooting

calcaneus fracture, *26*
ChatGPT, 190, *191*
chorioamnionitis, 94–95, *96–105*, 109
client-specific anatomy, 39, 42
closed head injury, *175*
colonoscopy, *36*
colorized radiology, 23–30
community strength, through social media, 179
complex medical information, trial presentation of, 21–23
computed tomography (CT) scan, 23, *26*, 28, 30
courtroom, knowing, 166
Covid-19 infection, *4*
craniotomy, right frontal, *174*
CT, *see* computed tomography (CT) scan
Cushing, Harvey, 19

dandruff, *11*
definition of medical illustrations, 1
DJO surgical, *7*
dry eye, *10*

ear, anatomy of, *2*
eczema, *11*
elbow injuries, *40*
endovascular aortic repair, *35*
expert witness directories, 164–165
external ballistics, 124
extubation, *90*

facial reconstruction, *see* forensic facial reconstruction
fatal condition, *70*
female abdomen, normal, *68*
femur fracture, right distal, *24*
fetal monitor strips, 37–38, *39*, *100*
fields of study, 15
fluoroscopy, 30

fMRI, *see* functional MRI (fMRI)
focus groups
  hiring, 168–169
  interview, 169–170
  medical artists, role of, 170–177, *171–175*
  for review of demonstrative aids, utilizing, 167–177
  during trial prep, advantages of, 167–168
forensic art, categories of, 149–150
forensic facial reconstruction, 149–161
  artistic phase, 153–154
  circumstances of, 151–152
  skull, three-dimensional facial reconstruction of, 150–151
  technical phase, 152
  tissue depth markers, 152–153
  tools and materials, 154–155, *154*, *155*
  using artificial intelligence, 156–161, *157–161*
forensic nursing, 113
format of trial presentation, 32–36
functional MRI (fMRI), 27
funisitis, *97*

gunshot wounds, 123–148
  atypical entry wounds, 125
  ricochet, 125
  Sutherland Springs Church Massacre Victims vs United States Government Department of Justice, 126–130, *128–130*
  tissue damage, 125
  trajectory, *12*
  see also apartment shooting; ballistics; mass shooting

hemorrhage
  brain, *25*
history of medical illustrations, 15–20

Imagine Art AI, *192–195*
interactive brain slice viewer, *185*, *186*
interactive injury summary application, *187*, *188*
internal ballistics, 124
interpersonal violence, 113–122
  diagrams for documentation, 114–122, *115–122*
  forensic nursing, 113

knee
  after fall, *34*
  amputation, left below the, *47*
  before fall, *33*

labor and delivery (L&D)
  timeline of, *37*, *99*
L&D, *see* labor and delivery (L&D)
law, 5–6
left internal thoracic (LITA) harvesting, *41*
left total shoulder arthroplasty, *8*
LITA, *see* left internal thoracic (LITA) harvesting
lordotic cervical implant, *83*, *86*, *89*

magnetic resonance imaging (MRI), 23, *25*, 27–28
  functional, 27
mass shooting, 131–144
  compensation and settlement for, 145
  multiple fatal injuries, *134–137*, *139*, *141*, *142*
  multiple traumatic injuries, *132*, *133*, *138*, *140*, *143*
  see also apartment shooting
meconium, 107–108, *108–111*
medical demonstrative aids to trial
  exchange, 165–166
  submitting, 163, 165–166
medical device, 7–8
medical illustration
  brief history of, 15–20
  definition of, 1
  gunshot wounds, 123–148
  interpersonal violence, 113–122
  for personal injury cases, 43–72
  trial presentation, 21–42
medical illustrators
  responsibilities of, 13–15
medical imaging/reports, utilizing, 165
medical malpractice
  defense, *see* medical malpractice defense
  Andrew Sibbernsen, 65–72, *67–70*
  Howard Thigpen, 59–65, *60–62*, 175–177
medical malpractice defense
  Christina Billiet, 93–107, *95–105*
  John Sly, 73–93, *75–91*
  Kiely Keane, 107–112, *108–112*
  see also medical malpractice
Mediceuticals, *11*
method of trial presentation, 30–32
Midjourney AI, 190, *191*, *195*
MRI, *see* magnetic resonance imaging (MRI)
multiple fatal injuries, *6*, 50–53, *60*, *70*
  bullet wounds, *134–137*, *138*, *139*, *141*, *142*
multiple sclerosis, *9*
multiple traumatic injuries, *35*
  brain, *25*
  bullet wounds, *132*, *133*, 134, 135, 136, 137, *138*, 139, *140*, 141, 142, *143*, *147*, *148*

neck, anatomy of, *20*

patient education, 2–4
pelvic exams, *121*, *122*
personal injury cases, medical illustrations for, 43–72
medical malpractice, 59–72, *60–62*, *67–70*
worker's compensation, 43–49, *45–47*
wrongful death, 50–59, *51–55*
Pioneer SlimFuse® plate, *84*, *87*
placenta
diseased, *109*
normal, *108*
size/weight, *112*
placental abruption, progression of, *5*
placental pathology, *96*
projectional radiographs, 29
psoriasis, *11*

qualified medical expert, finding, 164
qualified medical/forensic illustrator, finding, 163–164

ricochet, 125
right calcaneus fracture, *26*
right distal femur fracture, *24*
right elbow injuries, *40*
right frontal craniotomy, *174*

septicemia, pathogenesis of, *61*
shrapnel injuries, *144*
shoulder replacement, *8*
skull, three-dimensional facial reconstruction of, 150–151
skull fractures, 6, *25*, *136*, *139*, *141*, *142*, *175*, *185*, *186*
slice chooser, *25*, 185, *185–85*
social media, community strength through, 179
spine
appearance before surgery, *172*
injuries, cross section of, *171*
preoperative condition of, *12*
StereoLithography (STL), 40
STL, *see* StereoLithography (STL)

tech generation, immediate access of, 178
technology "wow" factor, 180–188, *181–188*
terminal ballistics, 124
teeth
extraction, *36*
interpersonal violence, in diagrams for documentation of, *118–119*
timelines of trial presentation, 37–38, *37–39*
trial presentation, medical illustrations for, 21–42 accuracy of, 39, *39–41*
client-specific anatomy, 39, 42
colorized radiology, 23–30
complex medical information, 21–23
fetal monitor strips, 37–38, *39*
format of, 32–36
method, 30–32
timelines of, 37–38, *37–39*

upper teeth extraction, *36*
uterus, bacterial infection at, *100*

worker's compensation, 43–49, *45–47*
wrongful death, personal injury and, 50–59, *51–55*

x-rays, 28–30